THE INNOCENT INVESTOR AND THE SHAKY GROUND FLOOR

ALSO BY SIDNEY MARGOLIUS:

THE INNOCENT CONSUMER VS. THE EXPLOITERS
THE CONSUMER'S GUIDE TO BETTER BUYING
HOW TO MAKE THE MOST OF YOUR MONEY
BETTER HOMES & GARDENS MONEY MANAGEMENT
   FOR YOUR FAMILY
YOUR PERSONAL GUIDE TO SUCCESSFUL RETIREMENT
PLANNING FOR COLLEGE
IT'S YOUR MONEY
NATIONAL TAX AND BUDGET GUIDE
PLAIN FACTS ABOUT SMALL BUSINESSES

THE INNOCENT INVESTOR AND THE SHAKY GROUND FLOOR

SIDNEY K. MARGOLIUS

Andrew S. Thomas Memorial Library
MORRIS HARVEY COLLEGE, CHARLESTON, W. VA.

TRIDENT PRESS · NEW YORK

82198

SECOND PRINTING

Copyright, ©, 1971, by Sidney Margolius

All rights reserved. No part of this book may be reproduced in any form without
permission in writing from the publisher, except by a
reviewer who may quote brief passages in a review
to be printed in a magazine or newspaper.

SBN: 671-27075-3
Library of Congress Catalog Card Number: 72-140570

Published simultaneously in the United States and Canada by
Trident Press, a division of Simon & Schuster, Inc., 630
Fifth Avenue, New York, N.Y. 10020

Printed in the United States of America

Acknowledgments

The author wishes to express his gratitude for expert help with what proved to be a massive undertaking.

To Mrs. Jean Toombs, who suggested this book and provided wide-ranging research and collaboration; Gordon Cole, for suggestions and encouragement; my wife, Esther, for perceptive copyreading and editing; Elaine Jessen, for alert editorial assistance and fact-checking; Sherry Zwerlein, for efficient help in manuscript preparation; Edwin Margolius, counselor-at-law, for careful review of tax facts and additional suggestions; Mrs. Dorothy Finkel, for observations of a certain investment promotion;

To a number of Better Business Bureau executives who helped enormously, including John L. O'Brien, St. Louis; Jasper Rowland, Akron; James W. Stephens, Atlanta; Robert B. Renwick, Birmingham; Theodore E. Lyman, Richmond, Va.; Ralph Smathers, Miami; and Mrs. Lori Laustrup, Roanoke;

To the government officials who devoted much time to our effort, especially Roland H. Cook, associate director, Office of Debt Analysis, U.S. Treasury; Stanley Sporkin, associate director, Division of Trading and Markets, Securities and Exchange Commission; Mike Taylor, legislative assistant to Congressman John E. Moss of California; Carl Lauderdale, director of criminal investigation, U.S. Post Office; Marty

Wolfe, special assistant to the postmaster general; Charles Molony, information officer, Federal Reserve Board; Bruce A. Craig, assistant attorney general, Wisconsin; Tim Ford, legislative assistant to U.S. Senator Harrison Williams of New Jersey;

To the investment counselors who advised on and reviewed investment information, including George Frazer, president, Leon Frazer Associates; Ferguson Taylor, vice-president, T. Rowe Price and Associates; Norman Freed, of Elkins, Morris, Stroud and Co.; Norman Mains, associate economist, Investment Company Institute; Paul Deacon and Beatrice Riddell, *Financial Post*, Toronto; Winston Dancis, Creative Programs Corp.; Samuel Braude, of Morris Cohon & Co.; R. Quentin Kramer, of Burton, Dana, Westerlund, Inc.; Martin A. Mersky, Gibraltar Securities Co.; Arnold Green, Bache & Co.

Viewpoints for Small Investors

"People sometimes drop remarks calculated to bring the little minnows into the net to be served up for the big fish . . . the longer I operated in Wall Street the more distrustful I became of tips and inside information. Given time, I believe that inside information can break the Bank of England or the U.S. Treasury."

—Bernard Baruch

"I never believe in taking a man's dollar unless I give him something for it, something in the way of rolled gold jewelry, garden seeds, stock certificates, shoe polish . . . to show for his money."

—A con man with standards,
in O. Henry's *Conscience in Art*

"Beware of a schemer with a smile."
—Chinese fortune cookie, quoted in full

Contents

PREFACE: The Innocent Investor and the Dawn of Knowledge   11

Section One: The Money Prowlers and Interest Nibblers

CHAPTER ONE: Are You a Potential "Reckus"?   17
CHAPTER TWO: "Catch 22" for Small Investors   31
CHAPTER THREE: Multi-Distributorships—How to Get Rich off Each Other   40
CHAPTER FOUR: Deceptive Franchises: Cloak for Unloading Merchandise   58
CHAPTER FIVE: From Rags to Riches and Sometimes Back Again via Gray-Area Franchises   74
CHAPTER SIX: Stock and Front-Money Gambles —and Sometimes Swindles   95
CHAPTER SEVEN: Meanest Hoax: Investments for Part-Time Earnings   107

Section Two: Making the Most of Your Investment Dollars

CHAPTER EIGHT:	New Opportunities and How to Use Them	123
CHAPTER NINE:	An Intelligent Lamb Among the Bulls and Bears	131
CHAPTER TEN:	Unloading Needless Mutual Fund Problems	165
CHAPTER ELEVEN:	The New Interest in Bonds, Preferreds, Governments, and Tax-Exempts	187
CHAPTER TWELVE:	Managing Fixed-Value Savings for Highest Return	200
CHAPTER THIRTEEN:	The Expanding Mortgage and Realty Trusts	207
CHAPTER FOURTEEN:	Tax Planning and Shelter for Small Investors	210

Appendixes: Agencies That Help Investors

A:	Better Business Bureaus	241
B:	Securities and Exchange Commission	245
C:	Federal Trade Commission	246
D:	Small Business Administration	247
E:	U.S. Commerce Department	249
	Notes	251
	A Glossary for Small Investors	255
	References	273
	Index	275

PREFACE

The Innocent Investor and the Dawn of Knowledge

This book has been written as a response to a need for frank, realistic financial guidance for wage earners and salaried people who today may earn a little more than just what they need for subsistence and think in terms of investing their extra cash.

The proliferating risks that inexperienced people face in investing in today's complicated money world came to light when Jean Toombs, a dynamic, experienced reporter and editor, wrote a series of articles for the *Machinist* newspaper on various investment promotions aimed especially at employed people with some extra funds. The extent of such half-world investment promotions as multi-level distributorships, referral plans, dubious and even outlandish franchises, and the number of people who get involved and often lose their hard-won savings, both startled and alarmed Mrs. Toombs. She communicated her concern to Gordon Cole, editor of the *Machinist* (newspaper of the International Association of Machinist and Aerospace Workers).

Cole suggested to me the need for a thorough report on these problems, and a guide to investing for wage earners and salaried people. For over a year Mrs. Toombs and I researched the entire problem of investments for moderate- and middle-income families—both the hard-sell pressures and the genuine opportunities. We interviewed some seventy experts in regulatory agencies, Better Business Bureaus, and the investment industry, and reviewed many advisory services and financial publications. We collected the individual experiences of a number of would-be small investors who had confided their own mishaps after reading articles on investment promotions in the *Machinist* and other trade union and credit union publications. We also posed as potential investors and employed other working people in this manner to see at firsthand how promoters of various investment schemes operated.

The result of this comprehensive research is this guide both to the pitfalls to avoid and the better investment opportunities for the small investor in a financial world mainly arranged for the benefit—and profit—of the big investor.

We found big traps of controversial legality and even outright illegality that can take a large slice of your savings at one swoop, but also many subtle little snares that can nick you a bit at a time for percentages of your potential investment earnings. Most of these latter are quite legal, and that is one of the most disturbing of our findings. There is a double standard of dealing for the small saver and the large investor, and the rule seems to be that the less sophisticated you are, the more you are going to be kidded and even exploited, whether in picking a place to put your savings, buying shares in mutual funds, or paying income taxes. Even the government participates in this game.

Knowing how to get the most for your money is as important when you save and invest as when you buy family needs. Knowledgeable management of your savings can make the difference between helping your children get additional education or inability to do so, between security in retirement and fear, between having a reassuring backlog of savings and having little or none. It is to this goal of maximum management, of making your money work as hard for you as you worked for it, that this book is dedicated. There are valuable opportunities today for increasing your investment income too.

We also tell you where to get help, and what agencies

can intervene if you are deceived. The key to the confidence man's swindle is that the average person doesn't want to know he's been a mark, and wants even less to have others know. If a deceived or mistreated small investor does not complain, both the swindles and the subtler legal deceits expand.

In a way this book is like Eve's apple. It may tell you some things you would just as soon not know about, but perhaps more that you do.

S. M.

SECTION ONE

THE MONEY PROWLERS AND INTEREST NIBBLERS

CHAPTER ONE

Are You a Potential "Reckus"?

In the language of high-pressure promoters, a "reckus" is a target for a deceptive scheme.

Today when many white- and blue-collar workers have some extra money above basic living needs, they have become reckuses for a growing number of high-pressure, if still legal, investment promotions, and even some outright frauds.

Some of the barely legal business opportunity schemes spreading across the country are startling, both for the large numbers of small investors who get involved and for the difficulty government agencies have in controlling them. Just as alarming is the innocence of the moderate-income investors. Reared in the folklore of moneymaking opportunities, they become ensnared in a wide range of promotions—from financially questionable, if still legal, multi-level distributorships to a growing array of foolish and even phony franchise, mortgage, real-estate, and other investments.

Investments in business opportunities have in fact become one of the ten leading problem areas, the Akron Better Business Bureau reported.

The stakes are high. In a typical modern pyramid investment scheme, thousands of families are lured into buying "distributorships" for "fabulous new products" on the promise of five- and six-figure incomes.

Similarly, as franchising has boomed—there already are

over 1,200 franchisors and 670,000 franchised businesses—misleading promotions have proliferated like weeds. They already have done severe financial damage to many small investors who can ill afford to lose their money, and especially to working people and the elderly retired, seeking additional income to withstand inflated living costs.[1] Housewives seeking to earn money to help with family living expenses also have become noticeably vulnerable to distributor schemes.

But if many thousands of people lose or stand to lose money in borderline investments, actually millions of small investors are sheared lightly, but often, in many more subtle ways by reputable mutual-fund promoters, Wall Street myths, hard-selling securities promoters, and even savings institutions.

Thus, believing in the ultimate wisdom of investment "experts," in 1968 the small investor may have paid $80 a share for a new conglomerate or a currently fashionable pollution, electronics, or computer leasing company and found that two years later his stock was worth only $20. He may rely on his government to regulate investment companies fairly, without realizing that political influence rather than fairness or even the public's welfare is responsible for sales commissions of 9 percent on mutual fund purchases, and severe withdrawal penalties if he discontinues such an investment plan.

Small savers are nicked even by their own government. For example, the government pays 5½ percent on E and H bonds bought chiefly by the small savers. But the government pays big investors as much as 6 to 7 percent on some of its borrowings. In contrast, the Canadian government pays its citizen savers 7 to 8 percent on its savings bonds.

At that, most E bond buyers get less than the advertised rate. Many who cash in bonds after a year earn only 4 percent. Some who cash in before six months get no interest at all. Revealingly, more $25 bonds, usually bought on payroll savings plans by working people, are cashed in the first six months than any of the larger denominations. Sixty percent of *all* savings bonds are cashed in the first year. Thus, the government has had the use of the money of these small investors for little or no interest.

The Money Prowlers and Interest Nibblers

Yet while large investors have fled to more profitable investments, families continue faithful to government savings bonds, in fact, even increasing their holdings after World War II.[2] Significantly, in this period the financial assets of large investors and institutions have increased faster than those of families, and you can begin to see why.

On savings accounts too, small savers often are nicked. They get only 4½ to 5½ percent while large investors get as much as 7½ percent from the same banks, and 8 to 9 percent on some corporate bonds, and even 5 to 6 percent on tax-exempt municipal bonds.

Again, as with E bonds, banks often get away with paying less than the stated interest rates because many depositors draw out funds before quarterly and semiannual dividend declarations. Actually banks who advertise that they pay 5 percent often pay zero percent, Professor Richard L. D. Morse, of Kansas State University, pointed out.

Here is a typical case of how the quarterly and semiannual dividend system trims millions of small savers out of a few dollars at a time, as reported by J. S. Oestreicher to his union's newspaper, the *RWDSU Record*:

> The average daily balance on my savings account was over $480 for the past quarter. I received only $3.35 in interest, instead of the $6 I figured I should get at 5 percent. I asked the bank about it, and was told that according to New York State Banking Law, deposits must remain in the bank until three days before the end of the quarter to receive dividends for the whole period. When I withdrew $250 on December 15 I became entitled only to the interest on the remaining balance for the whole quarter and lost all my interest on the larger part of my money that had been in the bank for eleven weeks of the thirteen-week period.

Yet this state's banking department permits banks under its supervision to emphasize in their ads that they pay interest from the day of deposit without also stating that amounts withdrawn before the end of the quarter yield no interest at all.

On some types of savings accounts such as Christmas and

vacation clubs, some banks may pay no interest even if savers do not withdraw before the end of the interest period. In fact, they even may charge you a late penalty if you don't keep up your club deposits, just like a teacher might give a child a black mark for misbehavior. This is probably one of the weirdest savings arrangements in recorded history. Yet millions of adults well above the age of consent each year submit to it.

As an example of the way government regulatory agencies often side with their client industries, when Congressman Benjamin Rosenthal of New York asked the Federal Reserve Board to consider requiring banks to pay interest on such accounts, the board refused. It claimed that such a requirement might deprive the public of a type of banking service it "apparently wants in spite of the lack of payment of interest." Yet some banks and savings associations do pay interest on Christmas accounts and still continue to make them available, as an increasing number did in the tight-money, high-rate year of 1970.

On almost every side the financially innocent family is kidded along and deprived of its rightful return on its savings. If you own a house, you probably pay part of your property tax and insurance ahead of time into an escrow account held by the bank. But you earn no interest on these deposits as you would if you put them into a savings account each month and then paid your taxes and insurance yourself. Nor can you even drop the arrangement when you do realize how much interest you lose over the years. The escrow requirement is a legal part of many mortgage contracts.

If you rent, you may be required by the landlord to put up a security deposit on which usually you get no interest. If you go on a vacation, you buy traveler's checks and pay the issuing company 1 percent for the privilege of letting them use your cash—without paying you any interest—until you use up the checks.*

---

* From two-thirds to all of the 1 percent fee for traveler's checks goes to the banks that retail them. The issuing companies such as American Express and First National City Bank make their profit on the "float"—the cash they

The Money Prowlers and Interest Nibblers 21

Even on their pooled savings, such as Social Security and Veterans Administration reserves and state insurance funds, the general public often has lost when these funds are borrowed by their parent governments at rates less than paid to private investors. (As one of many examples, the Washington State Labor Council complained early in 1970 that the investment portfolio of the State's Accident Reserve Fund was producing an overall return of less than 5¼ percent at a time when interest rates were commonly around 7 to 9 percent. One reason was that it was heavily invested in relatively low-paying municipal bonds.)

Similarly many families are persuaded to save through life insurance by some of the most glaring sophistry and figure juggling of any type of investment. The typical insurance buyer rarely checks beforehand as to why his so-called savings-type insurance policy may accumulate no cash value at all the first year or two, and, as shown in chapter 12, much less in subsequent years than if he had bought plain term insurance and put the difference into other fixed-value savings.

In fact, he can be convinced by salesmen that he is an immature dolt who would not be able to do any saving if he did not get a bill from an insurance company, and the insurance costs him nothing in the long run because at some future date his cash value will be as much or more than his total premium payments.

Once he does have some cash value in his policies, he lacks the realization that he could borrow on it at the 5 percent rate written into his contract, and invest these funds elsewhere at as much as 8 to 9 percent, as many large investors have done. In fact, the innocent investor is more likely to leave his own money in insurance policies while he pays

---

can use meanwhile for investment and loans. Sometimes banks offer a special reduced price on traveler's checks bought in the spring. They do you no favor. You lose more interest on the cash you pay in advance of your vacation needs than you save on the reduced price of the checks. Now you can understand why issuing companies advise that you can use leftover traveler's checks "anytime"; your next trip, for example.

true annual interest rates of 12 to 22 percent to finance installment purchases.

It is equally commonplace, of course, for a family in effect to borrow its own money from a bank and pay anywhere from 12 to 16 percent true annual interest while its savings remain on deposit at 4½ to 5 percent. This is called "How to Stay Poor or Where Are the Customers' Yachts?" But it is a trap that wage earners have walked into with both feet. Even while interest rates in 1969 reached the highest level since the Civil War, consumer debts rose to an all-time high of $116 billion—$11 billion more than the year before.

Equally questionable is the purchase, by hundreds of thousands of small investors, of hundreds of millions of dollars of face-amount certificates sold by Investors Diversified Services, the nation's largest investment company. As discussed in chapter 12, the yields on these fifteen- and twenty-two-year certificates as of late 1969 were 3½ to 4 percent, when many banks, associations, and E bonds paid 5 to 6, even on tax-deferred savings as are the face-amount certificates. Moreover these investors pay a sales load and would have to pay a penalty if they drew out their money before the end of the plan, but could borrow their own money at a higher rate than it was earning for them.

In buying stocks, too, the small investor is at a disadvantage. The brokerage fees he must pay on his small purchases were raised disproportionately in 1969—more than necessary in the view of some financial experts, as discussed in chapter 9.

Even worse, he lacks access to the same degree or quality of investment research that large investors can command. To many stockbrokers he is a nuisance. Nor does he have the ability to move quickly to grasp intermediate trends or get out of the way of disaster.

In fact, so notorious is the tardiness of the small investor that professional speculators often regard his decisions as a signal to do the opposite. An increase in odd-lot purchases (under 100 shares) is regarded by many professionals as time to unload stocks. A decrease is regarded as a signal to buy.

At least in 1970 the small investor could see that even the

large institutional investors as well as many mutual funds and investment advisers also could be trapped into believing that growth stocks were actually worth forty to fifty times their annual earnings, or that they always continue to grow, or that a stock such as Penn Central rationally could be valued by the stock market at $84 a share in 1968 shortly after consolidation and sell for as little as $5 two years later.

One of the most damaging developments adding to speculative excesses has been the rise and decline of so-called go-go or performance mutual funds operated by adventurous young managers now known in the investment trade as the gunslingers.

Such go-go funds sought spectacular results by investing in supposedly fast-rising new issues, new companies, new industries. They invested heavily, for example, in new chains of nursing homes organized to exploit the advent of Medicare and in similarly fast-expanding franchise companies whose profits for a while looked larger than they proved to be, because of the accounting methods used. The largest new nursing-home chain, Four Seasons, came on the market in 1968 with its shares priced at $11. That same year the shares spiraled to over $100, with go-go mutual funds among the largest investors. Less than two years later the company had applied for reorganization under the bankruptcy laws as both its earnings prospects and ability to secure financing dimmed.

Similarly stocks of some franchise companies doubled and tripled in price, but within months their values plummeted to a few dollars a share.

Yet many investors ran to get in on the ground floor of the go-go funds or bought directly into such overexpanded and underfinanced new ventures, attracted by the smell of the Medicare dollars and the roar of the burger stands. As culpable as the go-go funds are some famous-name brokerage houses that floated such overpriced and highly speculative stocks.

All through our investigations we found recurring political influences responsible for the second-class treatment of small investors and savers.

The influence of banks and savings and loan associations is the major factor in the lagging rate and sliding-scale structure of E bonds. A number of Treasury Department career officials often have privately urged their superiors to ask Congress to pay full interest right from the start as everybody else does.

But the banks and savings associations persistently pressure the government to hold down the savings bond rate to avoid greater competition for your savings. The banks no longer even make the effort to sell E bonds that they did earlier when they were not as interested as now in the deposits of small savers, even though the government pays them for handling bonds. At one time 80 percent of savings bonds were sold through banks and 20 percent through payroll deduction. Now 20 percent are sold through banks and 80 percent through payroll deductions.

In 1970 Senator John J. Williams of Delaware proposed a special retirement savings bond that would pay 6 percent. But Treasury officials resisted because they feared that a rate that high might lead people to remove savings from banks and savings associations. Congress did at least increase the E bond rate to 5½ percent if held to maturity, five years, ten months.

The theory of the sliding scale—that it encourages people to hold on to the bonds—has been long disproved by the high rate of cash-ins the first year.

Similarly, early in 1970 the government made it harder for small investors to share in the relatively higher rates paid on Treasury bills and notes by raising the minimum denomination to $10,000 from the previous $1,000. The minimum on securities of the Federal National Mortgage Association and Home Loan Bank was raised to $10,000 from the previous $5,000.

The alibi was that there was too much paper work for the government—a flimsy excuse for a bureaucracy that has raised paper work to a life style.

The real pressures came from savings banks and associations, who want to compel small savers to deal with them only, and also this time, from securities dealers who did not want to service small investments in government obligations. The savings institutions have been aided by the influential National Association of Real Estate Boards, which also pressed the Treasury and other borrowing agencies to fence off small investors from their high-rate bonds and notes. "Federal agency obligations [should] bear high enough minimum denominations to minimize competition with mortgage-oriented thrift institutions," the realtors' president told Congress.[3]

What the realtors want is to force small savers to subsidize mortgages. But such coercion is self-defeating and simple-minded while still injurious to small savers. The fallacy, or sophistry, is that the FNMA and Home Loan Board, which supply capital for mortgage lenders, also raised the minimum denominations on the securities they offer, so that the flow of fresh mortgage funds from moderate-income investors was actually reduced.

One of the most blatant efforts to force small savers into the savings banks and associations has come from the National Association of Mutual Savings Banks, especially surprising because these institutions began life as people's banks. Concerned that depositors had tripled purchases of federal notes and bills in 1969, the savings banks pressed not only for raising the minimum denominations but also asked the Treasury to time its offerings to avoid coinciding with interest-credit periods of the savings banks and associations.

The objective, of course, was to discourage small investors from drawing their money out of the bank to buy any higher-rate federal offerings, by making them forfeit their bank interest if they do. Even some Treasury officials I interviewed have been startled by the recent self-serving demands of the "people's banks."

Again, career officials within the Treasury Department argued that the government had an obligation to offer this investment opportunity to its moderate-income as well as rich citizens. But the government agency borrowings again have become a private club for rich investors, although some side doors now are opening for the working saver, as discussed in chapter 11.

The influence of savings and loan associations is especially effective on Congress and government agencies and has successfully restrained even the commercial banks from paying higher rates on moderate-sized accounts. Thus the Federal Reserve Board in 1970 permitted banks to pay any rate for certificates of deposits of at least $100,000 and up to eighty-nine-days maturity. Many banks then paid 7½ to 8 percent on such large deposits. But smaller depositors could get only 4½ to 5 percent on regular accounts, and only 6 percent on two-year deposits.*

The plea of the savings associations is that higher bank rates on regular accounts will pull savers away and so dry up funds for the mortgages in which the associations specialize.

But of all the political pressures that keep the small investor in an inferior and exploited position, the successful evasion by the mutual fund industry of major needed reforms is one of the most costly and scandalous.

For seven years beginning in 1959 the Securities and Exchange Commission (the government agency that polices the investment industry) investigated mutual funds. In 1966 it issued its report saying what impartial observers had long known: (1) the sales commission of 8½ to 9 percent charged investors by many mutual funds is too much, (2) the contractual-type of mutual-fund contract, under which you forfeit a large part of your investment if you discontinue before you complete the plan, excessively penalizes mutual fund investors and also encourages high-pressure selling, and (3) the management fees of some mutual fund investment companies are too high and so further reduce investors' yields.

Even though President Lyndon B. Johnson endorsed the proposed reforms, the mutual fund industry was able to stall

---

* Of course you also can get an inexpensive gift, which distracts small savers from the more important goal of getting the highest rates and best tax shelter. The government limits such account-opening offers by banks to gifts with a wholesale value of $5; for deposits of $5,000, the limit is $10.

off any changes. A diluted version of the proposed reform did pass the Senate but bogged down in the House.

The likelihood of reform and of strong SEC supervision of the investment industry was further threatened by the notorious letter Richard Nixon sent to several thousand securities dealers during his 1968 election campaign. Nixon promised to end the "heavy-handed bureaucratic regulatory schemes" of the Johnson administration if elected. The letter was not made public but newspapers subsequently secured copies.[4]

By late 1970 even the Senate's weakened reform bill was further diluted in the House by stubborn opposition from the mutual funds. Representative John E. Moss of California, chairman of the House subcommittee handling the bill, charged at a closed meeting of investment bankers that "never in my experience has a bill been lobbied so extensively." Members of the subcommittee have been "insidiously attacked in the press" and he himself had become "the subject of libelous insinuations" about his personal integrity, Moss complained.[5]

The objective of the mutual fund sponsors was, of course, further dilution of the already weakened reform bill. Pressure was especially intense on those subcommittee members from the Boston and New York areas, where some of the largest mutual funds are domiciled.

Curiously, the congressman who spearheaded the further weakening of the Senate bill was not one of the subcommittee members from the Boston or New York money centers, but was thirty-five-year-old W. S. Stuckey, Jr., from a rather poverty-stricken rural Georgia district.

Another opponent of reform, Representative Fletcher Thompson of Atlanta, based his opposition on the lack of public outcry. This is a revealing attitude. The apparent public silence in this case does not disprove the need for reform as much as it shows that many small investors are not fully aware of the disadvantages of the high sales charge and harsh penalties, and even when they are, have no organized voice to represent them in Washington.

At present, mutual funds using the front-end load contractual plan, usually charge you what they call an 8½ percent sales commission. The truth is, it would be an average of 8½ percent only if you complete the contract.

The contract you are asked to sign lets the fund sponsor deduct a disproportionate amount of your first year's payments to pay the salesman a large share of his total commission ahead of time. For example, if you sign a contract to invest $1,000 a year in a mutual fund with an 8½ percent sales load, 50 percent or $500 may be taken out the first year, and 4 to 6 percent or $40 to $60 a year from your payments in the following years—depending on the length and terms of the plan—to average 8½ percent a year. (Even the purported 8½ percent is really 9.3 percent, as explained in chapter 10.)

This is called the front-end load. It is detrimental enough if you complete the plan, because less of your money goes to work for you at the start to earn dividends. Over the life of the contract only 91 percent of your investment goes to work for you. But even worse, if you had to discontinue early because of some unforeseen problem, you lose a sizable chunk of your initial investment because it has been paid over to the salesman.*

Under the compromise law finally enacted in December, 1970, fund sellers are still permitted to deduct 50 percent of your first-year payments for sales commission. But if they do, you have the right to rescind in the first forty-five days. If you withdraw in the first eighteen months, you can get a refund except for a 15 percent commission, and during the first three years the commission would be limited to 20 percent for each year.

Unfortunately none of the bills sought effective reform of the even more important problem emphasized in the original SEC report—the sales fee. The SEC had recommended a 5 percent limit. The new law merely gives the dealers' association power to prevent excessive sales charges—little different

---

* Similar penalties are used in the life-insurance business, requiring purchasers to forfeit a large part of their "investment" in "cash-value" insurance such as ordinary life and endowment policies if they discontinue early.

The Money Prowlers and Interest Nibblers

from existing law under which the load-type funds have been charging the big commissions.

Revealingly, mutual fund sales fees usually are four or five times those charged on equivalent purchases of common stocks bought through the same brokers. Obviously there is no more effort or expense involved in filling one type of purchase order than the other.

The fees charged small and large mutual-fund purchasers again are disproportionate. The man who invests $50,000 pays only 4.9 percent; the $100,000 investor, 2.9.

But even without real reforms, a knowledgeable investor need not expose himself to contracts and penalties in buying fund shares. There are other ways to invest in mutual funds as discussed in chapter 10.

The former chairman of the SEC, Manuel F. Cohen, who left with noticeable suddenness in 1969 soon after Nixon arrived, has warned that the management fees (in addition to sales commissions) charged by mutual fund investment advisers also need regulation so that they are reduced proportionately as a mutual fund grows.

Even if you don't own a single mutual fund share, control of the management fee and other needed reforms and strong regulation are important to you, Cohen pointed out. Nowadays many pension and welfare funds, in which you share, are partly invested in mutual funds and stocks. The amount that can be diverted to the dealers and managers over the years can affect your retirement and other benefits.

In contrast to Nixon's blast against recent attempts at closer regulation, Cohen warned before his sudden departure that the investor has no organized voice, and government regulation of the investment industry really is his only protection.

The accuracy of this estimate was proved only too tragically in the excessive stock market slide of 1970. When both prices of stocks and the asset values of many mutual funds tumbled sharply, the disaster destroyed both some of the myths spread by securities salesmen and swallowed by small investors and much of the savings and unfounded expectations of these families despite even the partial recovery in late 1970.

Some of the mutual funds as well as individual investors had invested heavily in overpriced "growth" and "glamour" stocks, and even in "letters of acceptance" of future stock issues. These and sometimes other assets were valued at what later appeared to be inflated figures, which in turn inflated the prices investors paid for these shares.

Sharp market declines often are called shake-outs, meaning, the smaller, weaker investors are shaken out of the market. Declines, although not to the exaggerated extent of 1969–70, usually are inevitable when popular stocks are selling at excessive prices in relation to any possible growth in near future earnings as in 1968, and yielding 1 percent or less in dividends, including famed growth stocks then selling at forty-five to fifty-five times their current earnings. (Less than two years later most had lost one-third to one-half of their market value.)

For small investors, who had paid high prices in the late 1960s expecting gains or at least ordinary yields usable for children's college and other needs, self-serving industry slogans that the stock market was people's capitalism became bitter tea indeed. It also became clear, if you ever did believe it, that you do not really buy a share in America's future when you buy stocks. America's future is more durable than either Wall Street stock quotations or the profits of any individual corporation. Steep declines in the middle of inflations also show that the stock market is not as reliable a defense against inflation, especially over a short term, as securities salesmen habitually assert.

But even while there are more questionable and even irresponsible promotions and dangerous swings in stock prices, additional and even more rewarding savings and investment opportunities have developed for the well-informed, planning-minded small investor. This book warns about the dangerous areas, and on several of them posts off-limits signs for small investors. But we also report on the new opportunities and on how to make the most of your savings dollars.

CHAPTER TWO

"Catch 22" for Small Investors*

What you need to realize very clearly is that the government cannot fully protect you when you invest—no matter what you invest in. Subtle manipulations may not be controlled by any law at all, and even actual illegal tricks may escape the attention of authorities for a long time.

One reason is that in an age of a little more free money and heightened interest in getting in on the ground floor, investment schemes are proliferating faster than the authorities sometimes can keep up with them. The Post Office Department, which has taken on an increasing role in policing investment frauds, is investigating some two hundred pyramid investment schemes alone as this is written.

The postal authorities as well as state law authorities also have been running hard to keep up with dubious land promotions, especially in the Far West, Southwest, and Florida. From 1962 to 1970 this agency alone achieved sixty-nine convictions with other cases still awaiting trial.

But while the department estimates that its activities have

---

* In Joseph Heller's novel, the bombardier who tries to get out of the Air Force on the grounds that he is crazy, and according to regulations must be released, is confronted by a clerk with Catch 22. The catch is that if he is trying to get out of the Air Force he can't really be crazy. Small investors often are confronted by a similar catch: there may be a regulatory agency established to protect them, but for one reason or another it can't quite protect or it can't act in time.

saved the public more than $130 million, based on an estimate of the land still on hand to be sold by the promoters when they were hauled into court, innocent real-estate investors already had lost a known $60 million in lurid promotions (some advertised in our best newspapers). How much more has been lost and is still being lost by borderline promotions is unknown.

Another problem is that state laws vary and often are murky and difficult to use against some of the modern investment promotions such as multi-level distributorships. These involve selling a product such as cosmetics or household appliances through several levels of distributors, each supposed to get a large commission.

The catch is that the distributors must buy a quantity of the products from the promoters of the plan. Basically there is no law regulating the value of products or guaranteeing their salability. But because of the many disappointments, law authorities in several states have sought to assert that promoters' claims of large earnings in effect are deceptive, in a not always successful effort to control this type of investment.

Similarly the Better Business Bureaus do yeoman service in calling the attention of the public and the authorities to many of the investment schemes. But the bureaus, while probably the most valuable local sources of intelligence about dubious investment schemes, must run hard while undernourished. The business community expects the bureaus to serve as the voluntary or self-regulation answer to demands for more regulation but fails to adequately support these agencies with their expertise and alertness to deceptive investment promotions.

The Post Office Department has become increasingly active in policing investment deception, and where it can operate, it carries real clout because it operates under criminal law. But this itself is a limiting factor. The postal authorities can pursue effectively only those frauds covered by the criminal law, not the more subtle situations covered by civil law. Congress could strengthen the civil postal fraud statute by eliminating the need to prove that a promoter intended to defraud. Then the Post Office Department, by proving misrepresentation or falsity whether intended or not, could more promptly halt many deceptive schemes.

The real Catch 22 is that even when federal or state lawmen do manage to prove an investment promotion illegal and stop it, they may not be able to secure a refund of the money the would-be investors put up. Often it has been dissipated.

Or, as in the case of the Federal Trade Commission, the law provides neither redress for the aggrieved investor nor penalty for the promoter found deceptive. The law under which FTC presently operates makes it possible for a questionable practice to go on for a long time before the FTC can issue a desist order. It often takes two to six years from initial complaint to final order. Even then the order carries no penalty. FTC merely says, "Go and sin no more, at least not in exactly this way."

Even when the need is apparent, as in this case, a regulatory agency for many years may not be able to get the lawmakers to enact remedial legislation. Ever since 1962 the FTC and other experts on deceptive practices have recommended that the commission be given powers to seek a temporary injunction to halt deceptions early. Yet by late 1970 Congress still had not enacted this simple proposal.

Similarly, New York State Attorney Louis Lefkowitz each year since 1964 has asked that state's legislature to require that interest be paid on escrow and rent deposits and Christmas Clubs. The legislature finally did enact a law requiring landlords to pay interest on deposits in buildings with six or more tenants (the only state law of this kind to my knowledge). But the other bills have gone down the drain year after year in the face of stubborn opposition from the banks.

Perhaps of widest concern, the Securities and Exchange Commission has been weakened in recent years even as stronger regulation has become more urgent because of the massive increase in the number of people who own stocks. Some thirty-one million people now own stocks, a rise of 53 percent in only the five years from 1965 to 1970, the New York Stock Exchange reported.

The selling pressures are intensifying too, now that many insurance companies and their large sales staffs are also selling mutual funds; department store chains such as Sears Roebuck have organized mutual funds and are selling shares in their stores along with refrigerators and underwear, and even small loan companies such as Beneficial Finance and chain tax services such as H & R Block have formed mutual fund sales subsidiaries. Already over forty-six thousand insurance agencies are licensed to sell mutual funds and variable annuities (similarly based on stock equities) in addition to the many thousands of full- and part-time salesmen employed by mutual fund dealers.

Even the Army is involved in the mutual fund selling game, with shares being sold in its overseas post exchanges at the rate of $1 million a month.[6] The shares are sold by private companies but the PXs get a slice of the sales commission. Dismayingly, because overseas servicemen have little access to impartial guidance or opportunity to shop other investments, the plans sold to them through the PXs usually are the penalty-laden, high-commission front-end load-type described in chapter 1.

Although understaffed and under fire from the investment industry, the SEC is compelled to fight on many fronts to guard you against the intensified selling pressures and even manipulation of stock values that tend to trim the potential gains or deepen the losses of small investors.

During the late 1960s the SEC instituted a number of court cases and actions to make sure that insiders such as corporation officials and their associates do not exploit their special knowledge for personal gain in trading in their own companies' securities.

For example, in recent years officials of such large corporations as Texas Gulf Sulphur and the Glen Alden companies, and the big brokerage firm of Merrill Lynch, Pierce, Fenner & Smith, as well as officials of a number of mutual funds, have been charged with taking advantage of inside information in violation of regulations or of disclosing inside information to some large investors such as several mutual funds, without also telling the general public.[7]

The SEC also has sought to regulate more closely the so-called conglomerates, which buy up unrelated industries with shares of their own sometimes overpriced stocks. Unfortunately this policing action was not early or effective enough to prevent losses by many investors who rushed to get on the fleeting conglomerate bandwagon. Some of these modern conglomerates that sold for as much as $160 a share in 1968 were down to as little as $10 in early 1971.

Some of the conglomerates actually have been aided in their take-overs by large institutional investors, such as mutual funds, who were given inside information about the take-over plan and then bought stock in target companies. Ordinarily such a take-over bid drives up the price of the stocks of both the acquiring company and the target company.[8]

The public thus can be led to pay more for the stocks of both the conglomerate and the target than the market had previously indicated they were worth, while the institutions aiding in the take-over benefit from the higher prices of the shares they bought earlier. The SEC has sought to strip the secrecy from the arm-in-arm activities of the conglomerates and some of the institutional investors who get involved in take-overs.

The influence of large institutional investors often injures small investors in other ways. One of the most revealing incidents has been the effort of the treasurer of Harvard College, who also is president of the State Street Investment Corp. and a director of Middle South Utilities, to convince the SEC to approve a stock option plan for the utility's executives.[9] Such stock options, especially when unnecessary to stimulate management efforts, are detrimental to utility consumers and also to ordinary stockholders, as the SEC staff argued. (The commission overruled its own staff on this point.)

Although unsuccessfully so far, the SEC staff for many years also has sought to restrict the activities of the stock exchange specialists. These are the middleman brokers who specialize in specific stocks. The concern is that they also trade for their own account while helping to set the market price.

Another practice that may artificially affect how much you may pay or receive for a stock when you buy or sell, is short selling. In such transactions, speculators sell borrowed stock in the hope that it will go down. This, of course, is usually more of a gamble than a genuine investment practice. It has the effect af exaggerating declines. Of course short sellers eventually must buy back, which tends to stabilize prices but also sometimes inflates the price you may pay.

Artificial influences have been intensified by the development of hedge funds. These are mutual funds organized by speculators to sell stocks short as well as long. In recent declines these hedge funds were among the forces helping to push down stock values excessively, with consequent damage to small investors unable or afraid to hold on to their investments.

With these driving private influences always at work, you can see why it is urgent to maintain if not a truly strong SEC at least a courageous and adequate one. The SEC must protect both the thirty-one million individual investors in stocks and fund shares and the more than one hundred million who own stocks indirectly through pension funds, insurance companies, and so on. To this end, it must police insider relationships with the investing giants, and keep a watch for the whole country on the impact of these increasingly powerful institutional investors on the securities markets and the nation's economy itself.

Yet the SEC is a small Atlas indeed to maintain the stability of the huge investment world. On a budget of about $20 million a year, the SEC is responsible for regulating the buying and selling of over 20 million shares of securities a day with an average daily value of over $800 million. Any weakening of this agency could collapse many individual worlds.

There are other circumstances contributing to the shearing, whether lightly or heavily, of the innocent investor, one of them being the innocent investor himself. He has his critics as well as his sympathizers.

—He suffers from "inertia and lethargy," Saul Klaman, the chief economist of the National Association of Mutual Savings Banks, told a meeting of savings bankers in 1969, and that "works in our favor" in the early stages of competitive rate increases.

—He often seems to want a Big Daddy to make him save, and pays more than he realizes for such supervision. Christmas Clubs, enforced saving through life insurance, and contractual mutual-fund plans are notable examples. So is the custom of saving by having his employer deduct extra income taxes from his wages so he can get a refund at the end of the year. But on this windfall of accumulated funds the government pays no interest. Meanwhile, the moderate-income wage earner who practices this method often has installment debts on which he pays 14 to 22 percent annual interest.

—Sometimes he may not only be innocent but also greedy himself, and that is why he gets into trouble, some experienced observers think. "I feel that anyone who participates in a referral selling scheme or a multi-level scheme is engaging in something in which he knows he must con his friends to start," John L. O'Brien, president of the Saint Louis Better Business Bureau, commented during our survey.

Ralph Smathers, president of the Miami bureau, also questioned the innocence of investors in multi-level distributorships: "Most are seeking to get in and out with a profit before the pyramid collapses," he commented. "The phony franchises are generally characterized by promises of great returns with little effort and small investment. The small investor is little different from the large investor and is trapped by his own avarice, coupled with wishful thinking and often a mental lapse in utilizing sound practice and common sense. From time to time capable individuals have attempted to function as consultants to small investors [but] none have succeeded because they apparently are unwilling to pay a few dollars to obtain expert advice."

But the problem, as William J. Cotter of the Post Office

Department testified before a Senate committee, is that "the pyramid type chain promotion . . . is perhaps the most insidious devised to date. It provides schemers with a limitless sucker list and can reach enormous proportions [quickly]. Its most thoroughly vicious feature is of course its self-perpetuating nature. An honest victim once ensnared must become dishonest and sell to others in order to recoup his own losses."

As a psychologist told Mrs. Toombs, the easiest mark is the man who has lost some money: he can't let bad enough alone; he gets panicky about getting it back. The loss is a blow to his self-image. He can't stand to think of himself as a loser.

Too, the innocent investor today is up against a new breed of promoter: well spoken, using sales psychology with what has been described as hypnotic effect, employing the phrases and language of modern marketing, capitalizing on the great American folk myth of getting in on the ground floor and on the publicized financial successes of earlier house-to-house distribution and franchise organizations. If anything, the innocent investor is the victim of modern publicity and the lack of knowledge and irresponsibility of many of the publicity media and TV and radio personalities.

Today's investment promoters are no longer the crude fly-by-nights of a less affluent era. They are larger in scope, more organized, and represented by attorneys who seek out the legal loopholes, even sometimes professors from famous law schools.

A small investor living in today's investment world must realize certain facts of life.

You can be damaged in varying degree in three ways: (1) outright fraud, (2) borderline but still potentially dangerous investment schemes, and (3) subtle investment merchandising that nicks you for only a few percentage points at a time but does it regularly. This last is the most prevalent, ranging from churning (excessive buying and selling) by a broker bent on making a good living, or sometimes just a living, to the loss of interest by mishandling savings.

Actions or events that seem unfair to you may be entirely

The Money Prowlers and Interest Nibblers

legal under present law, or at least legal in your state if not in some others (state laws do vary).

Regulatory agencies are overloaded, and different administrations and legislatures may view controversial investment activities quite differently. The professional investment community is very influential—more than most people realize. When Wall Street sneezes, Madison Avenue blows its nose and Pennsylvania Avenue reaches for an aspirin.

To a large extent, and possibly decisively, you are really on your own. Your safest protection is your own knowledge, and especially, where to get information and guidance.

The trend to class-action court suits also can be an important help to deceived investors, especially for recovering damages that regulatory agencies can not always recover.

In a class action, an individual, group, or local government agency brings a suit to recover damages for all the aggrieved buyers. For example, in 1970 one stockholder filed a suit against a large corporation and a number of its directors charging that omission of some expense and loss items in the company's 1969 report inflated the company's profit performance and thus the price of the stock. Significantly, the suit was brought on behalf of all buyers of the stock after the date of the questioned report.

Such class actions help solve one of the most persistent problems moderate-income sellers have to face—that often losses suffered at the hands of deceptive or high-pressure promoters are not large enough to make it worthwhile for a lawyer to handle the case.

In fact, H. B. Montague of the Post Office Inspection Service estimated that, despite the rising number of complaints, not more than 10 percent of all instances of fraud even are reported, let alone redressed.

CHAPTER THREE

Multi-Distributorships— How to Get Rich off Each Other

Will Koscot Interplanetary corporation send you into financial orbit with its mink oil "kream" and other "kosmetics"? Can you find happiness as a "general" for Holiday Magic? Can "Hong Kong Executive Fashions" make you "independently wealthy" with "no risk"?

These are only a few of the hundreds of multi-level or pyramid-type distributorships that have become a widespread form of investment. They also have involved more people with unfortunate results than any other promotion recently, reported T. E. Lyman, executive vice-president of the Richmond, Virginia, Better Business Bureau.

Multi-distributorships have been especially tempting to moderate-income working people and housewives seeking to develop additional income. But it has been revealing to also see how some supposedly more sophisticated people, such as businessmen, officials of community organizations, and even lawyers, doctors, at least one university marketing professor, and even a state attorney general, have been attracted to these plans.

Typically, families with savings of from $2,000 to $10,000 are lured into buying a distributorship for a "fabulous new product," which, they are assured, can net them a five-figure income—at least. Often the investor must buy a quantity of the product.

The Money Prowlers and Interest Nibblers

These promotions have been built around many products and services, including cosmetics and cleaning products, "Hong Kong" suits, other clothing, vitamin products, housewares, tape recorders and appliances, even founderships for a discount store that the promoters say will be opened up in your town later.

Unfortunately in many of these plans once the would-be investor has bought a distributorship, he can recoup only by getting others into the scheme and collecting commissions on their investments. All the investors in such distributorships end up looking for working girls and housewives to invest in a kit of cosmetics to sell to friends and neighbors.

One of the classic multi-level plans is Holiday Magic Cosmetics. The promoters were active in a number of cities in 1967, leaving many unhappy investors with basements and garages full of cosmetics they could not sell. In 1969 and 1970 they renewed their promotion. The Miami Better Business Bureau reported that in Dade County alone an estimated one hundred investors had bought distributorships in 1967. By the time Holiday Magic returned in 1970, only three or four of these were still in business.

The Holiday Magic plan has four levels of distribution, ranging from the Holiday girl who must buy at least a $12 purse of samples or a large kit for $39, and an "organizer" who invests at least $91, up through the "master distributor" (at least $2,500), and finally to the "general distributor" who must invest at least $5,000 in cosmetics to resell to sub-distributors.

All these transactions are in cash. In fact, the written instructions for masters and generals tell them to have a blank check on hand if the person they are trying to recruit does not have cash or a check, and then to take any personal check to the prospect's bank "and obtain either a cashier's check or a certified check made out to Holiday Magic, Inc." You don't get much chance to change your mind.

The recruiters are shown in exact detail how to play psychologically on the prospect's emotions through Seven Emotional Keys or Ways to Sell.[10]

1. Assumptive Attitude—Assume they are going to participate. Choose close between General, Master, Organizer, Holiday Girl.
2. Subordinate questions; make them agree on minor issues. "Wouldn't you like to earn more money?" "Training is always valuable, isn't that right?"
3. Impending Event—"If you come in tonight, you will be among the first in this area."
4. Inducement—Give them something above and beyond the normal presentation. A General earns $3,300 totally for each one of his direct Master's promotion to General. A General maintaining a retail force of 50 to 100 Holiday Girls will earn $4,500 to $9,000 per month. (Example based on $300 average monthly volume per Holiday Girl.)
5. Physical Action—(a) Touch them; lead them to a seat with 3 fingers under the elbow. Don't push; be careful. (b) Help them fill out application.
6. Narrative Key—A story with which a prospect can identify. (a) Positive (story that stimulates hope of reward). (b) Negative (story that stimulates fear of loss).
7. Ask Them to Buy—(a) Be stronger than your prospect. (b) Don't give up too soon.

John O'Brien of the Saint Louis BBB calls this procedure a process of self-hypnosis. The recruiter is instructed not to ask you, "Do you want to come into this business?" but, "When can you get started with your training?"

It may never even be quite clear to the potential distributor that the application he is asked to sign also is an agreement to purchase the required amount of products. The prospect is invited to an opportunity meeting, at which the various levels and the potential percentages he will get on product sales are outlined. Then the prospect is asked, "Now that you have heard the advantages of the program, which position would suit you best?"

The Money Prowlers and Interest Nibblers 43

When the prospect obediently answers which would suit him best, the recruiter is told to enroll him in the first training class. The enrollment is in effect when his signature is on the application. The recruiter is then instructed: "When application is completed, fold and place in case or inside pocket of suit."

Apparently it would not be easy to take back that application-agreement from the recruiter. But Holiday Magic does not abandon you to any post-surgery depression. The company instructs recruiters: "Avoid buyer's chill; tell them they are going to be happier, healthier, wealthier and will receive what they want out of life with the Holiday Magic program."

The Holiday Magic manual suggests such rich earnings as "$25,000 extra a year." The recruiters are told to say, for example: "There are people doing this in our business (point to $25,000) . . . If you could conduct this business like many of our people are doing, making $25,000 and in many cases more . . . you'd want it, wouldn't you?"

A Better Business Bureau employee who attended a Holiday Magic meeting reported that the recruiters cited examples of people who had made as much as $76,000 in six months. On a blackboard the recruiters showed how salespeople could realize $601 in sales for twenty-four hours of work, of which they would get 40 percent, equaling a profit of $10 an hour.

But the application and agreement a distributor must sign gives the promoters a written escape hatch from any claim by disillusioned investors that they have been assured profits. This document says clearly, "I fully understand that Holiday Magic has made no guarantees of profit to me . . ."

Many investors have complained of heavy losses. A Saint Louis real estate man reported that he, his brother, and his sister had lost a total of about $18,000. He had invested to become a senior general, no less, expecting to profit on commissions from sales by distributors. "But no matter what training you gave, the salespeople couldn't push the product," he told the Better Business Bureau. He actually made $147 in the six months he remained in the program.

A Saint Louis doctor who had invested heavily even lost

his home. Another investor reported that he got rid of the merchandise he bought as distress merchandise and through gifts.

Despite the many losses, state authorities have had difficulty stopping the promotion. In several states authorities have tried, unsuccessfully, to bring the promotion under regulation by arguing that the investments in the plan really represent the sale of securities. The California attorney general did charge Holiday Magic and local distributors with placing misleading opportunity ads in newspapers. The corporation said it did not itself place or authorize such ads. But it accepted a $35,000 penalty on behalf of its distributors rather than submit to a restraining order. The attorney general agreed that future violations by distributors would result in actions only against them. (California later enacted a law barring multi-distributorships if the main objective is to sell distributorships rather than the merchandise itself.)

Finally the Federal Trade Commission in July, 1970, charged Holiday Magic, its chairman, William P. Patrick, and other officers with using an unfair and deceptive lottery-type merchandising program and with recruiting distributors and investors through misrepresentation. At this writing the final determination has not been made.

The use of employment-type ads by such companies and the lack of care of newspapers and national magazines in accepting them have led to such unforeseen involvement as that of a Saint Louis woman who answered an ad for a saleswoman with a cosmetic company. She told the recruiter she did not want to do door-to-door selling. According to her, he said to take their course because they had something better in view for her. While taking the course, he came into the classroom and whispered to her to sign a paper. She says she had no chance to read it but signed it anyway. Later she found she had signed to buy a kit for $139. After much pleading and appeals to the Better Business Bureau, the "senior general" agreed not to hold her to the contract.

An even more spectacular distributorship promotion is that staged by Koscot Interplanetary Inc. This company assembles potential investors at Koscot golden opportunity meetings to explain how they can make as much as $175,000 a year selling "Kosmetics [sic] for the communities of tomorrow." Most of these contain mink oil, "the most precious of kreams."*

These are sold at sales parties by a pyramid that includes "koordinators," "supervisors," and "directors." All of these people pay for the privilege of selling the "kosmetics." As with Holiday Magic they then try to recoup their investment by recruiting additional distributors who pay to get in.

The man behind Koscot is Glenn Turner, a former Holiday Magic distributor. Before that, Turner, who started his career as a sharecropper on a tobacco farm, was connected with various sewing machine companies in the South, the Miami Better Business Bureau reported.

One woman who attended a Koscot recruiting meeting at my request reported:

> It was like a revival meeting. The recruiters were mostly young fellows in their early 20s. They had a rapid-fire sales talk accompanied by a lot of activity such as pulling their ties off, flipping off their jackets, tossing chalk into the air. They talked fast, writing on the blackboard and erasing rapidly. They drew pyramids of various ranks of sellers and distributors, and had you making $100,000 in six months. The whole performance was an insult to my intelligence.

She told the distributor who tried to recruit her about the warning articles in the *Machinist*. He asserted that the reason for the articles was that the union was losing too many machinists to Koscot because they were making so much more money on the cosmetics than they had earned working as machinists.

In the Koscot plan, the retail manager invests $123 and

---

* Mink oil, of course, has no more cosmetic effectiveness than ordinary lanolin or any of the other oils used in toiletries, except possibly to another mink. It is scarce and expensive, and so sounds rich. Certainly mink oil is no less effective than other often promoted ingredients such as turtle oil, and minks are more beautiful than turtles.

recruits beauty advisers who invest $10 to $45. Or you can become a supervisor for an investment of $2,000, or a director for $2,500. Each of the people at these levels is supposed to earn commissions from the sales of everybody below him.

Promoters of multi-level plans often stage a dramatic campaign involving important local people when they come to a town. In Roanoke, Virginia, the vice-mayor gave Glenn Turner the key to the city in a ceremony. In Richmond, a number of state legislators attended a ground-breaking ceremony for a discount store (which has not been built at this writing) for which another multi-level promotion was selling founderships, as described later in this chapter.

In one Virginia city a savings and loan association president signed up for the foundership multi-level plan despite the arguments of the local Better Business Bureau manager that he should not, especially because he was a person whose financial judgment would be respected by others. He did make some money.

An auto dealer in the same city signed up too. Questioned later by the BBB manager about how he fared, he said, "Well, I got about five people interested but only two actually joined."

The BBB manager said the dealer should be glad the others had not invested.

"They were over twenty-one," he answered.

A reporter who attended a Koscot meeting in Charlotte, North Carolina, said that the appeal was that of "a surefire, get-rich-quick scheme for ordinary people if they are willing to work at it." He commented on the pressure for immediate decision: "Turner didn't have much use for the man who wanted to think it over. 'Show me a man who will make a spur-of-the-moment decision and I'll show you a winner,' he declared."[11]

A report by the *National Observer* of a Koscot meeting in Arlington, Virginia, shows how the recruiters in various cities all use the same sales talk and blackboard diagrams, reciting the story of Alice who holds sales parties at her home and sells $7,000 worth of cosmetics each month. The "koordinators," supervisors, and directors all get a commission.

The Koscot promotion has spread around the country, and at least as of now, is permitted in most states, although under specified restrictions in a number of them. The attorney general of North Carolina, for example, limited the number of directorships Koscot could sell to thirteen hundred. At the time the courts ordered Koscot to stop selling directorships and supervisorships, an estimated five hundred to six hundred North Carolina residents were directors. According to the *Charlotte Observer*, state accountants had figured out that if Koscot did get the maximum thirteen hundred permitted, and even if it cornered the market so that other cosmetics companies could not sell a single family there, the average director could expect earnings of only $1,400 a year.

In New York, Koscot agreed to a court order directing the company, among other admonitions, to offer distributors their money back. Frances Cerra, *Newsday*'s enterprising consumer writer, revealed that of 1,600 distributors in the state only 79 earned more than $5,000 in 1970, according to Koscot's own attorney.

Maryland, Wisconsin, Ohio, Michigan, New Mexico, and Louisiana also have acted to limit or prohibit the sale of distributorships, and other states are investigating at this writing, according to the Miami Better Business Bureau. In Indiana, Secretary of State William N. Salin served Koscot with a cease and desist order "for illegally selling securities." At the time he held a news conference and appeared on TV to explain why he thought this company was illegally doing business in Indiana. Koscot started a $2.5 million libel suit against Salin through attorney F. Lee Bailey. The suit was dismissed "with prejudice to the plaintiff," after "a sales plan completely within the framework of the law was approved jointly by my office and Koscot," Salin told me.

Wisconsin got a consent order against Koscot stipulating, among other points, that the company would refrain from selling distributorships, paying overrides to a director on the sales of a supervisor under him, or selling display racks to beauty advisers for purposes other than a bona fide sale. Interestingly, the order also provided for return, upon request, of escrowed payments of a director's release fee and return of funds for undamaged merchandise returned by distributors who did reorder or bring in another distributor.

But Virginia authorities found nothing illegal, the *National Observer* reported, and the West Virginia attorney general officially looked into the program, considered it to be legitimate, and then "bought in" himself.[12]

The Bestline Marketing System is another large multi-distributor plan operating in a number of states and selling cleaning products (Zif, B-7 Laundry Compound, and so forth). The general distributor can buy at a 60 percent discount, paying 40 cents for products that retail for $1, with three levels of subdistributors buying at proportionately smaller discounts. But they have to buy a lot of soap.

In Wisconsin alone, according to a legal action by the attorney general, from 1968 to 1970 at least 2,177 persons had invested over $2,869,000 in distributorships and mandatory inventory purchases. Among other charges, the state complained that a "director distributor" had to pay about $3,250 for inventory. To qualify as a "general" he had to pay an additional $2,750 of which $2,250 went to the general who sponsored the recruit. Then he too could recruit. The state also pointed out that if the pyramid recruiting plan worked as the company said it would, with the original investor recruiting forty-eight distributors in two months and they did the same, in ten months there would be three million distributors stemming from the one investor. Virtually the whole state would be distributors, presumably making their living buying soap from each other.

As a result of the legal action, Bestline did change its marketing plan, Assistant Attorney General Bruce A. Craig reports.

Another big promotion that has excited interest among many small investors is that for distributorships for discount stores, which the promoters say they will open later in that locality.

In one such plan, to become a distributor costs $320 for which the investor gets a specified article such as cookware, a sewing machine, or TV set, or can wait until the store opens to choose from a larger selection.

The Money Prowlers and Interest Nibblers

The next link in the chain is a "supervisor." He gets $70 of the $320.

The distributor also gets one hundred purchase authority cards, and then attempts to place these with people whom he expects to be potential purchasers. He then would get a sales commission of 12 to 20 percent on their purchases, and his supervisor would get commissions of 3 to 5 percent. If they do purchase, they in turn get cards to get other people to purchase and so on, only heaven knows where.

Certainly, the postal authorities, state attorneys general, and Better Business Bureaus don't know where. Some of these authorities are worried about these plans but apparently are not always sure how to regulate them. If the contracts to buy "founderships" could be considered securities, then they could be regulated by the states as such. The South Carolina Securities Division ruled that the contracts sold by Continental Marketing Associates did not constitute securities "inasmuch as presently we have no evidence of a sharing of profits." Tennessee state authorities and the Alabama Supreme Court also concluded that the contracts were not securities in cases involving CMA or its subsidiary, Alabama Market Centers, Inc.

But the Florida courts did rule that foundership contracts sold by Florida Discount Centers, Inc. (not related to CMA), were securities and could not be sold further unless registered with the Florida Securities Commission, but were also a lottery, so could not be registered anyway.

Moreover, some long-established companies operate on somewhat similar lines, selling cosmetics, brushes, housewares, costume jewelry, clothes, and other goods door-to-door or through not very merry parties for which the hostess gets a tablecloth, coffeepot, or other gift. (What she gets depends on what her guests buy.) These firms also often have chains of distributors and supervisors getting several commissions on the prices consumers pay. But while the goods sold sometimes are high priced, the emphasis is on selling the merchandise rather than on recruiting investors or distributors.

In the new plans involving the opening of a future discount store, a distributor also can become a supervisor by recruiting other distributors. He then would get an override or commission on purchases made through the distributors under him.

While some of the early founders or distributors in the discount house plans are reported to have made some money recruiting people, there are obvious investment uncertainties. First of all, in the plan sponsored by Continental Marketing Associates, the $150 foundership investment entitles the buyer to choose only from a limited number of items, such as a sewing machine, tape recorder, or cookware. Certainly no set of pots and pans is worth that price and many sewing machines sell for much less than that. Or if the investor buys a $750 foundership, he can get a portable color TV set. You can buy a portable color TV set for not much more than half that price.

As another example of the relatively low value of the merchandise promoted through such plans, the Florida Supreme Court found that a kitchen set that investors had to buy for $320 in another plan promoted by Florida Discount Centers actually had a wholesale cost of about $60. (Of course the buyer also received a founder's contract giving commissions of $60 for each unit if he could get others to similarly invest.)

Too, the promoters do not really guarantee to open an actual store in your locality, or not until a set number of founder contracts are sold. There is no real assurance they ever will (although at least one has). If they did, they would find it hard to compete in price with other discount or mass-merchandising stores while paying these additional sales commissions to distributors and supervisors. A well-run mass-merchandising store has a total retail margin of 28 to 30 percent of its receipts to cover all overhead, operating and sales expenses, and profit.

In the case of Florida Discount Centers, the contract said that when three thousand founders were secured, and perhaps sooner, a store would be opened. But the court found that "no effort has been made to acquire property" for the discount house advertised in the promotion and contract. Nor were prospects told what would happen if the store never opened.

The Continental Marketing Associates, which has blazed a

The Money Prowlers and Interest Nibblers 51

spectacular trail of sales of founderships through the South, selling over fifty thousand by 1969, did open a market center in Birmingham, acquired a site in Dothan, and also promised to build stores in other Alabama cities through its subsidiary, Alabama Marketing Centers.

The president of CMA, Edmond Randle, Jr., said in a sworn affidavit in February, 1969, that the prospective Dothan store "should open for business in June, 1969." But by August, 1970, no building even was erected on the property, Robert B. Renwick, general manager of the Birmingham BBB, reported. At that time CMA did have one other store in Alabama, a "mini store" in Muscle Shoals. But a bureau representative who visited it found the store was closing out many large items and planning to sublet at least half the store.

Randle also said that real estate for other stores had been acquired in other cities in Alabama, Tennessee, Georgia, Virginia, and North Carolina. A grand jury in Bibb County, Georgia, complained in 1969 that CMA had sold founderships in Albany, Georgia, for fourteen months and had not begun construction on a store there. In fact, by August, 1970, the company's activities in Georgia had virtually ceased, James W. Stephens, manager of the Atlanta BBB, told this writer.

Meanwhile CMA had used some of its funds to buy controlling interests in a number of other companies, including at least one bank and several electronics firms.[13]

When the CMA representative arrived in Missouri, the "show me" state, the Saint Louis Better Business Bureau immediately invited him to have an interview with the assistant attorney general. He promptly ruled that the sales talk violated Missouri law and issued a temporary order restraining the company from doing business in that state.

In Arkansas, too, CMA withdrew its sales program, at least for the time being, when officials told the company they believed it had violated state securities laws.[14]

CMA has based much of its argument that its contracts are not securities on an interpretation by a well-known Washington–Boston legal firm it retained, Gadsby & Hannah, headed by Edward Gadsby, a former chairman of the Securities and Exchange Commission. But the last time I spoke to a member of the firm, in July, 1970, he told me they represented CMA only on the securities question, had not done any work for them recently, and did not even know if they still represented them.

Another widespread multi-distributor promotion has been for the Gyro-Matic Safety Control. This is a metal box weighing sixty-four pounds with a moving weight, mounted in the trunk of a car so that it has an end-to-end motion.

Distributors sell the Gyro-Matic for $298 to $400. The claims for its performance have been controversial. The Missouri assistant attorney general stated that claims for the device's use of gyroscopic principles were not correct. The National Safety Council said its tests found no circumstances in which it significantly improved car performance. (In reply, Allstate has said the council's test "was a crude one," and claims that other tests show the device is of value.) In California, a consent judgment was entered enjoining the distributor from distributing literature making claims for performances not supported by independent tests, although it could continue to distribute genuine testimonials from actual users.

In those states where a multi-distributor plan is (or was) used to sell the device, the program envisioned big profits for distributors, but also big investments. An "executive safety distributor" had to buy one hundred units for $12,000, and makes $49.50 on each one sold to "direct distributors." The "direct distributor" got $30 on each sold to "distributors," who were supposed to make $40 a unit. All these commissions built up to a high retail price for the device itself.

Another auto stabilizer sold on a multi-distributor plan, is the Safe-T-Trac. In 1970 the FTC complained both about the claims of effectiveness the Cincinnati promoters made for the device and the claims of potential earnings from the multi-level marketing program, such as $7,920 a month.

The complaint charged that the company misrepresented that Safe-T-Trac is an effective safety device or will help in-

The Money Prowlers and Interest Nibblers 53

crease traction or prevent skidding, or functions as a shock absorber, or that the performance claims have been substantiated by competent, controlled tests, or that the lifetime guaranty is unconditional.

This program has four levels of investors whose investments range from $289.50 for an "associate dealer" to $10,000 for a "director." The directors could buy the units for $100. They were supposed to have a retail price of $289.50. The investors would get paid both commissions on sales of the unit by the lower ranks and fees for recruiting other investors.

But if Gyro-Matic will make you an "executive safety distributor" and Holiday Magic a "general," Hong Kong Executive Ltd. will make you a "board chairman" for just $1,000. Or if you are less ambitious, you can become a "president" for $400 or an "executive vice-president" for $200.

For this investment you get from one to five suits, depending on how much you invest, and one hundred cards entitling your friends to discounts on clothing made in Hong Kong, plus the "right" to sell chairmanships and presidencies to others.

Hong Kong Executive Fashions, Gyro-Matic, Holiday Magic, Koscot, and CMA at least do give the investor some merchandise for his money, in fact, a basementful of cosmetics if he is willing. But in one illegal multi-distributor promotion involving a liquid soap product called Terrific the investors did not get even some soap.

Edward Holt, a seemingly affluent businessman operating out of Oklahoma City, was convicted of two counts of mail fraud for this scheme. But the estimated loss to investors was more than $400,000.

In 1967, heading a company called National Marketing Association, Holt contracted with Terrific Products Company, a small chemical manufacturer to become its exclusive sales agent. Shortly after, the company learned that Holt had represented himself as an officer of the firm. They terminated their agreement. But he kept on, selling a product called Turific.

To provide an aura of success and affluence, Holt set up

elegant offices in a number of Southwest cities for what he called the Terrific Success Plan. Suggesting that a worldwide marketing plan was being organized to distribute the soap concentrate, he launched an intensive advertising program through radio, TV, and newspapers. (Eventually the cost of the ads had to be paid by the advertising firm that placed them.)

At this time he had as a prop the actual product. But as the Post Office's investigation showed, the advertising and the product were all sham to disguise his real intent.

Holt planned his operation with care. He induced respected members of the community to assume positions of prominence in the Success Plan. For example, a leading Oklahoma City personnel director got a free general distributorship in return for making a "few inspirational speeches" at some of the Success dinners that were integral to the whole scheme.

The dinners, now used in many real estate and other investment promotions, were impressive affairs. No pitch was made directly. The guest or potential investor left his name and address. A few days later a Success counselor called on him.

According to testimony, the counselor would ask the prospect whether he had met any new friends and whether he would enjoy coming to such a dinner meeting once a week, bringing friends with him.

If the answer was yes, the prospect was then told that as such a regular participant, bringing friends, he qualified as a distributor. The investment could be as little as $300 or as high as $8,000. But, the counselor pointed out, the more he invested, the higher his level, and the more money he would make.

He was assured that there was no selling involved as such. He would just invite friends and neighbors to the free steak dinner at a glamorous restaurant, introduce them to the Terrific Success Plan, and then watch the money roll in.

There would be no risk. His investment would be secured by an inventory of the product and the company would sign a written guarantee that, if he were not satisfied at the end of ninety days, his money would be refunded.

The Money Prowlers and Interest Nibblers

On questioning, the prospect learned that his inventory could be delivered to his home. But if this seemed cumbersome, he could get a warehouse receipt, certifying that his inventory was stored in a commercial warehouse. Where (or even whether) the inventory was stored was not vital at this point, he was told, because the product could not be marketed at the retail level until the complete sales organization was established.

While the investor could count on making a steady profit from the sale of the soap, he was told that the big money would come as commission on the amounts paid by others whom he introduced to the program. According to literature supplied by the counselor, this same organizational plan had been used by many fine companies and had a proven record of success.

In just a few months hundreds signed up, including a carpenter who mortgaged his furniture to invest $1,200. But the earlier ones got restive when nothing happened and started asking for the return of their investments. Holt used a number of stalling techniques, insisting on their requests in writing, quibbling over the time elapsed.

A month later he disappeared. Personnel at each National Marketing office thought he was at another office. Finally it was established that he was nowhere to be found and every National Marketing bank account was depleted.

Ironically, all that time Holt was already wanted by the FBI under the name of Robert Charles Collins. He was finally spotted in Phoenix operating the Chloratron Corporation of America. When arrested he said, "But this is a terrible mistake." At his trial, however, he pleaded no defense.

One of Holt's ploys shows how modern investment platitudes can be used to mislead. His brochures said, "Management is a company's most valuable asset. From its president down, Terrific [later Turific] is favored with top-flight management people having collectively more than 150 years experience in administration, finance, sales, etc." The forms invited the prospect to have his accountant, attorney, or banker call Holt.

Holt persuaded a Tulsa couple in their twenties to take $8,000 from a trust fund and invest it in a general distributorship. Six months later, he found another victim, a railroad worker. He went back to the couple and persuaded them to put in yet another $15,000, for which he would give them 10 percent of the entire operation and pay the young husband $1,000 a month as salary. This way, he removed them from the Tulsa distributorship and sold it to the railroad worker for $7,200.

A college marketing professor was another victim whose presence induced others to join. The local beauty queen was brought in as a social secretary to act as hostess at the steak dinners.

Holt even chartered a plane out of Oklahoma City, offering a free trip for investors if they would invite friends and relatives to the steak evenings in Dallas, Houston, and Memphis.

Holt is typical of the kind of modern high-pressure investment promoter described by the Post Office director of fraud investigation: "Plausible, low key, smooth, well speaking. Nothing of the spiv or shyster of earlier years. The men operating these rackets are educated, as a rule."

While some multi-level distributorships do provide diligent salespeople with a living, obviously they can not be regarded as investments, as tens of thousands of wage earners and small businessmen have learned in a heartbreaking way in recent years.

The clue to distinguishing between a reasonably sound sales program and an unreasonably risky multi-level investment is whether the program emphasizes earnings from selling the product or from recruiting others. If the plan "contemplates recruitment of an endless chain of distributors, [investors] would stand to lose their money," the FTC said in announcing a recent investigation.

The FTC told one manufacturer of household products that "a particular vice" of his proposed multi-level sales plan "is that part which provides override bonuses for recruited

The Money Prowlers and Interest Nibblers 57

distributors." Implicit "is the promise, rarely if ever kept, that the recruiting distributor can, without himself working, profit greatly from the work of others."

Even if the emphasis is on selling rather than recruiting, the product itself may not be competitively priced. Prices of the products in many plans we examined are inflated with combined sales commissions.

Cruelly enough, many multi-level promotions use classified ads resembling help wanted ads, to attract investors.

Claims that the product is a fantastic new development or invention are another warning signal. One more: if the promoters insist on cash or a certified check for a specified quantity order, you too can find yourself giving cosmetics or soap to everybody on your Christmas list.

CHAPTER FOUR

Deceptive Franchises: Cloak for Unloading Merchandise

The success of some franchises has meant new opportunities for high-pressure promoters drawn like flies by the vast publicity about legitimate franchises.*

Franchise deceptions are on the increase, J. R. Hoffman, vice-president of the National Better Business Bureau, told the Senate Subcommittee on Urban and Rural Development. Many promoters known to the bureaus from complaints in other fields have gravitated to franchising, he revealed.

New York State Attorney General Louis Lefkowitz sent a questionnaire to a number of franchisors. He had five hundred returns, and found a number of criminals identified with the five hundred as well as a number of other curious things. For instance some answered, "We're not in franchising." But when staff members wrote privately to the same companies, they would receive franchise offers at home. Authorities also have reported that a number of deceptive franchise salesmen are renegade stock and insurance salesmen with shady records.

In Nashville, which calls itself the franchise capital of the world and is headquarters for forty franchise companies, the Better Business Bureau has been called on to service thousands

---

* A franchise is an agreement with a business operator (the franchisor) to sell his products or product made to his specifications, under his brand or business name, and by the methods he prescribes. For this right and other benefits such as training, advertising, and supervision, the franchisee pays a royalty (in addition to his initial investment).

of inquiries and has stepped up its surveillance of ad copy. The Los Angeles BBB reported that during the first eleven months of 1969 it handled about 170 complaints and more than 7,000 inquiries.

In many of the deceptive variety of franchises today, franchising really has become a cloak for unloading either unsalable merchandise or an unconscionable quantity.

For example, three interrelated Colorado corporations operated by eleven promoters lured small contractors, plumbers, and cement masons to Denver by falsely promising an expense-paid trip. They were "given a chance" to become franchised dealers for glamorous-sounding Bermuda Pools, Cinderella Pools, and Town and Country Pools. But they had to engage to buy six pool kits for $12,000, consisting mainly of a lot of vinyl sheeting and filter equipment. If prospective investors could not raise $12,000, the promoters settled for advance deposits of $500 a pool.

The promised advertising and sales promotion never materialized, nor did the local families said by the promoters to have ordered pools, and the small investors were stuck with their vinyl sheeting and no customers.

Other serious recent areas of exploitation of would-be investors in deceptive franchises are in radio and TV tube-testing centers, some snack-meal franchises, "plastic" paints, and others. But the variety is infinite. One promoter even sold $750,000 worth of franchises for marketing cemetery mausoleums.

Even among the more legitimate if overpromoted franchises serious problems have developed.

There are four big risks for inexperienced small investors attracted by the franchise boom, as Robert M. Dias, president, the National Association of Franchised Businessmen, wrote in a letter to Senator Philip A. Hart of Michigan. In order of descending peril these are:

Outright Fraud: There is enough authority now in federal and local agencies to stop the wholly fraudulent franchises that have sprung up. "What is needed at both levels is determination" to act against the truly deceptive promoters.

The Great Gray Area: This is what Dias calls the growing number of situations where franchises are sold but the promised assistance and equipment are not immediately available nor may they ever be. The reason frequently is the franchisor's undercapitalization. If he and the franchisee are fortunate, the franchise may be able to get under way. If they are less fortunate, the franchisee loses all his money and has only a bankrupt corporation to turn to for reimbursement. While these situations may not have the requisite intent to prove a criminal case, they have the same effect, Dias pointed out. The proliferating problems of investors in gray-area franchises is shown in chapter 5.

Unfair Practices: Under threat of termination the franchisee is forced by the franchisor into practices that may be detrimental to business, such as directed purchase and price maintenance. The bitter controversy that has developed over such problems is analyzed in chapter 5.

Sales or Merger: The original franchisor may sell out to a third party even though the original agreement hinged on the franchisee's reliance on the reputation and expertise of the original franchisor. But despite payment of his, say, $20,000 fee, he can not control his own destiny—even to the choice of the parent company.

Some of the really fraudulent franchises are truly weird. Yet small investors, carried away by the glamour of the franchise boom, invest thousands of hard-earned dollars. A Texas promoter, Paul Hambly, operated quite a successful credit card franchise that even snared some experienced businessmen before the Post Office Department caught up with him and retired him to jail.

Hambly placed ads throughout the country. One in the *Indianapolis Star* read:

> Wanted at once by a corporation, now operating coast to coast, offering you an exclusive area franchise . . . a vital profitable prestige business, offering a needed service to businesses with over 80 million credit card holders. Persons selected should find excellent income the first month . . . a lifetime residual

income within a few months of operation. A minimum of $6,500 investment required. Other areas available for less.

Potential investors were told that the company—Universal Credit Card Inc.—honored all major credit cards and that the franchisee would be authorized to sell associated memberships to local merchants.

Merchants were told that they could sell their accounts receivable, representing charge sales of their customers, at a discount to UCCI for prompt payment. The franchisee was to get a commission of 1 percent of amounts paid to the merchants. It was estimated that franchisees paid in nearly $115,000, and merchants close to $30,000 for their associate memberships.

Eventually most of the merchants found that their accounts were not bought. In fact, the men who ran UCCI had some fifteen corporations that they used for the transfer of funds, thus keeping one step ahead of their creditors at all times.

Cited at the trial was the case of a Mr. Wise of Indianapolis who had invested $18,000. He had seen the ad with its promise of high income. The ad said to call a Mr. Avren. In the meeting between the two men, Avren indicated that the company was expanding, and that the holding company (Hambly Industries) had a successful record.

Wise, however, did not take it all in as gullibly as others had. He queried the Better Business Bureau and the bank references and asked for the names of some franchisees. But even when a prospective investor does try to investigate, the promoters have anticipated his moves.

First Avren told Wise it was not company policy to divulge their franchisees' earnings but he could phone John Hunter, a franchisee in South Carolina. Hunter confirmed he was a UCCI franchisee, and said he had more than one thousand accounts and his profits should be in excess of $25,000.

At this point Avren referred to the need for a good faith deposit, which would be refunded, while Wise made up his mind. It was demonstrated that "beyond mathematical doubt his earnings could soon reach $126,540 annually."

Wise also contacted another franchisee and the Dallas head office, which supported Avren's claims. Wise signed a contract and paid $10,000 for the Louisville, Kentucky, territory and options for other territories.

But later, when he found no Louisville merchants willing to join, he learned there had been another franchisee there who had left many unpaid bills. He also learned that Hunter was not a franchisee at all but an agent for another Hambly enterprise called Snak Bar.

Meanwhile lawsuits had begun to accumulate against Hambly and his various corporations. Curiously, the records show that the Texas Bank and Trust Co. had been dubious of the Universal Credit Card Inc. but still helped to finance Hambly.

Another franchisor who misrepresented both potential profits and exclusiveness of territory also has gone to jail, but not before he had fleeced small investors for $40,000. This was Manuel Homen, who promoted the Carol Lee Franchise for Instant Cocktail Mix.

Homen advertised in California and Hawaii:

> No selling required. Just service accounts. Cocktail Mix Industry sales are up 10 times . . . it's only the beginning. Carol Lee offers you a ground floor opportunity . . . Carol Lee offers to the qualified investor, an exclusive franchise. Our accounts are in liquor stores, supermarkets, drug stores, cocktail lounges. Investment from $2,500 to $15,000. Financing available.

If you had answered that ad, "Stoney" Homen himself would have called on you. Leaving nothing written, he would have claimed that Carol Lee had exclusive rights to the cocktail mixes in sixteen western states. Actually Wonder Bar had agreed to provide Homen with the products but had not given him a franchise. But he claimed that Carol Lee distributorships were being operated throughout the West and making great profit. Testimony supporting the indictment showed that in fact no distributor even received the product.

He claimed that a distributor would be provided with established outlets needing only weekly attention to replenish supplies. It turned out that no accounts had been or were established.

Promised profits sounded lucrative: you bought the mixes at $6 a dozen and sold them for $11.40 or $1.25 each. In reality, Wonder Bar products retail at 69 cents each. A full package—an exclusive distributorship—would cost $25,000. Even had Homen lived up to his bargain, he would have milked the investor of thousands: actual cost to him for the package was about $9,600.

The whole scheme was candy floss. No one got anything for his money. A typical example of those bilked was a Sacramento man who put up $7,800—and heard nothing more.

Unfortunately, the Postal Fraud Department can investigate but can not force restitution. In some cases, the court manages to effect the return of part of the losses incurred—but not in this one.

The Goal Trading Stamp promotion was an example of how fraudulent franchisors often tie into a current development or product in the news. During the investigation of this one, the postal inspector warned that "it is conceivable that a mammoth fraud against investors and the consuming public is in operation." It was eventually proved to be just that. Henry Bessesen was finally indicted at Minneapolis, convicted, and placed in five-year custody of the U.S. attorney after having defrauded hundreds of investors and merchants of more than $200,000.

Bessesen developed a plan for the distribution of trading stamps. The purported unique aspect was that these stamps could be redeemed for cash at the local bank instead of merchandise. He called his plan Goal Systems and the stamps Goal Points.

According to the indictment, Bessesen or an associate would ask for a deposit to secure a territory. The money, usually $300 to $5,000, it was said, would be used to promote the sale of the stamps to merchants. Investors were assured that the plan would be in full operation within thirty days, and they could expect immediate earnings.

It was the franchisee's job to sell pads of stamps to stores. Investors were told that 60 percent of the fees would be deposited in a trust fund to redeem stamps. The rest would go to pay investors until they had been repaid in full.

Actually, only $4,940 was paid back to investors. Except for a pilot operation, the investigation showed that Bessesen used the money to sell more franchises—not to develop the scheme, or redeem the stamps, or pay the investors.

Like most such schemes, Bessesen started with a franchise ad. The ad cited in the case appeared in no less a respectable investment publication than *Barrons*. It said, persuasively enough:

> WANTED: State and County Managers for an Absolutely New Sales Incentive Program. We have copyrighted a Goal Certificate premium with a cash value which is "bankable" and grows until redeemed for cash. This premium is similar to the mechanics of banking by mail and has the familiarity of trading stamps . . .
>
> We offer high commissions to managers chosen with generous overrides on the salesmen they supervise. If you are in between jobs or looking for something that has unlimited potential or at the peak of your ability but have been forced to retire because of age—look no further . . . we will mail you full details of our exceptional opportunity and arrange an interview so that you can see and taste the delight of the real deal.

Bessesen was the man behind still another operation—The International Credit System Inc. This ad also appeared in *Barrons*:

> *Discount Bonanza:* For persons with successful business backgrounds. State franchises available for a Credit System which enables business establishments not affiliated with Credit Card Companies to extend credit to any major Credit Cardholder. Persons qualifying will be given home office training plus complete finance format. This is a ground floor noncompetitive opportunity with high earning potential. We can help you raise operating capital if necessary . . .

A Saint Louis man was snared by both schemes. He paid Bessesen $3,000 for a credit card franchise as regional representative for the Missouri division. A few weeks later, while the Saint Louisan was setting up the selling program for this franchise, Bessesen showed him the ad in Barrons for the Goal trading stamp plan, and sold him the Saint Louis franchise for that program for $1,000 down.

Ultimately this franchise holder took Bessesen to court and got a civil judgment against him. This case later was used by the U.S. attorney in the criminal action against Bessesen.

Advisers always tell you to see a lawyer before you sign a contract. The Saint Louis investor did consult a lawyer all the way; in fact, paid him $900 in fees. Bessesen himself praised the contracts the investor's lawyer drew up. But the basic program was unsound and misrepresented.

The lack of caution of well-known investment magazines and newspapers in accepting ads for fraudulent or poorly founded franchise plans has played a large role in the bilking of many innocent investors. Leo Carl Martin, convicted in 1968 of mail fraud, advertised widely throughout the United States seeking investors in a process for manufacturing marble.

Martin operated on a seemingly professional basis. He hired an advertising agency to design and place ads such as this:

> Light Manufacturing: New process . . . Earn $8 to $12 an hour. Qualified applicants to have expenses paid while training at home plant. $4,500 investment secured by equipment and materials. Terms available with minimum $2,000 down.

An investor who saw the ad in the Minneapolis Star met with a salesman who persuaded him to go to Des Moines. There he met Martin and another salesman. They extolled the tremendous market for cultured marble. He was "getting in on the ground floor." They would train him, ship the materials and equipment, and buy his first ninety days' production, thus covering his original investment. If not satisfied, he would get his money back under the "sixty-day guarantee" they showed him. He gave them the $2,000.

For this he received a couple of pieces of equipment, eighty sacks of calcium carbonate, and three barrels of resin. He called Des Moines and learned the company had moved.

Another investor saw the ad in the *Chicago Tribune*. He paid Martin $2,500 as an advance. He was told that Martin Industries would set up distributorships to sell his product, that he could expect to double his investment within a year, that Martin would finance the $2,000 balance.

Back home, he waited for the papers covering the additional $2,000. When he phoned, Martin said he had misunderstood. No loan could or would be set up. The equipment was sitting on the dock waiting to be shipped but would not be until Martin received the rest of the money.

He mailed Martin a certified check for $1,900 and rented a shop. A few incidentals arrived but no major equipment and no molds. He finally went into business on his own, bought equipment, and actually set up a few accounts and sold some marble. He heard nothing further from Martin and eventually sold the business for $1,500.

At the trial, it was revealed that two victims received nothing, others waited months and even then vital pieces were left out, such as molds or the cement mixer.

One of the most notorious franchise frauds was operated by "Wild Man" Pritchard and the Chem-Plastics Corp. of Saint Louis and Las Vegas. Harold Pritchard renamed himself "Wild Man" in the 1940s when he was a fierce competitor in Los Angeles of "Mad Man" Muntz, a hard-selling car dealer who later promoted TV sets on TV.

Chem-Plastics (later National Chem-Plastics) distributed liquid floor coverings and concrete treatment material nationally through franchises. Previously Pritchard organized the Pylon Distributing Co. in Phoenix operating a similar business.

Chem-Plastics advertised all over the country offering exclusive franchises or distributorships. Prospects were told they could buy the products for $6.95 a gallon from Chem-Plastics and sell it for $13.90. The firm also promised sales assistance and training. The investors paid anywhere from $500 to $12,000 for their franchises, the Post Office Department later reported.

But, the postal authorities later charged, the firm did not provide the promised assistance, and the distributors found themselves with large quantities of the products, which they could not sell.*

The Saint Louis Better Business Bureau also reported many complaints from franchise holders in various cities complaining of overlapping territories, shortages, and even nondelivery of the product (these last may have been luckier than they realized). Hundreds of hopeful investors who had poured into Saint Louis also found to their dismay that the promised reimbursement of expenses really meant only if they bought the franchise.

In 1966, after nine years of painstaking investigation and file-building by the BBB, the postal authorities charged mail fraud, and Chem-Plastics itself went into bankruptcy. BBB manager John L. O'Brien reported that there were over two thousand creditors, the largest number in any bankruptcy on record in the federal court in that district.

In 1968, the Post Office Department reported, the wild one himself bit the dust. Pritchard and five other Chem-Plastics officials were sentenced to jail—Pritchard, for ten years. But the process took eleven years from the founding of the original Pylon company to the affirmation by the court of appeals of the convictions.

One promising development was that the court rejected the defense argument that the misrepresentations were made by salesmen and not by company officials. This claim often is made by company officials in such frequently deceptive businesses as franchises and home improvements. But the evidence showed that officials had been on hand at times when salesmen made their presentations.

The publications that had accepted Chem-Plastics business opportunity ads without investigation, again had paved the

---

* If the legal authorities can't figure out how to stop this kind of promotion early, they might at least consider setting up a merchandise exchange for investors who buy large amounts of goods from promoters of franchises and multiple distributorships. Unwilling owners of Chem-Plastics floor covering could trade some of it for cosmetics still owned by some of the Holiday Magic investors.

way for losses of hundreds of thousands of dollars by these small investors. The Saint Louis bureau itself publicly noted that such pillars of the business community as the *Wall Street Journal* and *Advertising Age* "should have known better than to take this advertising without screening."

This time many of the publications themselves were stuck. Among creditors listed in the bankruptcy proceedings were such large publications as the *New York Post, Baltimore American, Tri-City News,* and *Sacramento Bee,* as well as many small fraternal and monthly magazines hungry for every inch of paid copy they can get.

The interim activities of the Chem-Plastics promoters between first verdict and denied appeal vividly explains the eruption of the thousands of selling schemes that besiege small investors and consumers. One operation spawns many others. Pritchard organized two new promotions. One was Self-Hose, a leg spray for women. The other was known as Cardinal Liquid Plastics. It issued, for sales purposes, a forged Dun and Bradstreet report on the company, the Saint Louis BBB reported.

A Chem-Plastics vice-president teamed up with a bail bondsman, a marriage undoubtedly made in heaven, to develop the Litter-Vac Corp., selling a device to suck debris out of car interiors. This new enterprise also became the address of Quality Home Foods, a freezer-food plan operated by two other Chem-Plastics employees.

Meanwhile a plastic paint called Fabulous Liquid Coatings, with a label otherwise identical to the Chem-Plastics Pylon paint, appeared under the management of another former employee. Still another returned to his former vocation of selling cars.

While the Chem-Plastics promoters went to jail, sometimes fraudulent franchisors can steal a million and get off shockingly lightly. Two Los Angeles men who did business as U.S. Rustic Cedar Homes got only suspended sentences and $1,000 fines even though some twelve hundred distributor-franchisors had paid them an estimated $1 million for leisure home kits and plans that were never furnished.

A franchise that really put a hard-to-escape net around investors was the one promoted by Thermochemical Products Inc. of New York for water-repellent paints. The Federal Trade Commission charged that the franchisees—usually people who had small businesses other than paints—found the products "woefully lacking" in the claimed waterproof qualities. The paints and coatings were called Aqua-Chek, Vivilume, and Vin-L-Brush-On.

The FTC also found that the company's salesmen had falsely represented that Thermochemical was a division or subsidiary of Union Carbide Corporation or General Electric, that it would help dealers sell the products by providing advertising materials, that dealers would earn up to $18,000 a year, and other claims.

The net that the company wove around the dealers was its practice of assigning its invoices to the Wolmart Discount Corp. Under laws in most states, such finance companies that buy installment notes and invoices from the original sellers are considered to be the "holder in due course" and thus absolved from any complaint about deception or lack of performance by the seller himself. Meanwhile, the original seller has got his money from the finance company. The dealers might complain to Thermochemical but still had to pay Wolmart.

But this time the FTC attacked the theory of the innocent finance company, which has caused widespread injury to many installment buyers of other products. It cited Wolmart too, declaring that Wolmart's representation that it was an assignee of a holder in due course had the capacity to deceive the dealers into believing that Wolmart was an innocent purchaser of their invoices.

Widows and elderly people often fall victim to the wave of deceptive franchises. Jasper M. Rowland, Akron Better Business Bureau manager, told about a widow who sold her home to buy a display sign franchise. She lost her whole investment of almost $4,000 and had to go to work to pay storage on poor quality goods the franchisor shipped her.

She too had replied to a classified ad. The company representative invited her to a meeting with two other prospective franchisees—a seventy-two-year-old man and a small businessman who worked eight to ten hours a day and cared for a sick wife. They were shown well-made signs as samples. But those she received, she complained, were poorly painted and scratched.

She called the company and pleaded that she had no job and no money to support herself. An official said there was nothing he could do. At last report, the bureau was seeking restitution but with little hope.[15]

Sometimes franchisors go from one product to another, as did the Coffee Bar Manufacturing and the Royal Distributing companies of Richardson, Texas.

They sell eyeglass cleaners through franchised distributors and formerly sold coffee bars and stools. In a consent order, the FTC said that they promised profits of up to $1,000 a month. Few if any investors made any gain. The companies rarely established routes nor lived up to their guarantee of a return of 100 percent or any other percentage of franchisees' investments.

The ads sounded plausible in the style of this type of operator:

> We are looking for a sensible down to earth man [who] will with our whole hearted cooperation and our tremendous background . . . operate an agency from which he will supply drink packets of Maxwell House Coffee, Sanka, Hot Chocolate to offices, plants, stores. He will use our unique and highly unusual Coffee Bars, the cost less than $15 each . . . There is a necessary investment of $5,000 fully secured by inventory . . .

Another operator who set up a whole series of franchises was Roland Sockol of Miami. He had been a salesman for Aluminous Coatings, an affiliate of Ohmlac Paint and Refining Company, itself the subject of hundreds of complaints to Better Business Bureaus on its franchises.

Subsequently Sockol was connected with franchising All-Kote, a roof-coating paint; with Hydro-Mite Sports Boat, Inc., a franchise for amusement-ride boats (which went bankrupt);

then with a firm that sought to license auto-lease dealerships; and most recently with Universal Fiberglass of Hialeah, whose materials finally were confiscated by the Dade County Sheriff's Office.

One of the most ingenious franchisors was another Miamian, Harry Chereton, who also had companies in Illinois and Oklahoma. During the 1950s he was a principal in several finance companies and retail firms, all of whom went bankrupt. Then came the 1960s and the franchise boom. Better Business Bureaus started getting complaints about Silicone Products Corporation that Chereton managed, which franchised aerosol rack routes.

Since then he has been connected with at least eleven other companies, most of which sold franchises for aerosol rack routes and beverage dispensers. Again Better Business Bureaus started to get complaints.

One of the companies sold a product called Hangover Juice. Two of the most active were Silitronic Chemical Corp., domiciled in Miami, and Northeast Industries of Tulsa.

A number of judgments are known to have been secured—but not paid—in Maryland and Florida against Silitronic by its franchisees.

Another Chereton-connected franchise operation was the Peticare Insurance Co., which sold insurance on household pets. It was licensed in Oklahoma in 1966 but the renewal was denied in 1968.

But Chereton's boldest move was to set up his own "Better Business Bureau." In 1965 the Florida secretary of state actually issued a charter for the Better Business Bureau of North Miami, Inc. It was located in Chereton's office. Its only known activity was to issue a report stating that "Silitronic Chemical Corp. is a member in good standing of this Bureau."

One of the more persistent franchise schemes that attracts people seeking part-time income is tube-testing devices. In two prominent cases, the Federal Trade Commission got consent orders against the Youngstown Spectrum Corp. and International Distribution Center, and U.S. Electronics, Inc., of Pine Lawn, Missouri.

Both companies sold radio and TV tube-testing devices and replacement tubes, to be placed in hardware and drug stores. Youngstown sought an investment of $3,750; U.S. Electronics, $3,000. The FTC charged that the locations secured by U.S. Electronics were usually unsuitable and unprofitable—mostly service stations with little consumer traffic. In both cases, the FTC found, the franchisors would not accept return of the equipment, as they had represented.

The variety of franchises proven to be deceptive is amazing, as is the number of innocent investors who succumb to them. They include both products such as Lubri-Loy, Rite Baby Pants, and Mercury Automotive Products, and services such as the World Executives, Inc., which sold franchises for an executive job placement agency. All these collided with the postal authorities.

Most pathetic of all was the "exclusive franchise" sold by Greenheart Laboratories and Westex Enterprises to water and care for plants in the lobbies of large buildings. Postal authorities complained that the franchise buyers received nothing for their investment, not even water for the plants.

This franchise was rivaled for pathos by the one sold by San-Ad, Inc., of Chicago. It collected $85,000 for franchises for toilet-cleaning sanitation routes. Investors were led to believe they would get an established route and gross $16,500 a year.

Police and postal investigators also were appalled by the large number of elderly people who mailed in $100 down payments for a $6,000 exclusive franchise to sell Coty perfumes through local stores. The promoter, an international operator named Williamson, mailed an appealing personalized sales letter from Los Angeles to thousands of older people and they responded with no investigation and even no guarantee by the promoter.

How can grown people be trapped by some of the flimsy and even deceptive franchise investments reported here? Frank C. Hale, an FTC official, pointed out that they often are people who have had little or no business experience. "They may be elderly or retired persons with a small nest egg and little to do," he commented. "They can be tempted by inviting advertisements to try their luck at becoming successful businessmen. Often they are attracted by the promise of very substantial earnings. Frequently they do not recognize the importance of obtaining professional legal and financial advice. . . . They are prime targets. One of the most tragic aspects is the personal loss resulting from an unsuccessful franchise operation, particularly in the case of the elderly. Many of the individuals invest not only their life savings but all they can beg or borrow. Business failure can lead to total financial ruin and even wrecked lives. The young man can start again. But to whom may the elderly turn?"

CHAPTER FIVE

From Rags to Riches and Sometimes Back Again via Gray-Area Franchises

If little people can pay a few hundred dollars for a franchise to water plants, investors with somewhat more money can and do spend thousands on franchises that, while not fraudulent, as were many of those discussed in chapter 4, often are overpromoted or poorly worked out or simply not the right business for the investor.

The question often becomes one of whether the public can stomach still another Roadrunner Burger, Arkansas Fried Chickenbone, or peppermint-flavored pancake stand, even if a TV celebrity, athlete, or country musician is connected with it.

Even among some of the more successful franchises, increasing complaints are being heard from investors that they are in truth hardworking captives of the franchisors, who may require them to buy supplies at a higher price or can trade them almost like baseball players to another company or desert them in their hour of greatest need, which often arrives in the first year.

The National Better Business Bureau's J. R. Hoffman asked—and told—the Senate subcommittee investigating the franchise problems:

"Whatever happened to Pat Boone's Dine O Mat? Out.

"How many Hullabaloos are swinging? Not many.

"How many ended up in the Dog House? Most.

"How many were hit by Hit Parade records? All."

The list of well-publicized franchises, some sponsored by well-known people, that flared up brightly and then ran into difficulties is growing steadily. As this is written, the Securities and Exchange Commission is suing former U.S. Senator Albert B. Chandler and five associates, including two of his sons, seeking appointment of a receiver for Daniel Boone Fried Chicken, Inc., and its subsidiary Commonwealth Security Investors, Inc. Most of the charges involve alleged failure to file statements with the SEC, the Associated Press reported.

What is especially startling is the number of well-known stockbrokers, mutual funds, lawyers, banks, newspapers, magazines, and public figures who have recommended, invested in, got others to invest in, publicized, inspected, and otherwise participated in big franchise promotions that soon turned sour. If these be our investment counselors and guides, heaven help the small investor, because the authorities apparently can't.

Part of the problem, of course, is the swift rise of franchising. By 1970 it had become the fastest-growing industry in the country, with sales over $100 billion, reported Jerry S. Cohen, general counsel, National Association of Franchised Businessmen.

As noted in chapter 4, many of the skyrocketing franchise operations have been seriously underfinanced. Business columnist Elmer Roessner pointed out that a 1970 survey of 191 franchising companies by the National Industrial Conference Board found 34 percent admitted a shortage of working capital.

In addition to the well-publicized categories such as fast-foods and specialty eating places, an investor or small businessman can now obtain a franchise for pet shops, computerized financial services, wig shops, fast-reading institutes, travel agencies, diet training, amusement devices, nursing homes, child care, temporary help agencies, home alarms, indoor tennis, data-processing schools, duplicating services, auto transmission shops, and others. One sales organization alone —Dimensions Consultants of Ohio—represents some eighteen hundred franchises. There now are franchises for success motivation institutes and even the ultimate—a franchise for selling franchises to other people.

Apart from the deceptive franchises reported in chapter 4, some of the larger and well-intentioned franchise operations flounder because of sudden overexpansion and/or inexperience.

One of the most dramatic examples of rags to riches and almost back again in only three years was that of the National Pizza Corp. Two young men of Saint Louis, Hershey Moss and Stuart Hoffman, self-styled swingers, launched their skyrocketing business in 1967 with $5,000 of borrowed capital, $2,000 of it on a bank credit card. They bought fifty tabletop pizza ovens and placed them in taverns, bowling alleys, snack bars, and similar locations. (The ovens were do-it-yourself cookers that warmed up a frozen pizza for about $1.25.) They soon started franchising, and by 1968 had seven hundred distributors and $4 million a year in sales. They now were manufacturing their own pizza ovens and other materials. A franchise cost about $4,000 and included an oven and other materials needed for setting up pizza stations. By June of 1969 they were offering stock to the public at $6 a share.[16]

By now they were branching into other franchise businesses. These included Leisure Time Films (franchising rear-projection color movie devices for bars and so forth); a One-Hour Carpeting Cleaning franchise; National Pok-O-Golf, for which they sold both the coin-operated golf game machines and the distributorships; and Vel-Vett, a franchised process for shooting nylon fiber on walls and other surfaces to achieve a velvet effect.

National Pizza also took over the franchising for Wig Chateau, which called for an investment of $16,000 for hair goods, spray, and other materials and equipment, and training in wigging.

But by 1970 the roof fell in. There were complaints from franchisees that some of the equipment was faulty, that—in some cases at least—the company did not secure enough or satisfactory locations, and that the ovens were overpriced and

The Money Prowlers and Interest Nibblers 77

the pizzas inferior to those demonstrated by sales representatives. A Michigan high-school principal, who expected a second income from a string of pizza-oven locations, demanded full reimbursement even for pizzas that had spoiled in cold storage. There were complaints that some salesmen had misrepresented. The background of some of the salesmen indeed was questionable.

Only in America can you start a multimillion-dollar business on a credit card. But also in America the faster the skyrocket, often the faster the fizzle. By the spring of 1970 National Pizza's young heads had sold their 70 percent stock interest to a restaurant chain. The stock was now quoted at $1.25 a share.[17] They also had closed several subsidiaries and announced they would concentrate on marketing frozen pizzas through stores, but would no longer franchise them.

Not all the National Pizza ventures had unreasonable prospects and some are continuing today. But the rush to expand had resulted in some faulty equipment, some untested and unworkable business ideas, and had lost much time and money for many of the investors both in the franchises and the corporation's stock.

Another skyrocketing franchise developed by an energetic young man that attracted even some of the largest Wall Street firms before it sputtered was AAA Enterprises, Inc., of Atlanta. Like National Pizza's young officials, Jackie G. Williams had started with a $7,000 loan, buying and selling mobile homes. By the time he was thirty-two he was a multimillionaire with his own jet plane and parklike offices decorated with beautiful secretaries, and was franchising Bonanza and Upside Down Charley's mobile-home lots, *The New York Times* reported.

Williams then started offering franchises for mobile tax-service offices and carpet stores, and committed his company to come up with a "new franchise concept" every month. A syndicate of brokers headed by Francis I. duPont, A. C. Allyn, Inc., floated a stock issue at $13 a share in May, 1969. Five months later the stock was selling for $26.[18]

But ten months later it was down to $2, as the company

began to suffer losses. In what is now becoming a familiar sequence, controversies developed over whether AAA was living up to franchise agreements, and future franchise fees already reported on the company's books as income began to turn delinquent.

Like the two young Saint Louisans, Williams and AAA have retrenched and now are concentrating on making and selling mobile homes, not on franchising.

The difficulties franchisees may encounter is shown by the testimony of Dr. Victor Nitti during the investigation conducted by the Senate Subcommittee on Urban and Rural Development.

Dr. Nitti, a New Jersey dentist, and his brother-in-law put $27,000 into a franchise for renting tools and equipment. The franchisor, A to Z Rental Inc. of Chicago, was a subsidiary of Nationwide Industries, a publicly owned company. The rental service offered everything from dinnerware for a party to snowplows.

Nitti and his brother-in-law agreed to pay a fee of 3¾ percent of gross income for ten years. In return they were to be provided with necessary expertise. They bought $30,000 worth of equipment as inventory with a $7,500 down payment, financing the balance with A to Z at 8½ percent over five years. It also was necessary to prove that they had backup money of $6,000 to help over the initial period.

Nitti testified they had twice as much money as they were told they needed. And they lost it all. He said, "The franchisor projected our first year's gross income at $39,000. We actually grossed a little over $20,000. What went wrong? We had followed the training instructions to the letter." They had a location on a main shopping street.

But when they got down to the nitty-gritty of making sales, they found that three or four months after their grand opening there were days that failed to produce a single dollar. Gradually they learned that this also was the experience of some of the other A to Z franchisees. Dr. Nitti's testimony goes on to point out that on December 2, 1969, A to Z Rental Inc. and the parent Nationwide Industries went bankrupt.

The company's stock, the testimony cited, had been floated at $13.75 a share. With over $14 million in capital it embarked on acquisitions, buying one company after another, including Prescription City System, Inc., to sell medicines and rent or sell medical equipment. The stock soared to $54. An earlier book on franchising—*The Franchising Boom*—had spoken glowingly of Nationwide as exemplifying "the new trend in second-generation franchising which is to become a holding company conglomerate of other franchised business."

But within twenty-one months of going public Nationwide declared bankruptcy.

Nitti had gone over the agreement with his lawyer. Unfortunately, he said, there are not enough attorneys familiar with the inadequacy of legislation supposed to protect franchise investors.

Nitti's complaints are instructive to others interested in franchises, as clues to what to investigate.

——They were permitted to open just before winter, acknowledged to be the worst period for this type of service.

——They were promised nationwide TV promotion. It came seven months later, but on a much smaller scale.

——The business development manager supposed to help them get started did not turn up until four months later.

——They paid list price for inventory. When Nitti's brother-in-law and his wife went to Illinois for their one-week training, they were given the lists of equipment to be bought from A to Z. Most was available on the open market for less, Nitti testified.

——When a director of A to Z visited them in the spring of 1969, he informed them that a $30,000 inventory in fact was too small to sustain a business, let alone produce a profit. (They had found this to be true. Often they had to refer customers to a competitor or borrow from another center and split the rental.)

Throughout that summer and the next fall, other A to Z centers were failing, including one on Long Island, New York (later to carry the name of Ed McMahon Center after the TV personality whose picture appeared in A to Z advertising).

When Dr. Nitti fell behind in payments, he testified, the

treasurer told him that forty out of four hundred A to Z franchises were in trouble, which the company did not consider too bad. But, Nitti complained, nowhere in the promotion material was this failure rate mentioned. While the SEC requires that prospectuses for new stock offerings spell out the investment risk, this is not so with franchising.

Now, as in other burgeoning franchise conglomerates, retrenchment has taken place. Some of the franchises have been taken over by longer-established rental firms.

Fast-food and highway restaurants have become the most hyperactive franchise businesses following the success of such giants as Howard Johnson, MacDonald's, Kentucky Fried Chicken, and several others. The *Pilot Directory of Franchising Organizations* lists over two hundred major fast-food franchises, screened (usually successfully) to eliminate those that have proved troublesome. There is an investment range from as little as $3,500 for "secret formula" Heavenly Fried Chicken, to $65,000 for a Benihana of Tokyo Japanese Steak Restaurant.

But even with the established successes, and for one reason because of them, an investor attracted by the fast-food boom can not assume similar success for other franchises. The risk is illustrated by the fate of franchisees of the Jolly Giant drive-in restaurants. In a consent order against Meal or Snack System, Inc., the FTC reported that all the franchisees who used its methods and took its training were out of business by 1969.

The FTC charged that the franchises cost much more than the represented $8,500 to $9,500; franchisees investing $9,500 did not earn $30,000 a year; the companies did not have national contracts to provide supplies at less than those charged other restaurants; the training was not complete but actually inadequate; and the promotional program was not at all extensive but consisted of one plastic advertising mat and one cloth banner.

While there is no reason to doubt either the sincerity or taste buds of Minnie Pearl, the country singer, or John Jay Hooker, Jr., a leading Tennessee politician, thousands of people who bought franchises or stock in the past three years are still wondering if Minnie can outfry eighty-year-old Colonel Sanders well enough to retrieve their investments.

Hooker, a lawyer and occasional candidate for the governorship, organized Minnie Pearl's Chicken System. Of about 1,600 franchises sold during the three years, by 1970 only 260 were in operation; many others had been delayed by inability to obtain operating funds; and some 12 others closed because of unprofitability.

Hooker sold stock to his friends and acquaintances at 50 cents a share. According to R. W. Apple, Jr., in *The New York Times*, these included leading Tennessee newspaper publishers, judges, congressmen, and many small politicians and family retainers. Six months after the stock was publicly offered in May, 1968, the shares were selling above $60, even though only five chicken stands were built when the stock went on the market.[19] But six months after that, the shares in the company (now known as Performance Systems, Inc.) had dropped to $33, on an adjusted basis, and by mid-1970, to about $9.

Both the SEC and the Senate subcommittee investigating franchises now were looking into the company's problems, including the frequently used practice of counting receipts and notes for sales of franchises as current income. Hooker's friends who bought shares at 50 cents made money, some of them a lot.

The prospectus was obviously frank. It pointed out the speculative nature of the shares, if any of the investors had really read and heeded its warnings. But the combination of franchise industry glamour, Wall Street enthusiasm for a quick buck, success of other fast-food franchises, and publicity generated by the celebrities involved in the venture apparently had overcome needed investment caution and outweighed the obvious inexperience of the promoters. Hooker himself still hopes for success. He and his brother pledged several million to provide new capital.

Even some of the well-established franchise organizations can be quite severe in dealing with franchisees, as some of the government agencies and businessmen's organizations have come to realize.

Dias, head of the Association of Franchised Businessmen, told about these misadventures reported to him by worried and disappointed franchisees.

> *From Little Rock:* A year ago I bought a dry-cleaning franchise as an investment. One month after opening I found that the dry cleaning machine was six months old. It was a model that sold in 1963 for $2,900. I paid $7,000 plus freight and installation. The rent that they negotiated was far out of line, and parts of the installation were inferior. I lost $12,000 in ten months.

> *From Omaha:* We purchased a franchise for $8,700. The company did not fulfill the contract we signed with them, would not answer our letters or calls, sent equipment that didn't work . . . and THEN sent us a letter canceling our contract as they were organizing a new company.

> *From New York:* My mother, owner of this store (bakery and doughnut) put a mortgage on her home to give her children a business and a good future retirement. Last summer she had to remortgage her home for an additional $10,000 so the franchisor wouldn't take legal action to close our shop since we could not afford to pay their commissions. We have had thirty-two failures of equipment in twenty-nine weeks of operation. I have asked the franchisor for help on how to make this a profitable business. His representative said: "Clean shop; good display of product; pleasant sales girls. You have all these." That was the last help we received.
>
> Here is an expense example for one week: register reading average during first year, $2,800. Expenses: salaries, $1,200; rent, $263; commissions, $196; milk, flour, doughnut fills, other ingredients, $608; paper goods, $90; loan, $163. Balance of $280 has to cover utilities, insurance, accounting, maintenance, baker training.

> *From Los Angeles:* I paid $8,500 for a territorial franchise involving sale of advertising on filmscreens. After investing $4,600 on filmscreens I ceased to receive communications from the

company and had to function without their support. I have subsequently terminated my business at great loss.

The "unrestrained pitch handed out to potential franchisees through advertising and so-called franchise consultants and brokers" has become a major problem in the fast-foods field today, reported Thomas H. Murphy, publisher of *Continental Franchise Review*. He told about a Pennsylvania franchisor who made an intrastate stock offering (thus avoiding SEC disclosure regulations). The company was selling its own securities, telling potential stockholders that they were experts in the fast-foods field.

Their program consisted of a menu of "honey fried chicken," a hamburger developed by a Pennsylvania Dutchman who had been successful in marketing it, and a series of flavored hot dogs. This company had never actually developed a single product. Their honey fried chicken was a name only. They had not developed the technique of producing the Dutch hamburger. They were planning to cook the hot dogs in a $1,200 microwave oven that, Murphy said, sounded like a great engineering innovation but would have created a bottleneck in serving and increased production costs.

These people really knew little about the fast-foods business and were mainly merchandising food names.

In the case of a new and untried franchisor, your franchise fee may not pay for management experience at all but simply for trying out an idea on your capital, Hoffman warned. At the least every franchise should have a pilot operation that a careful investor can study.

Some franchisors also are too willing to take chances on unsuitable franchisees. A leading operator-franchisor, Herbert Wetanson, publicly criticized franchisors who have said to him, "If this guy goes bankrupt, we have another one on line behind him." Obviously you need to be careful about franchise ads that say no experience needed and of promoters who try hard to sell you instead of also evaluating your abilities.

Wetanson also charged that many franchisors establish

dummy real-estate corporations that guarantee leases. Or the franchisee has to guarantee the lease. The safer way for the franchisee is for the franchisor to find the location and guarantee the lease, and even sometimes get the building built.[20]

Another troubled franchise business is auto transmission repair services. For some years the Federal Trade Commission and several state attorneys general have issued complaints against a number of franchised outlets of AAMCO Automatic Transmission, Inc. (as well as some transmission centers of other companies).

A frequent complaint was that the AAMCO centers cited would advertise a low price for dismantling and inspecting transmission. But the complaints said, the price did not include reassembly. That cost extra.

In one case cited by the Minnesota attorney general, a Saint Paul car owner complained that he answered an AAMCO ad for transmission overhaul for $75. After work started, he was quoted $230. When he ordered the firm to stop work, his transmission was given back to him in pieces in the trunk of his car.

Then in 1967, the parent AAMCO company, headed by a former Boston dance studio operator, wrote to all Better Business Bureaus that it was discontinuing its national TV and other ads for "$23 tear-down and inspection." These had featured Zsa Zsa Gabor. Saint Louis television stations and newspapers had refused AAMCO price advertising even before 1967.

AAMCO shops by no means have been the only transmission shops cited by government agencies. AAMCO itself pointed out to the bureaus the hard-sell practices of other companies too, which was true enough.

But in 1970, despite the previous announcement of the change in business methods, the FTC lowered the boom. Up to now the citations had been against individual franchisees. Now the commission charged that the parent franchisor had used deceptive advertising to lure customers, then itself had directed centers to refuse to reassemble a customer's transmission if no further work was ordered, and also failed to disclose the use of old parts.

While the motel industry has the fewest problems in the franchise industry, they have invaded even this area. Murphy reported that Dutch Inns of America sold franchises throughout the country at $12,000 a motel. Then the franchisee had to sign a lease back to them for operation on the basis that financing would be readily available because of the long-term lease signed by Dutch Inns. Nearly any franchisee realizes that financing does come easy if he can get a major long-term lease on his motel. But this was not true with Dutch Inns, because of the company's insolvency.

The terms specified that Dutch Inns would furnish operating capital, furnish the motel, and staff it with expert personnel. Dutch Inns stated that they had sold over seventy of these franchises in a very short time. The SEC reported that they had in fact sold seventy of this type contract in 1968. By simple arithmetic, Dutch Inns had incurred approximately $14 million in liabilities by signing these contracts. A financial statement issued in Wyoming (after one of their sales to a franchisee) showed that total assets were $250,000 and liabilities approximately $2 million.

The amazing thing is what happened when the company took over Congress Inns and some of this franchisor's personnel. Congress Inns similarly had sold franchises for the same $12,000. Congress Inns was unable to perform and most franchisees lost their investments. Congress personnel who went to work for Dutch Inns went back to former Congress franchisees, knowing they were prime prospects because their motel dreams were still vacant lots, and sold them a Dutch Inn franchise for another $12,000. Their motel dreams are still vacant lots, Murphy reported.

Perhaps the most shattering experience was that of distributors for the Success Motivation Institute of Waco, Texas. The FTC complained that the institute recruited distributors through ads, but courses were difficult to sell, the institute made "no bona fide effort" to determine whether the prospective distributor had the appropriate personality, verbal skills, and other attributes, and "a substantial number" did not achieve success in selling the Success course. No doubt they were not properly motivated.

The role of celebrities in franchising also came under the cool eye of the Senate subcommittee investigating franchising headed by Senator Harrison Williams of New Jersey.

Zsa Zsa herself had been assessed $1,000 by the New York State attorney general in 1967 when he enjoined ten AAMCO franchised shops from alleged fraudulent and illegal practices. "We're not too happy with personalities lending their names to companies many of them know nothing about," Barnett Levy, head of the Attorney General's Bureau of Consumer Frauds, commented at the time.[21]

Celebrities who have lent their names and at least varying measures of talent and activity to franchised operations include Edie Adams' Cut and Curl; Al Hirt's Sandwich Saloons; Eddy Arnold's chicken shops; Johnny Carson's Here's Johnny's food shops; Mickey Mantle's Country Cookin' and men's shops; Tennessee Ernie Ford Foods; Arnold Palmer driving ranges and putting courses; and many others such as Trini Lopez, Al Capp, Sammy Davis, Jr., and Arthur Treacher.

The Gabors are big in franchising. Sister Eva promotes the Eva Gabor International Wig Boutiques owned largely by two Kansas City industrialists.

The Senate subcommittee was concerned by charges that celebrities collected royalties on the use of their names without actual familiarity with the soundness of the businesses.

"When a man picks up a check, in one instance in seven figures, what has he done other than lend his name?" Senator Marlow Cook of Kentucky demanded to know. "Don't you think the real answer is to see that when somebody goes into the franchise business he not only lends his name, he also lends money and his effort [and] assumes the responsibility of seeing that it is a success?"

Johnny Carson and Joe Namath (Broadway Joe's restaurants), among others, assured the senators that they observed operations and did participate. Namath pointed out that many of his football friends invested in Broadway Joe's, and as the largest stockholder, he was concerned about the safety of their money too. (Obviously Namath would not want to antagonize opposing linemen who might be investors.) But, it later developed, apparently he had overextended himself in franchised restaurant investments and he himself was dropped by Broadway Joe's as the chain encountered financial problems.

Jackie Robinson, vice-president of Sea Host restaurants, told about his own active involvement but also added his concern that investors may be "duped by a name" rather than investigate the product and the company.

Minnie Pearl, who had been asked to go into the chicken business by her old friend, John Hooker, Jr., told the senators how she cares:

> I was assured right from the beginning that I would be part of the business. I have an office and a secretary and I am there every day I am in town. . . . I have had the pleasure of knowing our franchisees . . . and of going to our openings and signing autographs. I feel I should take an interest in the stores and go over there and I always give them a picture and autograph it and I say on one side of it: "I care." And I do care. It means a great deal to me that our business should be operated in a clean, safe, sanitary, courteous manner with quality control. . . .

The regulators too have come under fire. John Young Brown, president of Kentucky Fried Chicken, criticized the FTC and other agencies for inadequate protection of "small businessmen who often scrape up every dime they can and put it all on one dream of a franchising concept that could be misleading."* He warned of a "tremendous influx of fast-buck promoters" in many fields outside the basic franchise industry (car, oil, drug, and bottling companies), almost to the extent of a "carnival atmosphere." He candidly told the subcommittee:

> For example, in the Wall Street Journal, New York Times or Washington Post, you see a number of franchise ads promising

---

* Subsequently the FTC indicated its concern by launching, in May, 1970, an investigation of franchising, ordering fifty franchisors to file special reports on their activities. On the basis of the data obtained, the commission will establish guidelines for contracts and for advertising franchise opportunities.

that a man can make $50,000 on a $10,000 or $20,000 investment. The slick promoters dream up a roadside franchise, and the next day advertise that it is a proven franchise with a trademark that is a household word. They overexaggerate performance statements when in fact they have no stores in operation. The Small Business Administration has a responsibility and ought to take a more active role to fully inform the small businessman before he makes a commitment. . . . The Department of Commerce could be helpful in offering more information. . . . As a last resort I would even recommend that the franchisors themselves offer some type of service.

The neutral position taken by government agencies in the explosion of franchise problems also has been criticized by Dias, although he did credit the FTC as "the only government agency which has taken a realistic position and made it known."

Even among the famous, well-established franchises, bitterness has erupted. Nearly one-third of all franchisees have had legal disputes with their franchisors, according to Professor Donald M. Thompson of the University of Alberta.[22]

Most of the legal disputes involve either agreements requiring franchisees to buy supplies from franchisors or territorial rights of franchisees.

Legitimate franchising undoubtedly has become a permanent part of American business and investment life, especially for smaller businessmen. Already an estimated one-fourth of all small businesses are franchised operations.

But if you are attracted to franchising by the stories of success and the undoubted successes, you do need realistic insights into the troubled side of paradise too. Here are the problems with which you may have to cope, as reported by critics of present franchising practices in asking Congress for remedial legislation:

Exaggerated Advantages: "The media have published stories unwittingly magnifying the advantages of franchising to the investor," Dias charged. "They have helped create the prevailing opinion that there are few failures; that it is the ideal way for budding entrepreneurs to get started, or for retired businessmen to invest their nest egg . . . [they] either gloss over or completely ignore the other side of the story."

But Dias also asserted that some studies of returns on this investment, such as the 15 percent reported by the Boston College franchise study center, are exaggerated.

Another claimed exaggeration, according to Harold Brown, Boston lawyer and author of *Franchising: Trap for the Trusting*, is the often quoted figure that franchisees have a failure rate of 10 percent or less compared with 50 percent among independent businessmen. These figures were taken from a master's degree thesis by a graduate student and were based on seventy carefully selected franchisors, not on a random selection. (Other estimates of franchisee failure are as high as 40 percent.)

Exaggeration of Earnings: A leading deception is false statements or exaggeration of earnings to be expected by the franchise, Hale, of the FTC, reported. Claims such as "earn $20,000 per year" and "you can earn $8 per hour" would be deceptive unless justified by the facts. Too frequently these facts are not to be found, he said. The fact that one, two, or several franchisees are earning the amount claimed is not enough to justify the claims.

Advertised earnings must be customary, usual, and typical of those earned by other franchisees, Hale pointed out. Even if a large number of franchisees are earning the amount claimed, the claim is deceptive if the present franchisees are located in prime locations and the franchises now offered are in less desirable locations.

Representations such as "in your spare time" and "several hours each evening" should mean just that, Hale warned. If the franchisee must spend more time than that advertised, the claim probably is deceptive.

Demanding Work: Often the franchisee must work harder and longer hours than he had anticipated. There is "constant pressure, and control by the company to impose mandatory working hours and high sales quotas," Cohen charged.

Franchisor's Inadequacies: The franchisee also may find, in gray-area operations, that the franchisor has poor management, insufficient capital and cash flow, and ill-conceived marketing concepts.

One-Sided Control: Should he overcome all other problems and make a financial success of the franchise, he still may have trouble, Dias warned. If he has a short-term franchise, it may be terminated and the franchisor may take over the operation. If he has a long-term franchise, it can be canceled for a score of reasons contained in small print. Or he may find he has a new competitor in his own exclusive area—his own franchisor. This is often coupled with loss of cooperation from the franchisor and frustration in getting supplies, advertising, or other services the franchisor is expected to furnish for him.

Angry charges of one-sided control, and severe at that, have been voiced by a number of experts. There is a noticeable disparity in the positions of the two parties.

"The franchisor inculcates the franchisee with the necessity of being taught, guided, and controlled not only through the initial training period but throughout the existence of the franchise," Brown told the Senate subcommittee. "This control is buttressed by the contractual requirements . . . upon pain of losing the franchise if he does not. Upon termination or failure to renew, the franchisee is confronted with the covenant not to compete and forfeiture of his equity."

Many franchise agreements permit the franchisor to cancel a contract even if the franchisee is operating profitably, David B. Slater, president of the Mutual Franchise Corp., told the 1969 International Conference on Franchising. Thus, a franchisee who, without competent legal guidance, signed such a contract can be forced to negotiate a new contract at a higher fee.

But while the franchisee often must live with fear of loss of his investment through cancellation or termination "for minor contract infringements," he himself has only limited or even no rights to transfer his franchise, Cohen pointed out.

Roessner pointed out that the dream of independence as owner of one's business really can be an illusion for franchisees as "most must agree to run their business exactly as the franchisor demands, [building] to his specifications on a site he helps them select."[23] Often also his selling prices and product offerings are restricted, regardless of local competitive situations.

Prices of Supplies: A frequent complaint of franchisees is that they are required to buy supplies from designated companies, but the prices negotiated or charged by the franchisor may be higher than from other suppliers. Sometimes franchisees have complained about discrimination—that some franchisees are charged less than others.

Franchisees already have won several court victories over this issue. In a 1970 case, expected to be appealed, a jury found that a requirement by Chicken Delight and its parent Consolidated Foods, Inc., for the purchase of packaging, dips, cookware, and so forth was an unlawful tie-in.[24] In another instance, involving the right of Midas Muffler franchisees to bring suit against the franchisor for full-line forcing, the court was impressed "by the fact that the dealers had to pay more when buying exclusively from Midas," Commissioner MacIntyre pointed out. Further "the court was unimpressed by a favorite justification of franchisors that exclusive dealing [benefits] dealers because of consumer acceptance of the franchisor's brands."[25]

On the other hand, some franchisors are reported to try to make savings for their outlets on supplies, which can help offset some of the royalty fee. In any case, the comparative cost of supplies is an important point to investigate.

Take-overs: A growing worry is take-overs of franchise systems by large corporations. A "trend toward concentration of franchising among America's largest corporations," John Buffington, FTC general counsel, called it.

"The great importance presently attributed to franchising's renewal of opportunities for businessmen would be a grievous error if these men, financed by Small Business Administration loans or from their own life savings were eventually absorbed by large corporations," Buffington warned. "Instances where franchise systems, which owed their success to the hard work and investment of the franchisee, have been taken over by giants include Burger Chef, now owned by General Foods; Shakey's Pizza, owned by Great Western United, the Colorado-based conglomerate; Stuckey's, bought by Pet, Inc."

Fees: Cohen called them "exorbitant" and "out of proportion to sales volume." (They usually are 3 to 5 percent.) Complaints of discrimination also have been made in royalties charged.

Even with all these problems, a well-informed investor able to negotiate a fair contract with a reputable franchisor can still find franchising a rewarding endeavor, Dias advised. But a franchise is not a license to mint money at someone else's risk, one franchise-system president said. "For their $13,000 to $20,000 cash investment and eighty hours of hard work [a week] we expect the first year, all that franchisees can expect is a fair reward for their labor and a reasonable return on their capital investment," he candidly warned.

In defending franchisors, Philip Zeidman, counsel for the International Franchise Association, conceded that there are abuses. He agreed that franchising will not save a small businessman who does not have "the basic ingredients required for success in business today," nor will it win acceptance for a product that does not meet a felt public need. But, quoting a U.S. court in the case of *Susser* v. *Carvel*, he argued that "the franchise method of operation has the advantage . . . of enabling numerous groups of individuals with small capital to become entrepreneurs." Instead of additional regulatory legislation (introduced in 1970 by Senator Williams) Zeidman urged "greater restraint and cooperation" and increased use of existing laws to eliminate the abuses "of the few un-

The Money Prowlers and Interest Nibblers   93

principled or misguided franchisors who fail to perform as they promise."

Robert Metz reported in *Franchising: How to Select a Business of Your Own* that a University of Minnesota study found that successful dealers usually had management experience before they came to franchising, some competence in a technical or professional area such as bookkeeping, or substantial experience in a related field.

But critics insist that laws providing for more equality in transactions between franchisor and franchisee are needed. From all the evidence Mrs. Toombs and I studied, there seems no doubt that presently the franchisors are more equal than the franchisees.

The two points of greatest concern are the frequent lack of full disclosure of the franchisor's financial status and the fear of termination that haunts not only mom-and-pop teams running a roadside hamburger stand but also large, successful franchises.

"On the termination of a franchise, the assumption of many franchisors seems to be that the franchisee has contributed little to the business and that the only intangible asset of any value is the franchisor's trademark which automatically reverts back to the franchisor," reported Rufus E. Wilson, chief of the FTC's Division of General Trade Restraints. "There is little recognition of the fact that the franchisee's investment of effort, time, and money may have enhanced the value of the franchisor's trademark in the particular area and that the franchisee may be entitled to a fair compensation when the franchise is terminated or transferred to another franchisee. An equitable franchise agreement would take into account contributions made by the franchisee to the business."

In fact, compulsory reversion to the franchisor of all rights without adequate compensation could be construed by the FTC as an unfair practice or unfair method of competition, Wilson warned.[26]

The legal changes sought by the franchise critics offer useful clues to potential investors as to what information to look and ask for. In general the reformers want these requirements:

———Provision for full financial data from franchisors such as is required by the SEC for securities, including balance sheet, profit and loss statement, and working capital schedule. (The reformers want this data required without regard to the present controversy over whether a franchise should be considered a security like stocks.) A franchisor, who does not adequately disclose, can collide with present laws. Section 12 of the FTC act specifically prohibits false advertising. Commissioner MacIntyre warned franchisors, "Not only must the franchisor give accurate information . . . he also has the affirmative duty to reveal any unfavorable news concerning his system."[27]

———A statement of the company's chronological development and expertise, with all sales material and brochures filed with appropriate government agencies.

———Some provision—arbitration, for example—for evaluating the franchisee's contribution and recompense if terminated.

———Biographical disclosure on directors and officers, detailing experience and company's chronological development and expertise.

———More exact information about the nature of the training.

CHAPTER SIX

Stock and Front-Money Gambles— and Sometimes Swindles

Government authorities have had to combat a surprising number of high-pressure promotions exploiting interest in livestock and oil lease participations, and highly speculative and sometimes even fraudulent stock and other investments. The speculative climate and unusually high interest rates again provided an opportunity for law-skirting promoters and actual swindlers.

The Case of the Vanished Herd

Several leading Midwest businessmen, including three officials of two Illinois banks, already have been found guilty of mail fraud in promoting cattle investment clubs. The clubs supposedly provided a way an investor could own—without putting up any money—a herd of cattle being fattened for market. The investors, who lost a total of $1.5 million, included doctors, lawyers, bankers, and stockbrokers—the authorities small investors are supposed to look to for advice.

Each investor was allowed to buy one hundred head of cattle. Instead of laying down cash, the bank loaned him his entire investment on a two-hundred-day note taking a 100 percent mortgage on the cattle as security.

Western Testing Inc. and Better Beef Inc., both of Illinois, then were to buy the cattle for the clubs, fatten them in a feedlot operation, and sell them before the two hundred days elapsed.

Unfortunately for the investors, their financial castle collapsed when almost half of twelve thousand head of cattle the firms were supposed to be feeding could not be found.

Western Testing and Better Beef went into bankruptcy—and the investors became liable for mortgage repayments. Some lost heavily when the notes fell due with no cattle to sell.

In the spring of 1970, the operator of Western Testing and Better Beef was found guilty of mail fraud and securities violations, along with the former president and board chairman, the assistant vice-president of the State Bank of East Moline, and a farm loan manager for the Moline National Bank.

Front Money and the Penalty of Leadership

Perhaps because of the general climate of high interest rates in the late 1960s and 1970, a number of schemes have developed based on high interest rates, sometimes also promising shares in business along with return of the money.

In Saint Louis, in a typical but big front-money scheme, the Diversified Brokers Co. snared some 4,400 investors for an average of $1,800 by selling them promissory notes with promised returns of 40 to 100 percent. The company sold these notes to investors from Indiana to California. The brokers claimed they bought distress commodities and government surplus which were resold at a huge profit.

The investors destroyed themselves by their own greed in the hope of an impossible gain, and were also seduced by expensive entertainment provided by the firm. At the trial, the company's auditor testified the firm owed investors and lenders a total of $15 million.

All that was left was about $1.5 million in cash in banks and an assortment of art, antiques, and expensive office furniture, including a framed motto, The Penalty of Leadership.[28]

In this case the penalty of leadership proved to be jail sentences: Donald P. Smallwood, the president, for thirty-five years, Vice-president Roy Lay, for twenty, and Harold Connell, the secretary, for five.

The Money Prowlers and Interest Nibblers

But the final tragedy, John L. O'Brien noted, was recorded in April, 1970, when a young housewife who had lost $10,000 to Diversified Brokers bought a store, to try to recoup and have funds to educate her children, and was murdered in a holdup.

O'Brien's comment on this widespread disaster is that "time and again people come to the bureau to inquire, often after they have invested, not to really find out the facts but to gain our reassurance on their good business judgment."

The Oil Venture Frauds

Publicity about oil lease ventures used by large investors for both gains and tax loopholes also has attracted promoters with their own brand of win-nothing, lose-all promotions (at least, an unquestionable tax deduction).

Two Louisiana men doing business as Rebel Drilling Co. already have been convicted of making numerous misrepresentations in selling almost $3 million worth of fractional interest in oil and gas leases. One official of another Louisiana firm, Underwriters Investment Corp., has been sentenced, and six others are awaiting trial at this writing for the sale of worthless oil stocks and other securities. Another oil stock promoter awaiting trial even promised each investor he would be named to the board of directors.

In another case two Colorado promoters doing business as Paramount Oil Co. and U.S. Geological Service got jail terms for inducing investors in oil and gas leases to buy geological evaluations, representing falsely that the leases were valuable and would be bought by Paramount.

Puffery in Commodities Trading

Another type of venture formerly reserved for the well-to-do but now reaching for moderate-income investors, is commodities trading. There is nothing fraudulent usually in such trading, but exaggerated promises of return are. The FTC already has charged one Chicago trading company with misrepresenting potential profits and minimizing the "substantial risk" of trading in commodity futures.

The Worrisome Insurance Investment

One new type of promotion worrying Better Business Bureaus and the insurance industry, and under investigation by a number of state officials, is the recently organized charter insurance companies. This new type of company includes in its insurance policies an agreement entitling the policyholder to share in company profits.

What concerns the public and private agencies is that salesmen, many of them former salesmen for food-freezer plans and utensils sold door-to-door, emphasize the speculative profit-sharing side of the offer.

Too, most of the charter insurance promotions have been in states with relatively weak state insurance departments. Unfortunately, as in some of the multi-distributorship promotions, some of these companies have had the names of leading citizens associated with them.

Some states now have prohibited such insurance plans on the basis that, as the statute says, they are "misleading" and "unable to perform as claimed." One Better Business Bureau manager reported that he was dismayed at the rapid-fire sales talks he monitored, and his own inability to follow the figures that included a suggestion that an estate of some $50,000 to $60,000 could be built by investing $500 to $600 for perhaps twelve years.

One company promised a "guaranteed cash return" of $200 a year, which sounds impressive but is really only a return of part of an excessive premium.

The Classic Case of the Shaky Ground Floor

While such newer schemes are coming to the fore, misrepresentation and illegal sale of stocks and other securities is still the major problem plaguing the innocent investor, who is not necessarily always a small investor.

The case cited by Stanley Sporkin of the SEC Trading Division as the classic one involving investment fraud through promotional material was that of First Standard Corp., with offices in New York, Miami, and West Montreal. The entire operation was a beautifully presented house of cards, Sporkin said. It should be instructive for all investors eager to get in on the ground floor of new products.

First Standard had described some fascinating-sounding products indeed in a handsomely printed annual report that it distributed to prospective investors until enjoined by a U.S. district court.

But, the SEC charged, the company had no marketable product, was not engaged in any production activities, did not intend to, and had no present assurance of income or anticipation of earnings.

The prospectus described a transistorized record player, Discomatic, in glowing terms. In actual fact, the company had neither contracts nor patents for its production or distribution. It merely had a sample. With respect to "radio sunglasses," the corporation had samples but no contracts for production or distribution.

For the Electronic Shinemaster the company described, it had distribution rights in Canada, but had not engaged in distribution or done any market analysis to find out if the product would have any acceptance.

With respect to Playboy Corporation, a company of that name was formed in Panama, but no plans existed for establishment of any such clubs. The SEC said there was no relationship to Playboy International Clubs Ltd., which had challenged the use of the name.

With respect to the manufacture of coats and dresses under the Louis Jerome label, neither First Standard nor Louis Jerome Fashions actually manufactured any garments.

With respect to the video tape recorder, First Standard had a prototype under test. But it did not intend to manufacture the item, had no orders, and did not know whether the product was suitable for production.

One division, the Lucey Corp., had done some business but at a loss. First Standard also did have a 50 percent interest in a motorbike company but no dealerships had been set. It did not have any tobacco division as stated; and the self-lighting cigarettes it told about actually had not been manufactured, and it was not even known if they were practical. The company also had a Helipod division but no operational Helipod.

Interestingly, the company had used a famous firm of auditors, two leading New York banks as depositories, and a large New Jersey bank as transfer agent for its stock.

The letter from the president to the stockholders actually told the truth: "First Standard Corp. was engaged . . . from its inception in research and development to market a product under the trade name Aplo Therm . . . First Standard Corp. with its present limited capital is not desirous of owning physical assets such as factories, land, or maintaining a large personnel staff. The company feels that through the purchase of patents, product developments, and research and interest into growth potential fields and through subcontracting for manufacture and franchising sales, the same control can be maintained . . . thus eliminating the need for considerable working capital and a large permanent staff . . ."

Now comes the part that fooled by implication: "The following pages will in detail explain each corporation's activities . . . and the diversified areas in which your company will operate. We are pleased to inform you that recently Acme Missiles and Construction Corp. (ASE) and Transcontinental Investing Co. acquired a substantial stock interest in your company. It is hoped that the continued assistance and cooperation of these two firms will contribute materially to the progress of your company."

Products were introduced like this: "Your company has procured the services of Japanese and American Associates to obtain products which could be produced in Japan and mass marketed in the United States. Presently your company has purchased a completed prototype 'Discomatic,' a fully transistorized record player.

"Your company has incorporated Playboy Corp. in Panama and is in the process of forming Playboy Facilities . . ."

Inexperienced investors often succumb to questionable stock investments because they fail to examine or understand the prospectus, Ralph Smathers, president of the Miami BBB, warned.

The Sound of Respectability

Solid-sounding names may hide some serious misrepresentations nowadays. Nothing could sound more conservative than the Arkansas Loan and Thrift Corp. Yet four principals were found guilty of misrepresenting the safety of the firm's common stock and bond certificates, and its financial condition.

Aldridge International Associates, Inc., also sounded impressive. But Jack Aldridge, Indianapolis, was found guilty of manipulating the sale of securities through fraudulent representations and promises so that he got the proceeds of the sales without benefit to the investors.

Equally impressive were such names as General Income Distributors, Inc., General Income Sponsors of Iowa, and Mortgage Investors of Iowa. The principals sold preferred stock in these firms, then diverted the assets to another company they controlled and converted the money to their own use.

Hot Tips and Great Expectations

Many cases in which the SEC has had to act involve concerted high-pressure sales campaigns to sell highly speculative securities by brokerage firms themselves. These campaigns usually include the use of false and misleading representations and—note well—predictions. In recent years the SEC also has had to revoke the registration, as market advisers, of a number of publishers of overenthusiastic stock-market-tip newsletters. In the case of Marketlines, Inc., the SEC complained, and a court of appeals affirmed, the content and tone of ads for the publication "was designed to whet the appetite of the unsophisticated." In another case in 1969, the SEC accused the editor of two stock market letters of buying certain stocks, then recommending them in his letters and selling them when the prices had risen.

Sometimes a new company still not in operation can become the objective of speculative stock trading even by established securities dealers. This happened in the case of Chill Can Industries, formerly known as Interstate Development Corp., a Florida company. In 1970 the SEC ordered temporary suspension of trading in the securities because the only known financial information about the company was a balance sheet dated August 15, 1969, showing that the main asset was the patent rights to a self-chilling beverage can. The company valued the patent rights at $890,000 and issued 890,000 shares of common stock. There was no information on the method used in valuing the patent rights and therefore no assurance that the reported valuation had any relation to the real value, the SEC observed.

Despite the dearth of information—let alone any assurance that the container is commercially feasible—and lack of any known manufacturing and marketing facilities, the stock had been traded on the over-the-counter market from $8 to as much as $14 a share.

The Corporate Shell Game

It is fantastic to see how often various stocks attract trading interest even before any operations are under way and with little or no assurance they ever will be. Another trading suspension ordered by the SEC involved Les Studs, incorporated in 1969 with only nominal assets. Les Studs exchanged 75,000 shares of its stock for 75,000 shares of an empty shell, which was a subsidiary of Atomic Fuel Extraction Corp. This company spun off the Les Studs stock, and public trading developed in the over-the-counter market, ranging from $1 to $4.25 a share. But the Les Studs company's actual operations during this time consisted of two purported franchise-consulting agreements (one was with a Yonkers pizza parlor managed by the brother of the company's president). The only other possible asset appeared to be certain undeveloped timberland in Tennessee.

In another case the corporate shell of the Kachina Uranium Corp. changed its name and business to a theatrical agency, then was acquired by another company. The principals of that company took over still another company and managed to develop trading in its shares. They also took over another uranium corporate shell and developed still an-

The Money Prowlers and Interest Nibblers 103

other company from that. Its shares traded as high as $1.88 but in late 1969 were down to 25 cents. All told, seven different companies were involved, mostly stemming from the two old uranium corporate shells.

Ultra Jet Industries is another shell that distributed millions of low-priced shares. When the SEC ordered a temporary suspension of trading, it noted that the company had no operating income and its only business, "if any," was that of acquiring other shell companies in exchange for its stock.

The Sonics Boom and the Deaf Salesmen

While the U.S. Sonics Corp. actually was an operating company that developed a ceramic filter, it encountered financial difficulties when the Navy canceled anticipated orders for hydrophones. Unable to find merger partners, Sonics finally went bankrupt. The SEC charged, and the U.S. Appeals Court affirmed, that five salesmen employed by Richard J. Buck & Co., a New York area broker-dealer, enthusiastically recommended Sonics stock to customers even though they knew of the company's problems and that it had never earned a profit. Among various claims made by the salesmen were that Sonics would make Xerox look like a standstill, that its market value could double (increase eight to ten points) within four to six months, and so on.

One of the points made by the court, which is helpful to investors, is that whether or not there is any proof of intent to defraud, a securities salesman can not deliberately ignore events that he has a duty to know or recklessly state facts about matters of which he is ignorant.

The Canadian Mining Promotions

At times working people and small businessmen have been bombarded by phone calls from Canadian telephone boiler-room operators urging purchase of penny mining stocks or have succumbed to hot tips or heavy publicity about new ventures, often related to glamour industries and products in the news.

Ivan Shaffer in *The Stock Promotion Business* illustrates the risks of mining promotions with the case of a promoter who first got Canadian newspapers excited about a nickel ore find on the basis of one drilling. Then he came to New York where he and his salesman put up at the Waldorf-Astoria. There they used the phones to sell stock at 25 cents a share. But the company did not have enough money in its treasury even to drill another hole. In any case whatever land in the area that had real mining possibilities already was optioned to large companies.

A frail old prospector was the front man for a scheme that posed him as a company's expert who had "supervised the staking out." In the midst of the promotion, he landed in the hospital to recover from a spree. That did not deter the promoters. They photographed him in bed, wrapped in his mackinaw. His five-day beard added a note of authenticity. He and the promoters were finally convicted of other frauds in the U.S. and Canada. That did not deter him. He ultimately sold an article to a popular American magazine—on mining fraud!

Shaffer believes there is no way Americans can be successful buying Canadian mining stocks. The American "investor complex" does not relate to the necessary speculative concept, he thinks. Nor is there any way American investors can get information fast enough to act on it.

Another maneuver reported by Mrs. Toombs shows how the market prices of penny stocks are sometimes rigged, although in this case the maneuver finally failed.

A Toronto promoter gained control of a company with assets in the hundreds of thousands of dollars that included a portfolio of high-quality stocks. He had arranged to buy the controlling shares from a small group of professional men, borrowing $850,000 to do so.

On gaining control, he got permission from the gullible directors to exchange the portfolio valued at $460,000 for other stock he allegedly owned. He then sold the stocks in the portfolio, realizing $460,000 and using it to pay off part of his loan. Now he set out to wash trade the 300,000

The Money Prowlers and Interest Nibblers 105

company shares in his possession through brokerage accounts he set up in Toronto, New York, and other cities.

His aim was to fake trading to force the price from 20 cents to $3 a share. Had he succeeded, he would have paid off the rest of the loan and ended with nearly half a million over. The maneuver failed because he couldn't meet the spiraling brokerage commissions. To solve this problem he asked his New York broker to "consolidate his holdings" by selling $700,000 of other stocks and "to buy his company's shares" with the proceeds. When he failed to deliver the other stocks to New York, the authorities stepped in. He was convicted of theft of $460,000 and given a nine-year prison sentence.

The Advance-Fee Trap

In times of tight money, promoters fraudulently seek advance fees from businessmen having difficulty raising capital or mortgage money. For example, the Post Office Department reported it had sixty-three advance-fee schemes under investigation at the end of 1969, double the number of four years ago.

In reporting upon the investigation that led to the conviction of a Los Angeles investment firm, the postal inspectors noted that the principal in this scheme was not the head of any close-knit criminal group, "but rather a very active promoter with nationwide connections among self-styled money brokers and other types of confidence men."

In a sophisticated version of the advance-fee scheme, this firm offered a loan guarantee service for a fee. The company had a bogus Dun and Bradstreet report on its credit standing, and bank references were supplied by a dishonest branch bank manager.

In a representative incident, the promoters asked a businessman seeking a loan to "show his good faith" with an advance fee of $5,000. The executive seeking capital to expand his business did not receive the loan, and never got back his good faith payment.

In another advance-fee promotion, a finder's fee of $600

was required for a loan to develop some New England property. In exchange for this fee, the developer was put in contact with an insurance company executive willing to make the loan at 6¾ percent plus a bonus, and an advance payment of $1,600.

However, problems developed. Interest rates were raised and the insurance company could not go below 8 percent. When the developer refused to accept these terms, he was led to believe that, with an advance payment of $7,500, the interest rates could be cut to 7½ percent.

As is often the case in advance-fee schemes, the developer neither received his loan, nor was he refunded his advance fees of nearly $10,000.

In Chicago an attorney has been indicted at this writing for making false representations to secure advance fees for getting loans. A man in Wheeling, West Virginia, operating as World Wide Mortgage Corp., pleaded guilty to an advance-fee scheme in which he collected $100,000.

The difficulties of securing mortgages also have stimulated exploitation of homeowners. An Indianapolis promoter induced homeowners, mostly elderly and low income, whose homes needed repair, to sign papers purportedly covering loans. The papers were really legal instruments conveying ownership of the property to the promoter.

CHAPTER SEVEN

Meanest Hoax: Investments for Part-Time Earnings

The many misrepresented vending machine promotions are the most widespread of an array of heartless hoaxes masquerading as part-time earnings or investment opportunities.

Deceptive vending-machine sellers alone have taken literally millions of dollars from such investors as widows and elderly and handicapped persons hoping to supplement their incomes by servicing vending machines.

Other such persistent hoaxes include rack distributorships, chinchilla breeding, and referral plans for the sale of vacuum cleaners and other merchandise (the poor man's multiple distributorship). Another burgeoning modern investment hoax involves import business opportunities.

The role of newspapers in accepting without investigation the ads that find the potential victims for these deceptions is, in my judgment, a disturbing chapter in American journalism. Better Business Bureau leaders, who seek to use persuasion rather than the legislative bludgeon, are deeply concerned about the need to close this well-traveled avenue to investment victims. The *Bulletin* of the Saint Louis bureau, in June, 1970, observed, "We have noted over the years that as false advertising laws . . . against bait advertising are passed in the various states, almost without exception media are exempted from responsibility under such laws in what they accept."

In the same vein, the Akron bureau has suggested that media should require documented proof before accepting business opportunity ads making claims of sizable earnings.

Postal inspectors have found that the typical bait is an ad in the help wanted columns seeking men or women to service coin-operated machines on either a full- or part-time basis. You have seen many such ads. You may not have realized how effective, and brutal in their results, they can be.

Those answering the ad are then approached by salesmen who induce them to purchase vending units by falsely claiming they can earn big profits. Salesmen often promise that a trained factory representative will arrange suitable locations. Locations, if obtained, are generally the poorest sort, and the investor discovers the company did not pay the applicable license fees. Sometimes flimsy vending machines are sold at exorbitant prices. And sometimes investors do not get any vending machines at all.

One promoter alone extracted $350,000 by selling cigarette, ice, nut, and other types of vending machines. This was the Federal Distributing Company of Tulsa. Its operator, Gordon Adkins, finally was convicted of mail fraud.

Postal authorities reported that the victims were paying $100 for vending units that cost the promoter $17. The $100 seemed small to investors. They were promised profits of from $2,000 to $4,275 per machine, depending upon location.

None of the vending machine operators, of course, made the promised profits.

An order by the FTC hearing examiner in 1969 against three related firms cited the following as typical of what he charged were their deceptive ads. Older people attempting to pad threadbare Social Security payments are especially attracted by the lure of a few hours of work a week.

SPARE TIME INCOME
Refilling and collecting money for NEW TYPE high-quality coin-operated dispensers in this area. No selling. To qualify you must have a car, references, $600 to $900 cash. Seven to twelve hours weekly can net excellent monthly income. For personal

The Money Prowlers and Interest Nibblers

interview write WINDSOR DISTRIBUTING COMPANY. Include phone number.*

The difficulty an individual faces in investing in vending machines is that in real life the large operators usually have good locations and only the unprofitable ones may be available. Often the sellers indicate in their ads that they help place machines. But the FTC often has complained that already established routes are not available and the sellers almost never help place machines.

If you do not realize the difficulty of placing vending machines, you can satisfy yourself by asking the proprietors of the most popular businesses in your neighborhood if they would let you place your machines there.

A classic example of how vending machine promoters manipulate prospects is shown in the operations of Global Distributors, which bilked such victims as a railroad worker, a routeman, and an invalid woman and her husband of surprisingly large sums—an average of over $2,500 each.

In every case the manipulation was the same, and was remarkably successful. A North Carolina man named Samuel Satterwaite saw the ad seeking "a man or woman to service coin-operated dispensers; $500 to $4,800 required as an investment." He answered, and a month later received a letter signed by a Mr. Allison saying that the company had thought it had made arrangements for that territory, but these had fallen through and a representative would call shortly. Meanwhile would he send in the enclosed preliminary application.

A month later Allison appeared. Global Distributors, he said, had surveyed locations and arranged for twenty-eight. Satterwaite "could count on $7,200 annually."

By now it had become clear that the purpose was not to service dispensers but to sell them. But this seemed to involve little risk. If dissatisfied, Allison said, Global would buy back the machines. Satterwaite, enthused, decided to start with ten machines for $3,600. He drew a cashier's check.

---

* The other two firms cited were Pentex Distribution Co., Dallas, and Pen-Ida Distributing Co., Salt Lake City.

A month later Satterwaite had heard nothing. There was an exchange of letters and anxious phone calls, with reassurances by Allison, then a postcard indicating that Global had moved headquarters to Oklahoma City, and finally another letter stating that because he had been so patient, the company would pay the freight charges and give him five Multi Vendors free.

Satterwaite finally sent a certified letter saying he wanted to cancel his order and get his money back. He got a reply from another man, a Mr. De Herrara (who will appear again) sending literature on other machines, and saying that the company would try to work out something to his satisfaction. But Satterwaite wanted his money. Finally a lawyer wrote that Allison had been unable to liquidate his debts, and proposed to have the company withhold 20 percent of his salary to pay his creditors. Satterwaite never received a cent—or the machines.

Testimony from other victims at Allison's subsequent trial for mail fraud showed the same pattern. The ads invariably suggested that employment was offered. Allison also promoted a hot-nut machine claimed to produce net earnings of $2,000 to $4,300 annually from ten units. None of the victims who did finally receive machines made even a reasonable profit.

The sales methods used were insidious and deliberate, Mrs. Toombs pointed out. The application form included many unnecessary questions about the respondent's financial and personal status. "If you were accepted as one of our operators," the form read, "would you be willing to invest profits back into the business?" Testimony by a salesman for Allison showed that the mention of credit standing and financial position on the application was part of a shrewdly designed plan to keep the prospective purchaser on the defensive; he would find himself trying to prove his suitability instead of investigating the Global company.

In fact, the salesmen were instructed: "Always have the respondent fill out the application first. This puts you in the picture as an interviewer, not as a salesman. You must be

The Money Prowlers and Interest Nibblers

negative, but friendly. Calm. Reserved. Analyze slowly everything your prospect says and does. Use eye contact."

An unexplained slightly sinister element appeared when a semi-invalid California woman put down $500 and set out to raise the additional $3,100 required for machines. When she encountered difficulty in raising the money, she was told by Allison, in confidential tones, that he "could trust her to keep her mouth shut and do what she was told, because they were dealing with a syndicate." This frightened her, and she tried repeatedly to get her down payment back. Again, it was a matter of lulling letters and the postcard indicating a change of address. She never got her money back.

An Ohio bakery route salesman and his wife saw the ad and thought it would make a good job for her to supplement their income. Allison told how they could make $10,000 a year. He spoke of thirty-six locations, promising that earnings would pay for the machines in six months. He suggested that they be located "in bowling alleys and other respectable places" so the wife could service them.

This couple took more precautions than most. They queried the Better Business Bureau in Tulsa but received no derogatory report. They ordered ten nut machines and sent a certified check for the whole amount. Months later they had heard nothing except to receive the change-of-address postcard and several delaying letters. Then came the letter from De Herrara. They hired a lawyer who got a judgment against De Herrara, who turned out to be Allison's brother-in-law.

Sometimes you can be fooled by what seems like a well-known name. Two Dallas men operating as Howard Johnson Distributing Co. advertised for persons interested in servicing vending machines. Investors soon discovered the company had no connection with the Howard Johnson restaurants. Appeals for assistance with the poorly located machines or requests for the guaranteed refund were ignored, postal authorities reported.

The Texas Southern Distributing Co. leaned on the Nabisco name. Its ad read:

Spare-time income collecting money and restocking company accounts dispensing Nabisco Snacks. Must be bondable, able to devote 8 hours a week. Starting inventory $500 to $1,400 required. For personal interview call or write Nabisco Snack Varieties.

In a few lines of type, several psychological devices are used, for example, the suggestion of selectivity: "Must be bondable."

The Nabisco company had nothing to do with the promotion. While the machines did dispense Nabisco biscuits, they also could handle any number of other brands.

Some of the ads cited $15 to $20 as the weekly average income for each machine. Two victims who actually received machines found the weekly income to be $3 or less, according to the indictment for mail fraud of Russell Lee Hildebrand, who operated the company.

His two-year sentence was suspended and he was placed on probation even though most of the victims, who paid between $500 and $1,400 for machines and locations, testified that they received no machines.

Another effective manipulating promotion by Hildebrand sought "distributors for brand-name coffee products." This time $799 was required for inventory. Respondents got a letter that said in part, "Because of the many facets of our program, information supplied by mail could not be thoroughly understood . . . therefore we are placing you on our schedule for an interview."

The salesmen made bigger promises orally than in writing. They showed charts of profits and promised good locations. After sixty days, when customers had recouped the cost of the first machine, the company would sell them additional machines at a 50 percent down payment.

To show the extent of overpricing in many such promotions, the investors paid $40 for machines for which the factory charged $20, and $150 for models that cost $50.

True to pattern, Hildebrand stopped furnishing machines and sent this letter: "We apologize for the time needed for delivery. There has been an increase from $149.95 to $179.95. The factory has back-ordered several of our orders . . ."

But, the trial disclosed, the factory involved had no backlog, had not increased the price, and could have furnished any machines Hildebrand would have paid for.

Similarly, a Saint Louis promoter promoted Vend Ur Gas coin-operated gas stations, using without authorization the name of the well-established Petro Vend self-service pumps. Previously he had sold investments in Chrysler Turbo Jet car-wash devices, which had no connection with the Chrysler Corporation.

The sale of chinchilla breeding stock with the promise of large profits is a widespread and persistent promotion. TV advertising has given the promoters a new way to reach the public. In 1969 the FTC issued citations for deceptive practices to chinchilla ranches at the rate of almost one a month.

In a typical case, a consent order barred the largest producer in the East—the Young Bennett Chinchilla Ranch of Louisville—from advertising that large profits can be made from breeding chinchillas in homes or outbuildings. The usual claim is that each female will produce four live offspring a year, and successive litters of one to six, FTC citations indicate.

In various cases the FTC has pointed out that (1) buildings used for raising chinchillas need adequate space and environmental control, (2) breeding chinchillas requires specialized knowledge, (3) chinchillas are not hardy but susceptible to disease, (4) some of the pelts will not be marketable at all and others would not sell for $20 to $70 and even up to $120 as is often claimed, (5) purchasers will not realize annual incomes of $10,000 to $20,000 in five to six years, (6) the "unconditional guarantees" of replacement actually are subject to many limitations, (7) there is not a great demand for the pelts, and (8) chinchillas are not odorless.

The Hurley Chinchilla Ranch of Omaha advertised that a breeding stock of seven females and one male would result in twenty-one offspring the first year, thirty-six the second, seventy-eight the third, and so on. But, the FTC pointed out, the claimed figures did not allow for deaths, culls, fur chewers, and other problems that reduce production.

Too, the FTC said, seldom if ever does the company or its agents buy, through Hurley's Purchase Plan, any of the offspring raised by purchasers of its breeding stock at the claimed prices.

A dangerous new business opportunity deception has developed in the import business—dangerous because promoters have snared young people looking for careers as well as mature ones previously in business.

In one case in which two of the principals were found guilty of mail fraud, the firm of Morgan And Keys Associates, Jacksonville, advertised:

> PART OR FULL TIME.
> LOOKING FOR YOUR OWN BUSINESS?
> BE A WHOLESALE IMPORT DISTRIBUTOR
> Not a selling job. No experience or warehousing needed. We establish retail accounts and furnish training. You simply collect for sold merchandise and replace items. Income begins at once. Items such as transistor radios, tape recorders, jewelry, novelties, hardware, and many, many more to cover all retail stores.

According to the indictment, Marcus Morgan claimed that earnings would be $400 monthly at least; that distributors in Florida, Arizona, Texas, and California were all successful; and that he and a wealthy Florida businessman, James W. Keys (a backer), would obtain five, ten, twenty, or more locations for investors to sell imported merchandise that they would obtain on a consignment basis.

A building supply salesman in his fifties was one of those snared by Morgan's ad in the *Jacksonville Times*. He met with Morgan and a man called William Dill, in Saint Petersburg. Morgan, a pleasant-looking businessman, described himself as president of the Morgan And Keys Associates importing business and said his company had a few profitable distributorships for sale at this time with the fee secured by inventory.

He pictured the success possible with this kind of distributorship, using his son's case as an example. Dill volunteered

The Money Prowlers and Interest Nibblers

that he owned a successful route in Jacksonville and had recently joined Morgan And Keys as a salesman at Morgan's invitation.

Morgan mentioned that a James W. Keys, a Jacksonville Beach businessman with substantial holdings in motels and cocktail lounges, was backing the enterprise.

Morgan displayed jewelry, clocks, and radios as the type of merchandise available. It all sounded valid. The building-supply salesman signed an agreement and put up his money, demonstrating that even salesmen can get hooked by salesmen.

What followed was disillusionment. He got no training. The merchandise was virtually unsalable. The outlets named would not handle it. Comparable merchandise was offered elsewhere for less than he paid. Morgan refused to refund his money.

Such confidence-building words as "We invite your banker's investigation and can furnish plenty of references," all proved false. So were such claims as:

"Earn $400 monthly." (No known investor realized anything near this amount.)

"Others with distributorships enjoy great success." (Investigation established that all known distributors were unsuccessful and dissatisfied.)

"Merchandise will turn over in ninety days." (None of the victims accomplished this.)

"After ninety days of operation, unsold merchandise could be exchanged." (In fact, victims always were told merchandise they wanted was out of stock. Anything they returned was not paid for or replaced.)

Dill was a shill. It was proved that he had no distributorship but was simply a salesman. It also turned out that Keys was not an officer of the company, had invested no money, and had stock only to secure a bank loan he had guaranteed for Morgan.

One of the most persistent and extensive deceivers, often masquerading under help wanted ads or operating through personal contact, is the referral plan. It promises bonuses if the purchaser refers other customers who buy the product.

A New Hampshire housewife, for example, was told she would get a $250 vacuum cleaner called a home cleaning system virtually free. The salesman, who got her name from another buyer, explained that instead of spending millions on advertising, his company helped families earn bonuses through owner recommendation.

The husband hesitated. But the salesman said he had strict instructions and the offer was good "tonight and tonight only."

This hard-driving closing is typical of the high-pressure seller and is disturbingly effective. The couple signed the papers and paid $19.90 down. They didn't realize that they had signed a contract to buy the vacuum outright for $250. They did not know that the machine had a wholesale value of only $60 and that their contract would be turned over immediately to a finance company that would press them for payments.

The housewife thought ten other customers would be easy to find. She wrote and phoned all her friends and relatives. Only two were willing to buy. Later, when they were dunned by the finance company, they sought out the Postal Inspection Service. Eventually the U.S. attorney charged five promoters and three corporations (manufacturer, franchisee, and finance company) with mail fraud, use of a fictitious name, and conspiracy. The men involved were fined $11,250.

The cleaner was the Compact, made by Interstate Engineering Corp. of California. To show how long such selling methods can go on, it was in 1961 that I first called this company's attention to complaints about the price of their machines and the referral selling method. The vice-president assured me that their complete cleaning system represented good comparable value, because it was not just a vacuum cleaner. He also cited payments made in various cities for referrals.

It took seven years, but after the New Hampshire incident, Interstate finally announced it was discontinuing its owner-

The Money Prowlers and Interest Nibblers 117

recommendation program in the sale of both its cleaner and its Vanguard home fire alarm.

At times the Post Office Department alone has had as many as one hundred such referral schemes under investigation in addition to the hundreds of citations and suits by the FTC and state attorneys general.

Kirby vacuum cleaner salesmen have been cited by various agencies a number of times. In 1969, the Detroit Better Business Bureau reported that it had received so many complaints that it was forced to report its findings to the Wayne County prosecutor. Previously the Kirby division of the Scott and Fetzer Co. had told the prosecutor and the bureau that it would remedy such practices by its salesmen. The bureau cited this as a typical complaint:

> I am writing to you because of a gross misconception of a company for whom I worked part-time. I replied to an ad in a suburban paper which read, "Men Part-Time $3.75 Hourly Guaranteed." . . . I was employed by a Kirby distributor . . . they led me to understand that buying a Kirby at a reduced rate was a prerequisite of employment. They gave me a set commission rate which they did not live up to. I have not seen any of this guaranteed salary that they promised.

At about the same time the California attorney general instituted suit against Scott and Fetzer and its eighty-nine distributors of Kirby cleaners in the state, charging sales misrepresentations.

In Denver five salesmen for the Airway Sanitizor have been indicted for mail fraud as this is written. They placed help wanted ads for women. A prerequisite was the purchase of a vacuum cleaner at what the Post Office Department called "an exorbitant price." Buyers were assured they could meet payments by making appointments for the company, the postal service charged. But few, if any, earned enough to meet the payments. Some one thousand persons in this one city were allegedly induced to buy "these often unwanted vacuum cleaners."

Another vacuum cleaner company whose dealers have used

help wanted ads to attract job seekers is Fairfax Industries of Washington, D.C. (The referral device also is used to sell central vacuum systems, often for $1,000 or more.) In Fort Dodge, an indictment against officials of Charles Harold Enterprises charged they used a two-step plan, promising commissions on each system sold to someone referred by the original purchaser, and additional commissions on sales made by subsequent purchasers stemming from the original purchase.

Startling amounts are taken from buyers by referral plans. In Danville, Virginia, a salesman for Eastern States Enterprises, Inc., pleaded guilty to mail fraud. He too had represented that buyers would be able to pay for central vacuum systems through referrals. This one salesman sold $89,000 "worth." In Flint, Michigan, a so-called consumer marketing firm pleaded "no contest" to charges of fraud in a referral selling plan in which the public loss was estimated at $244,000.

Many other goods sold this way are unconscionably priced too. The Post Office Department found a Yonkers, New York, salesman had used a referral plan to sell color television sets for about $1,000 over the going price and electric broilers at $200 extra. He took in over $400,000 from his victims. A Utah firm sold color TV sets for $995 that stores sold for $695. Other goods sold at exorbitant prices by the referral method have included water softeners, and home movie equipment for $350 that retail stores offered at $250.

In Seattle, some twelve hundred victims lost over $500,000 in excessive costs over normal installation prices for home intercoms and fire and burglar alarm systems sold through referral plans by the Monarch Electronic Corp. But the company's president was merely placed on probation for five years, fined $1,000, and ordered to pay $4,000 in investigative costs.

Previously the Lifetone Electronics Co. had taken $315,000 from families in the same city through referral selling of intercoms and fire and burglary alarms.

Referral sellers often arrange with banks and finance companies to take over the installment notes. Some leading banks have been involved in financing such plans in Texas, Michigan, and other states. In one case, the owner of Modern Floor Fashions, Riverside, Connecticut, was found guilty of mail fraud for referral selling of carpeting at $25 to $30 a yard that the company bought for $5 to $7. The public's loss was estimated at $500,000. But of particular interest, an official of a New York bank was charged with accepting a $10,000 bribe from the rug company to arrange to buy the installment contracts.

Perhaps the cruelest trick is the worker's opportunity advertising for women seeking homework such as addressing envelopes. In a typical case, the Post Office Department caught up with a Fort Worth man who had operated under such names as Home Worker's Guide, Ramsey Enterprises, Home Worker's Opportunity, and Co-Op Mailing Association.

In response to the ad, the work seeker received three pieces of literature. The first asked for $1 for a list of three hundred firms hiring homeworkers. The second asked for $3 for manuscript instruction. The last paragraph said, "You can't lose a single cent . . . complete satisfaction is unconditionally guaranteed." The third piece said, "Mail these proven successful big-pulling letters from your own home. Get $12 in every mail, keep $8 for yourself."

Instead of assignments to address envelopes, the respondents got merely a list of firms to contact to apply for work. For $3 they received a twelve-page Merchandise by Mail Sales Plan, primarily a mail promotion for making perfume at home and selling it through mail solicitation. Respondents who returned this booklet, asking for their $3 back, were advised that the refund did not refer to this particular order.

The sentence received by the operator, Ernest Wade Ramsey, is indicative of the penalties too weak to discourage deceptions. He had taken about $40,000 from several thousand work seekers—and was placed on probation for one year.

SECTION TWO

MAKING THE MOST OF YOUR INVESTMENT DOLLARS

CHAPTER EIGHT

New Opportunities and How to Use Them

Never before have there been so many pressures on ordinary families to invest in risky ventures. But also never before have there been so many opportunities for alert savers and investors to increase their income. Yields of 6 to 9 percent in relatively secure and even wholly secure savings and investments are available for those who know about them. So are capital gains, sometimes in media not ordinarily used by small investors. Moreover, the tax amendments effective in 1970 actually have increased tax-saving opportunities for small investors.

The fact is, even as some financial interests try to bar these richer opportunities to small investors, new ways to use them have opened up, such as mutual funds and syndicates for investing modest amounts in government obligations, tax-exempt bonds, and mortgages. Similarly, no-load mutual funds are better established and more widely available. Investment clubs are more numerous and have developed increasing expertise.

The small investor faces disadvantages but has strengths too, in his flexibility, greater realism, and longer view of his needs.

First you need to work out an investment plan and philosophy tailored to your investment needs and goals, one that maximizes a small investor's advantages while minimizing his disadvantages.

Here are policies to follow in working out your plan.

Balance Your Plan: No one way to save and invest is best in all respects. Each has its own advantages and disadvantages.

For example, in 1968 stock investors openly sympathized with people who owned E bonds and pointed out that the annual increase in their value barely kept pace with the increase in living costs. In 1970 after the stock market plunge, people who owned E bonds openly sympathized with people who had bought stocks. But despite the exaggerations, over the long run stocks actually are one of the ways, if not wholly dependable, that moderate-income families can hedge against inflation. You simply need to keep a foot in both camps—inflation hedging and fixed-value savings.

Tailor It to Your Objectives: While all have their own usefulness, some forms of investments and savings do have particular advantages for families in different situations. Your plan should be tailored to your own goals and needs.

In general, a younger family more often seeks growth of capital. It is more willing to trade higher income now for capital gains later—for tax purposes among other reasons. Younger people also can take more risks. Older or retired people can not wait for growth. They need highest possible income now and can not take risks. At retirement they are less concerned about taxes. These differing needs affect what proportion of savings a family may decide to invest in stocks or mutual funds and how much in investments that fluctuate less.

Earmark Short- and Long-Range Funds: The savings you expect to need within three to five years can be considered short- and intermediate-range funds. These can go into fixed-value and relatively less fluctuating investments. Only longer-range funds should go into more speculative forms.

The short- or long-range nature of savings also would help influence you in choosing immediate income or investment income that can be deferred. As one example, which is explained in detail later, short-range savings should never go into E bonds whose main usefulness is for long-range tax shelter.

Look for Highest Yield: Consistent with your investment

Making the Most of Your Investment Dollars

objectives, consider forms of saving and investment outside of the standard methods of stocks, mutual funds, savings accounts, and E bonds. Corporate bonds and preferred stocks, federal agency obligations, tax-exempt municipal and state bonds, new kinds of mutual investments, and mortgage trusts —some of these less common methods discussed in later chapters may actually suit your needs more than the standard forms and pay higher yields.

The charts in this chapter show how money grows at different compound interest rates. A family that saves or invests $1,000 a year (about $20 a week) for fifteen years at an average net yield after taxes of 4½ percent accumulates a fund of $21,700. A family that gets an average of 6 percent after taxes accumulates $24,700. Note also the chart of comparative yields of different investments and savings.

Tax-Shelter Your Savings: As much as possible, seek the investments and use the methods that will provide at least some tax shelter for the yield your savings and investments earned. Many tax-minimizing methods usable by moderate- and medium-income families for different objectives are outlined in chapter 14.

Be Alert to Change: Yesterday's favored savings media may not be today's or tomorrow's. Even a decade ago few moderate-income families invested in corporate bonds, preferred stocks, or tax-exempt municipal bonds. Now some alert small investors are taking advantage of the recently higher yields on such investments. In some future year, tax-exempts again may not be suitable for small investors.

Pick Your Investments: Because these are times of increasing sales and advertising pressure on behalf of specific investments, keep in mind that no one salesman, even if quite sincere, has the whole truth. You have to first select among different types of investments and then select among the institutions or investment companies offering that type, for example, among a number of different mutual funds whose performances vary considerably or among different types of savings institutions whose interest payments and ways of paying vary.

As you have seen in earlier chapters, you also need to be

skeptical and check and compare. No one investment channel can be depended on to be completely regulated by law—certainly not to the extent that the regulations can not be breached verbally or shaded either by overstatement or by omission of some facts important to you.

Finally, few savings or investment institutions are really fair or sportsmanlike. As we have seen, even the government treats its small savers a little unfairly.

Following a balanced program, a family savings and investment portfolio of $12,000 might be invested like this to achieve an average yield of 6 percent at 1970 yields, while maintaining both the safety of fixed-value savings and the growth possibilities of securities investment, with of course some of the risks.

```
$2,000 in stocks @ 4½ percent ............... $ 90
$2,000 in mutual funds @ 4½ percent .........   90
$1,500 in E bonds @ 5½ percent .............    83
$1,000 in savings account @ 5 percent ........   50
$1,500 in savings certificates @ 6 percent ......   90
$4,000 in corporate bonds, preferred stocks,
     or mortgage trusts @ 8 percent ..........  320
                                               $723
```

There can be variations. A family concerned about job stability or a growing family's immediate needs may want to start with a larger proportion in easily retrievable fixed-value savings. But in general, a balanced plan somewhat along these lines provides some tax shelter, some defenses against disaster, relatively high income, and moderate growth. At this yield, the fund would build up to $24,000 in twelve years simply by the reinvestment of dividends and compounding of dividends.*

---

* A simple formula for determining how long it would take a given capital to double at a given rate is to divide the rate into 72. Thus, at 4 percent money doubles in eighteen years; at 5, in fourteen; at 6, in twelve.

Making the Most of Your Investment Dollars

TYPICAL YIELDS OF VARIOUS SAVINGS ACCOUNTS AND INVESTMENTS*

Fixed-Value Savings

	Typical Yields
Credit Unions	5–6%
Savings and Loan Associations	5–5½
Mutual Savings Banks	5–5½
Commercial Banks	4½–5
Long-Term Savings Certificates	5¾–6
U.S. E and H Bonds	5½

More Speculative Investments**

Mutual Funds	3–3½
Closed-End Investment Companies	3–4
Common Stocks—General	3½–4
Growth Stocks	1–2
Liberal-Income Stocks	6–7
Preferred Stocks	7–8
Utility Stocks	5–7
Bank Stocks	4–5
Corporate Bonds	7–8
Tax-Exempt Bonds	5–6
Real Estate	10–12
Mortgages, Mortgage Participation	7–8½
Treasury and Federal Agency Obligations	5–7
Insurance Company Stocks	3½–4

* As of January, 1971.
** Dividend income, not including potential capital gains or losses. Combined dividends and value increase of stocks is estimated at 9 percent over a forty-year period.

HOW MONEY GROWS AT DIFFERENT RATES

This compound interest table shows how one dollar saved or paid each year accumulates at different interest rates. To determine how much you will accumulate if you save a specified amount for a specified number of years, multiply the figure for that period and rate by the amount saved each year. For example, if you save $500 a year for twenty years at 5 percent yield, multiply $500 by 34.719. The result is $17,359.

Years	3½%	4%	4½%	5%	6%
1	$ 1.035	$ 1.040	$ 1.045	$ 1.050	$ 1.060
2	2.106	2.122	2.137	2.153	2.184
3	3.215	3.246	3.278	3.310	3.375
4	4.362	4.416	4.471	4.526	4.637
5	5.550	5.633	5.717	5.802	5.975
6	6.779	6.898	7.019	7.142	7.394
7	8.052	8.214	8.380	8.549	8.897
8	9.369	9.583	9.802	10.027	10.491
9	10.731	11.006	11.288	11.578	12.181
10	12.142	12.486	12.841	13.207	13.972
11	13.602	14.026	14.464	14.917	15.870
12	15.113	15.627	16.160	16.713	17.882
13	16.677	17.292	17.932	18.599	20.015
14	18.296	19.024	19.784	20.579	22.276
15	19.971	20.825	21.719	22.657	24.673
16	21.705	22.698	23.742	24.840	27.213
17	23.500	24.645	25.855	27.132	29.906
18	25.357	26.671	28.064	29.539	32.760
19	27.280	28.778	30.371	32.066	35.786
20	29.269	30.969	32.783	34.719	38.993
21	31.329	33.248	35.303	37.505	42.392
22	33.460	35.618	37.937	40.430	45.996
23	35.667	38.083	40.689	43.502	49.816
24	37.950	40.646	43.565	46.727	53.865
25	40.313	43.312	46.571	50.113	58.156
26	42.759	46.084	49.711	53.669	62.706
27	45.291	48.968	52.993	57.403	67.528
28	47.911	51.966	56.423	61.323	72.640
29	50.623	55.085	60.007	65.439	78.058
30	53.429	58.328	63.752	69.761	83.802
31	56.335	61.701	67.666	74.249	89.890
32	59.341	65.210	71.756	79.064	96.343
33	62.453	68.858	76.030	84.067	103.184
34	65.674	72.652	80.497	89.320	110.435
35	69.008	76.598	85.164	94.836	118.121

Making the Most of Your Investment Dollars

This table shows how one dollar left in savings grows at different rates of compound interest. To find how much a specific sum will

Years	3½%	4%	4½%	5%	6%
1	$1.035	$1.040	$1.045	$1.050	$1.060
2	1.071	1.082	1.092	1.103	1.124
3	1.109	1.125	1.141	1.158	1.191
4	1.148	1.170	1.193	1.216	1.263
5	1.188	1.217	1.246	1.276	1.338
6	1.229	1.265	1.302	1.340	1.419
7	1.272	1.316	1.361	1.407	1.504
8	1.317	1.369	1.422	1.478	1.594
9	1.363	1.423	1.486	1.551	1.690
10	1.411	1.480	1.553	1.629	1.791
11	1.460	1.540	1.623	1.710	1.898
12	1.511	1.601	1.696	1.796	2.012
13	1.564	1.665	1.772	1.886	2.133
14	1.619	1.732	1.852	1.980	2.261
15	1.675	1.801	1.935	2.079	2.397
16	1.734	1.873	2.022	2.183	2.540
17	1.795	1.948	2.113	2.292	2.693
18	1.858	2.026	2.209	2.407	2.854
19	1.923	2.107	2.308	2.527	3.026
20	1.990	2.191	2.412	2.653	3.207
21	2.059	2.279	2.520	2.786	3.400
22	2.132	2.370	2.634	2.925	3.604
23	2.206	2.465	2.752	3.072	3.820
24	2.283	2.563	2.876	3.225	4.049
25	2.363	2.666	3.005	3.386	4.292
26	2.446	2.773	3.141	3.556	4.549
27	2.532	2.883	3.282	3.734	4.822
28	2.620	2.999	3.430	3.920	5.112
29	2.712	3.119	3.584	4.116	5.418
30	2.807	3.243	3.745	4.322	5.744
31	2.905	3.373	3.914	4.538	6.088
32	3.007	3.508	4.090	4.765	6.453
33	3.112	3.648	4.274	5.003	6.841
34	3.221	3.794	4.466	5.253	7.251
35	3.334	3.946	4.667	5.516	7.686

grow at a specified rate, multiply by the figure in the interest-rate column for any given number of years. For example, $5,000 earning 5 percent for twenty years grows to $13,265 in twenty years.

CHAPTER NINE

An Intelligent Lamb Among the Bulls and Bears

If you expect to invest in stocks with some degree of safety and worthwhile return, you really need to know at least as much as larger investors, not less.

In truth, small investors are being pushed more and more into group types of investment such as investment clubs, mutual funds, investment syndicates, and indirect investment, as through pension funds and variable annuities.

For one reason it is not as easy for an inexperienced small investor to get needed up-to-date investment information, let alone inside information as the SEC had charged some large investors do, or even expert professional advice.*

The very growth of mutual funds and investment conglomerates sponsored by banks, insurance companies, and other institutions itself has made it difficult for the small investor to compete for information. As the SEC has pointed out, such institutional investors are staffed by professional managers who avidly seek out and analyze all available information. Thus, it is harder for an individual to gain equivalent access to relevant information.[29]

While some small investors make themselves as knowl-

---

* Judging from the sheeplike performances of some brokers, mutual fund managers, and other professional money managers, in this respect the small investor is not always worse off than larger ones. There really are more sheep in Wall Street than bulls or bears.

edgeable as some of the professionals about buying securities, others who have become interested in investing are alarmingly confused. In our research for this book, one of the largest bond firms reported that it even has small investors come to it seeking mutual funds because they confuse mutual funds with municipal bonds.

Nor can a small investor always rely on the advice of brokers' salesmen. Many, although not all, are really more salesmen than counselors and may as well be selling any other commodity. Those more soundly investment-oriented usually are not able to give much time to a small investor, because they earn less commission on his infrequent buy and sell orders. Some brokerage houses no longer even give any commissions to salesmen if the brokerage fee is under $10 or $15, and some no longer want the small, infrequent investor at all.

Under these circumstances the small investor also may become the victim of churning. This is the practice by some brokers of overly frequent buying and selling of shares for accounts under their supervision in order to earn more commissions. The practice is frowned upon by the more careful brokerage houses and has been the subject of SEC punitive action in flagrant instances.* A variation that is harder to police is the tendency of some stock salesmen to pressure customers into unnecessarily frequent turnovers from one stock to another.

Even though he usually gets less service, the small investor must pay more for it in terms of the larger percentage of investment he pays for executing his orders. He has always paid higher commissions. Recent and pending increases raise the charges on small purchases disproportionately, as shown later in this chapter.

The small investor actually is the chief victim of the investment industry's archaic methods and its many small firms and specialists. Every transaction must be handled by several

---

* Norman Freed, a long-time broker, advised that the amount of churning has been reduced in the past three years and that both the New York Stock Exchange and the more scrupulous firms are trying to cut it down. In that respect, the investment industry may be gaining in dependability.

Making the Most of Your Investment Dollars

brokers and go through several computers. These paper handlers include the buyer's broker, sellers, the specialist in the stock, and the stock exchange. Then individual certificates must be issued even for a few shares, each signed, handled, and delivered. The many brokerage houses, specialists, and transfer agents themselves become a vested interest against greater efficiency.

Another problem the small investor must learn to deal with is excessive swings in prices. The stock market is something more than a high-stake bingo game but something less than a rational investment and capital-formation medium. But more than ever, the prices you may pay or receive when you sell may be at the mercy of the new breed of stock market swingers, whose recklessness recently infected even some long-established brokerage houses.

The swingers particularly include the performance mutual funds and their followers who, as the United Business Service said, indulge in "furious trading, buying new issues of little value for a fast ride, following fads in the market; pushing up hundreds of thinly capitalized stocks to the stratosphere."

In recent years such large speculative investors, by buying and dumping large blocks of stocks, have caused stock prices to perform erratically. The effect on small investors is twofold.

———You may be seduced into paying more for temporarily fashionable stocks than they are really worth. Larger investors who accumulated these stocks earlier, distribute (unload) them on small investors like you.

———You may be frightened into unloading stocks prematurely by the excessively low prices that follow periods of speculation, or you may be forced into selling because you need your cash.

The chairman of one medium-sized national corporation confided that he has become more worried now than he formerly was pleased when a mutual fund or other institutional investor buys a large block of his company's stock. While the purchase does lift the price, he has learned to fear the disproportionate depressing effect when such a buyer unloads the stock in one large block on the open market instead of waiting until another large buyer can be found, or instead of selling part at a time.

Many small investors have followed the swingers into overpriced speculations such as the recently deflated franchise companies, data processing companies, aerospace companies, conglomerates (a number of unrelated companies owned or controlled by the same corporation), nursing home chains, electronics, and even science-oriented companies at too high prices. As an example of ill-founded fever to get in on the ground floor, a few years ago when drug companies were the glamour investment, there was a spurt in buying of shares of Park Chemical Co. It sounded like a drug company but really manufactured automotive chemicals. Years before, and perhaps the story is more legend than truth, some investors who believed mining stocks were due for a rise bought shares in the Gold Dust Co. Actually it made a soap product. More recently, and there is nothing legendary about these events, frantic investors rushed to buy when companies even in unrelated businesses such as dresses merely announced they were going into the nursing home business. Even more stable industries have had their temporary bandwagon upsurges followed by declines.

Small investors often can not act rapidly enough to compete in this kind of speculation. It can be temporarily successful because it is self-fulfilling. When some new development occurs many brokers and advisory services assemble lists of companies with, for example, a stake in pollution control, such as producers of air-cleaning equipment. Sometimes such recommendations really are sound. Unfortunately, often by the time they trickle down to the small investor, many brokers have recommended the same stocks and prices may have risen unduly. The immediate effect on earnings of companies affected by new trends may be overestimated and then the prices sink unduly. That often is a good time to buy—when nobody is looking.

The increasing domination of the stock market by large institutional investors such as mutual funds, pension funds, banks, and insurance companies, even when they act more responsibly than the swingers, also affects what happens to you. At times in recent years stock prices have been unduly high in relation to values simply because of strong investment demand from pension funds, mutual funds, life insurance companies, and other institutional investors in relation to the availability of stocks. This occurs especially in periods of lower interest rates when corporations prefer to finance expansion by borrowing, because interest costs are a fully tax-deductible business expense, rather than by offering additional stock on which they must pay nondeductible dividends.

For example, the statistics on the available supply of stocks and other equity issues compared to institutional purchases of stocks show that in 1968 institutional buying of stocks was nearing an all-time peak at the same time that new equity issues were falling to their lowest point in twenty years. The result was that stock market prices were high in 1968.

But institutional purchases started to drop in 1969 just as new equity issues were rising to their highest level in twenty years. As demand fell off, so did the stock market, in fact, to an exaggerated degree as many heavy investors and plungers were squeezed. Especially hurt were speculators who bought stocks on margin, i.e., they put up part cash and borrowed the rest from the broker. They had to pay 8½ percent on borrowed money while they had to put up additional funds as their equity in the stocks drained away. If not, they were sold out, adding to the downward pressures.

Given these problems, should a moderate-income family invest in stocks? The answer is yes if you understand the risks and particular disadvantages and adapt to them. Under the following circumstances, the answer is yes.

1. If the funds you risk on stocks or mutual fund shares are not part of your basic budget and you can wait through temporary dips. (You would not, for example, buy stocks with money earmarked for children's tuition or even your own minimum retirement needs.)

2. If you are prepared to give the time and attention needed for research and continuing review of your holdings. (You cannot just buy stocks or even mutual fund shares and put them away; there are times to sell too.)

3. If your purpose is long-range investing, which means conservation of capital while seeking gains. (The stock market attracts both investors and speculators. The speculators buy stocks for a quick move and then get out. The investors look for long-range solidly based value. They continue to watch the performance and results of the companies in which they invest and are prepared to revise their investments if satisfactory performance is not forthcoming. Because they did not commit funds they expect to need in a year or two, long-range investors are able to wait through dips if their holdings have basic value and even use the averaging techniques described later in this chapter.)

4. If you want to take advantage of the special tax benefits that the investment industry lobbied Congress into giving owners of stocks and mutual fund shares, as described in chapter 14.

5. If you want some protection against inflation, even though the capacity of stocks to keep pace with inflation at a particular point is often exaggerated.

But the answer is *no* under these circumstances.

1. If you have heavy overhanging debts. (Family installment debts usually command true annual interest rates of 14 to 22 percent compared to the 9 to 12 percent typical annual return—including both dividends and long-term increase in value—of stocks and mutual fund shares.)

2. If your main investment purpose is conservation of what funds you have now and high immediate income, as it may be in the case of people nearing retirement or already retired. (The main purpose of investing in stocks is the possible increase in value over a period of years. Higher immediate income is available today from many less fluctuating investments. And retired persons usually do not find the tax benefits of long-term investing as useful as do younger investors.)

3. If your job is at all shaky and you may need to retrieve your money for basic living needs.

4. If your housing situation is not settled and you may need your funds for new housing.

5. If you are out to make a quick killing. (This is the kind

Making the Most of Your Investment Dollars

of speculation in which the small investor is at a real disadvantage.)

Three Ways to Buy Stocks

If you have decided that you are able and want to invest in stocks, there are three ways to do it.

——Buy stocks yourself.

——Invest through a group method such as mutual funds or closed-end investment company, as discussed in chapter 10.

——Join or organize an investment club, which is a compromise between direct investment and buying mutual fund shares, discussed later in this chapter.

Investing in stocks yourself, rather than through a mutual fund or investment club, requires a larger amount of capital and more attention to the necessary research for selecting and watching your investments. Some small investors do become quite capable and successful investors, but they devote a good deal of time to it.

In *The Battle for Investment Survival*, Gerald M. Loeb pointed out that "one must devote some time every day to investing. Nothing is more logical, yet nothing more surprising to most people. They must devote months to earn a net savable profit . . . and then in a few minutes toss a large part of it to the winds because they look at investing very much as buying tickets to the theater."

More capital usually is needed for solo investing than investing through a mutual fund or club because you should have enough to diversify your investment in at least three or four different companies and avoid committing all your funds at one time. If you have a reserve you can average your investment downward by buying additional shares at a lower price if one or more of your stocks drops, thus averaging your cost at a lower level.

It usually is difficult to achieve some measure of diversification in buying stocks by yourself without an initial risk capital of at least $3,000 to $4,000. Very small purchases also involve proportionately higher broker fees. For example, 20 shares of a stock selling for $20—a $400 investment—would cost you a buying commission of $13.50, at this writing, or about 3½ percent of the $400, and another commission when you sold the shares. For a purchase of 40 shares of the same stock—an investment of $800—the broker's commission would be $19.50, or 2½ percent.

Mutual funds provide greater diversification for small investments more readily than do direct purchases because the fund managers pool the funds of many investors and buy stocks in many companies. Such diversification does not guarantee you against risk. In fact, the very diversification means that the asset value of a mutual fund's shares inevitably will rise and fall with the general market, advised Arnold Green. But the mutual fund method does cushion a major risk often faced by small investors who buy just one or two stocks—the possibility that unforeseen disaster could strike those particular stocks. Even that number one favorite of small investors—A.T.&T.—lost almost half its market value in several years and started melting away even before the 1970 decline.

There are several ways to minimize risks of buying stocks even without enough initial capital for diversification.

One way is called dollar averaging. For a number of years the New York Stock Exchange sponsored a plan, which some brokers still offer, called the Monthly Investment Plan. You choose the stock or stocks and invest at least $40 a month or quarter. You do still pay larger brokerage commissions on such small investments under $100 than if you accumulate cash and then buy stocks for a lump sum. However, you can reduce this cost by investing a larger amount quarterly or even twice a year and still achieve the benefits of dollar averaging at lower commission costs. You can work out such a plan to accumulate stocks whether or not brokers in your area will accept the regular MIP plan.

A second way to achieve some diversification even with small investments is to buy shares in corporations that own shares of a number of other companies and possibly also have investments in mortgages and real estate. Among these are banks, insurance companies, and so-called closed-end investment companies described in chapter 10.

Take note, however, that at some times bank and insurance stocks are better value than at others, because they too enjoy a special period of popularity among speculators and professional money managers. At such times the professionals may push prices of these stocks beyond a reasonable level of value.

Many small investors have combined dollar averaging with diversification by using an MIP or similar periodic investment formula to accumulate shares in closed-end investment companies (their shares are sold on the stock exchange like other stocks, but unlike mutual funds or open-end investment companies).

Dollar averaging or periodic investing is less speculative than investing a lump sum. If you invest the same amount each quarter or other period, you level out the fluctuations of the market or of a particular stock, because you buy at an average price.

In fact, because of a mathematical quirk, the average price you pay will be a little less than the average at which the stock or fund shares sold for during the period of investment.

For example, you decide to invest $400 every four months for one year in XYZ stock. Because you will invest the same amount each month, in some periods your level investment will buy fewer shares as the price rises, and in other periods more, as the price drops. But you would get your shares at an average price. For example, if you invest $400 each period in a fund or stock whose shares sell for $20 at the start, the first time you will get 20 shares. If the market price of the shares drops the second time to $16, your $400 would buy 25 shares. If the price the third time was $25, your $400 would buy 16 shares.

Even though the average price of the shares at those three periods was $21.33, you bought at an average of $19.67.

Many large institutional investors such as college endowment funds use dollar averaging.

Of course, while you reduce the risks of bad timing, you also forfeit the opportunity to time your buying for low points and the possibility of maximum gain. But for an investor seeking to minimize risks and willing to settle for a smaller potential gain or over a longer period, the exchange is a reasonable one.

A third way to reduce risk, if knowledgeably handled, is through convertible bonds and preferred stocks, discussed in chapter 11. These can be converted to the company's common stock at a previously established price. Thus, if the common rises, so will the related convertible security.

A fourth and increasingly popular way to secure diversification, gain assistance in research, and also reduce commissions is through an investment club. These often are established by employees of the same company, teachers' groups, or members of a fraternal, professional, social, family, or other organization.

The club can achieve greater diversification and members can share the research. Clubs usually can get more assistance from brokers than do individuals. A club also can buy round lots (100 shares) at less commission.

Investment club advisers think it is quite possible for small investors to accumulate $20,000 to $30,000 worth of stocks in a twenty- to thirty-year period by budgeting $10 to $30 a month to invest through a club.

There now are some sixty thousand such clubs, about fourteen thousand of them members of the National Association of Investment Clubs, reported Thomas E. O'Hara, chairman of the NAIC board. About one-fourth are all-women's clubs.

Membership in NAIC costs $10 a year for the group itself, plus $2 for each member for a subscription to the association's magazine *Better Investing*.

Most clubs are small groups of perhaps ten to twenty members who meet once a month. Some of the older clubs have accumulated rather large portfolios of stocks through steady investing over the years and by plowing back their gains. A number now have over $100,000 of assets, and some as much as $400,000, although their members usually pay in more than the average investment of about $20 a month.

NAIC's own surveys indicate the average affiliated club has been able to achieve about 15 percent greater earnings than the 425 stocks in the Standard & Poor's Industrial Average.

You can get information on how to organize and run an investment club from the National Association of Investment Clubs, P.O. Box 220, Royal Oak, Michigan 48068.

The NAIC material, or a broker experienced in counseling investment clubs, can explain the different kinds of agreements used to form clubs. Usually a partnership has most tax advantages for moderate-income investors, while an incorporated club may be more useful for upper-bracket taxpayers.

NAIC also sponsors local councils who give help to both new and established investment clubs and groups interested in forming clubs.

As you develop additional investment funds, through accumulation of dividends or other savings, there is no reason not to combine several of these methods of investing. Many investment club members also have their own portfolios. Similarly, over half of the nine million holders of mutual fund shares also own stocks or other securities, the New York Stock Exchange reported.

Selecting Stocks

Usually brokers and advisory services classify stocks according to the investment objectives, as in this classification by United Business Service:

——Income and safety (as good income return as possible with relative stability of principal).

——Growth (long-term capital appreciation with current income return secondary).

——Businessmen's risk (capital gain and moderate income from medium-risk securities).

——Speculative (profit is the primary aim and the investor is willing to accept a high degree of risk).

Most brokers and advisory services will provide lists of stocks classified according to these objectives. Often small investors are criticized for rushing to buy stocks with no clear plan or idea of their investment objective. On the other hand, such classifications should not be taken too literally. There are many overlaps and exceptions. Such income and safety stocks as public utilities in some cases and at some periods (as when interest rates generally are rising) may not be safe. In other cases and at other times, they may offer potential growth as well as good current yield.

Similarly at times the growth stocks are so overpriced as to discount for years ahead their potential growth.

Actually sometimes the businessmen's risks, when carefully evaluated, offer values for small investors too.

Any of these three groups offer investment possibilities depending on your age and broad objectives. The real job is to buy good value.

You can not just buy any stocks, even if the companies are well-known, and expect that you will share in a rising market. The averages may go up but your stocks may not. They may even fall. Of one hundred stocks in fifty industries followed by *Johnson's Charts*, the average gain from 1960 to 1969 was 63 percent. But thirty-five were above average, and sixty-five below average. Of these sixty-five, forty-one actually declined during this period of generally rising prices.

The basic criteria of good value are the present price at which the stock is selling compared to its earnings and the prospect for growth of these earnings.

The first yardstick for determining value is the price-earnings ratio. This is the price at which the stock sells in comparison to the company's latest twelve-months earnings per share of stock outstanding. The per share earnings figures are reported in newspaper financial pages and financial magazines, and also are available from brokers or compilations such as *Moody's Handbook* and the Data Digests *Monthly Stock Digest*.

To figure the price-earnings ratio (P/E), you divide the annual earnings into the price of the stock. Thus a stock selling for $20 and earning $2 a share net (after taxes) has a P/E of 10.

The P/E ratio usually has more influence than the dividend rate on investor interest in a stock, and consequently the

Making the Most of Your Investment Dollars

price at which it sells, although older people often will be more interested in the dividend rate than younger investors usually are. The dividend rate is determined by dividing the price of a stock into its annual dividend. For example, a stock selling at $20 and paying a dividend of $1 has a dividend rate of 5 percent.

A high dividend rate does not necessarily mean a stock is good value. The rate may be high because of a relatively high payout rate. Some corporations may pay out in dividends as much as 50 percent or even more of earnings; others, very little or none. Many so-called growth companies tend to pay out less in order to plow back the earnings into research and expansion. In any case, the P/E ratio is the more vital figure for investors seeking capital gains.

There is a wide variation in P/E ratios. Some stocks may be quoted as low as ten or eleven times earnings. Others may have a P/E of fifty or even sixty. The very low ratios may occur because the company is considered to have little growth prospects or is in a cyclical industry with earnings affected by ups and downs, or because it suffered a recent profits decline or is expected to. Stocks quoted at low ratios may or may not be good buys.

Often brokers and counselors steer small investors into so-called blue-chip stocks or recognized growth companies even when they have a high P/E. This is considered safe. Sometimes it is, but sometimes disasters have occurred when the P/E ratios have been unrealistic because many other investors, brokers, and institutions also recognized the growth.

Because of the same sheep syndrome, other stocks may be selling at lower prices than their earnings and prospects really should merit, due to a temporary interruption in a normal growth rate or because they are not considered to be in growth industries.

For example, in recent years the market generally has tended to place a relatively low value on stocks in many cyclical industries such as autos and parts, machine tools, steel and other metals manufacturing and producing companies. Oil and some food chain stocks often sell at a low P/E

COMPARING P/E RATIOS, YIELDS OF DIFFERENT CLASSIFICATIONS OF STOCKS*

		Range of Yield	Avg. Yield	Range of P/E	P/E Avg.
33	Top-Quality Growth Issues	0.8–6.6%	3.28%	9–29	18
33	Medium-Grade Growth Stocks	0.5–6.4	3.16	9–29	16.7
18	Better-Grade Stocks for Profit	1.6–6.5	3.9	8–27	14.2
26	Speculations for the Venturesome	0.5–8.5	2.4	6–24	14.3
23	Stocks with Rising Dividend Patterns and Stocks for Above Average Yields	4.5–8.9	6.57	7–15	10

* Developed from listings by United Business Service, August 3, 1970.

because earnings in those industries are considered to have flattened out, although with exceptions. Or the market may value most conglomerates at a low P/E because some had a weak financial base. Similarly, utility companies have fallen to a low ratio in recent years as yields from competing investments have risen.

Yet within most low P/E industries there are companies that show a trend of increased earnings and yet often sell for less than fifteen times earnings and sometimes less than ten.

The real goal of research-oriented, independent-minded investors is to find undervalued or at least reasonably-valued stocks that have reasonably good future prospects and to find them before the brokers and advisory services all start recommending them again. The fact is, the market's evaluation of specific stocks often is tinged by extremes of optimism and pessimism, and bandwagon psychology. There is not always a valid business reason for the very sharp differences in market valuation of stocks of the same growth character, with a range of twelve to forty times earnings, or the phenomenon that one year a stock may sell for twenty times earnings, another year for ten, often with no important change in its earnings trend.

Nor should a high dividend rate be downgraded excessively. While professional investors give much greater emphasis to growth, and correctly so, a high dividend, if the company is

Making the Most of Your Investment Dollars 145

able to maintain it, is a form of growth too. This return can be reinvested and compounded. Too, in times of declining or sidewise markets, a high dividend return makes waiting at least financially tolerable.

Nor is it always true that high dividend payers are necessarily greater risks, advised George Frazer, a leading Toronto investment counselor. Their investment qualities vary depending on their productivity, earnings, and management.

One of the reasons why well-to-do investors prefer growth stocks to high dividend payers, and also a reason why the popular ones are often overpriced, is that plowing earnings back into expansion usually results in long-term capital gains. Only 50 percent of such gains are taxable. Tax savings are important for small investors too, as shown in chapter 14. But until a couple have $200 of dividends, which are wholly exempt from federal tax, dividends need not be a tax concern. Nor are they in most cases for children and students, retired people and widows.

Here is a table showing how long you would have to wait for a worthwhile yield if you now buy a stock yielding 2½ percent, on the basis of different assumed rates of annual dividend increase (calculated by First National City Bank of New York from Moody's Investors Service):

PURCHASE OF STOCK YIELDING 2½%

Assumed Annual Dividend Increase	Years to Equal Return at Top of Column			
	5%	6%	7%	8%
3%	23½	29¾	35	39¼
5%	14¼	18	21¼	24
10%	7¼	9¼	10¾	12¼
15%	5	6¼	7¼	8¼

It is not difficult to find stocks with a reasonable P/E ratio. But to evaluate their future prospects requires more research and experienced advice. In fact, you really need to compare recommendations from several sources and then decide on the basis of your own judgment and research. Even research directors for some of the large brokerage houses can be dreadfully wrong.

The first task is to determine the company's earnings trend for at least four or five years to see whether it actually has been able to increase earnings and at what rate. Usually a genuine growth stock is considered to be one that has increased earnings 10 percent a year. A lower growth rate may be a rewarding long-term investment if the price is correspondingly lower and the yield relatively high.

Often industries and individual stocks have assigned to them a "normal" P/E. For example, professional investors may feel that an industry or company currently may have a normal P/E of only ten to twelve times earnings. You can determine the typical range of P/E valuation of the stock or industry by consulting a broker or checking through *Moody's* or *Data Digests* for several years back. Often undervalued stocks can be found among companies and industries currently unfashionable among large investors. Such stocks, however, may find resistance for a time in pushing through the barriers of normal valuation, unless new developments or good news changes the investment industry's concept of the worth of those stocks.

When prices of good-quality issues fall well below their customary P/E multiples, they may be in a buying range.

For example, Edmund Brown Jr., an experienced analyst, pointed out that among the food chains one (Grand Union) has a historical multiple of twelve to thirteen times earnings and another (Safeway) has a usual multiple of thirteen to fourteen times. Multiples for such leading oil companies as Jersey Standard and Shell usually are fourteen to fifteen. General Electric has a customary multiple of about twenty-four, and Westinghouse, about nineteen. Natural gas companies have customary multiples of thirteen to sixteen, and some of the leading paper companies, seventeen to eighteen. When such stocks reach prices one-fourth to one-fifth below their usual multiples, Brown considered they merit investment support.

From the defensive view, there are obvious dangers in buying a stock when it is priced much higher than its average multiple over the past three to five years, unless its prospects are definitely improving. This kind of buying often is the cause of losses by small investors.

Similarly, an industry group may vary considerably from its normal multiple. For example, life insurance stocks a decade ago had a customary multiple of nineteen. David L. Babson pointed out that in the early 1960s the multiple increased to thirty-six, representing a doubling in the average price of these shares, while their average earnings increased by only 18 percent. The inevitable decline in prices developed and the life stocks returned to their more customary multiple later in the 1960s.

How much are stocks in general worth? In periods of stock market booms, the P/E ratio of the widely used stock averages had multiples of twenty to twenty-five. That means the average stock sold at twenty to twenty-five times earnings. At those times so-called growth stocks have sold for thirty to ninety times earnings.

In declines, the averages often have fallen as low as thirteen times earnings before recovering. Here are P/E ratios of the Dow-Jones Industrial Average in recent years, taking the midway period of the year: 1961, twenty-four times combined earnings of the stocks comprising the average; 1962, sixteen times; 1963, eighteen; 1964, nineteen; 1965, sixteen; 1966, fourteen; 1967, seventeen; 1968, sixteen; 1969, fourteen; 1970, fifteen.

Even within a few months there can be a decided swing in the market's valuation. At the beginning of 1966, the Dow-Jones P/E was nineteen; midway that year, fourteen.

Keep in mind that the stocks comprising the Dow-Jones are blue chips. The broader Standard & Poor's averages show even greater swings.

Noticeably, the long-term P/E trend has been downward from 1961 to 1970. In the intermediate trends, usually recovery starts within three to six months.

A stock should be able to double its per share earnings in five years to justify a price of more than twenty-five to thirty times earnings. That would mean an increase in net earnings per share of about 15 percent a year. Not many growth stocks have been able to achieve that rate. Yet many have sold in recent years for much more than thirty times.

At a continued growth rate of 15 percent a year, a stock for which you pay thirty times earnings in five years would have a more reasonable multiple of fifteen times the price you originally paid. The fact of business life that buyers of the most popular growth stocks with a record of rapid earnings increases but high P/E ratios must take into account is that such growth usually can not continue for many years without slowing down. Very profitable businesses finally attract very strong new entrants, for example, IBM's entry into the photocopying business dominated by Xerox, the entrance of many new cosmetics sellers into Avon's backyard, and new entrants into the "miracle drug" business.

You can use as a rule of thumb the yardstick that if a company is selling for ten times its per share earnings, that means it is earning 10 percent on your investment; if twenty times, only 5 percent.

In evaluating future prospects of possible stock investments, experienced investors consider both the industry's prospects and the individual company. It is not enough to determine that a company is in a successful industry or one with good prospects or one that has enjoyed favorable news recently. Each company has to be considered on its own merits. As the chapters on franchise problems showed, there was a boom in franchise stocks but some companies were successful while others proved to be disasters.

David Norr, who won a contest of the Association of Customers Brokers by selecting five stocks that rose 92 percent in less than ten months, told me:

> I always ask myself, Will this company be significantly bigger in five years or more? I consider its past growth, its likelihood of further growth, the return it earns on its invested capital, its predicted future earnings, and the ratio of price to earnings.
>
> I ruled out very speculative ventures. Investors should weigh the possibilities of loss as well as the possibilities of gain. The

Making the Most of Your Investment Dollars

worst mistake anyone with small savings can make is to go overboard on investments that may go up tenfold.

But my stocks weren't all blue chips either. They were carefully thought out selections. They either were priced low on the basis of present earnings or had an excellent outlook for increased earnings. An investor should apply all the yardsticks.

Large investors and brokers often are able to visit company plants and offices and obtain on-the-spot information about future prospects. They make these reports available to their customers.

Some successful investors go further. They do their own informal but practical research into the market and consumer interest in a company's products. They often can do this quite successfully in the case of companies manufacturing consumer goods. It is not unusual for professional analysts to visit drug and food stores to learn how well a company's products are selling.

One prize-winning analyst, who had managed to select the stock of an undervalued auto company just before it made a profit turnaround, told me he visited the company's local dealers to find out how well its new compact model was selling.

Other yardsticks that professional analysts often use, which you will find defined in the glossary at the end of this book, include current ratio, net quick assets, book value, the margin of profit, ratio of sales to fixed assets, and cash flow. As with the earnings trend, this data needs to be reviewed for several years back.

You will find most of this information in companies' annual reports or in the various investment manuals and digests available in public libraries.

The most difficult factor to assess, and one which professional analysts are constantly trying to judge, is the quality of management. Recent performance and reputation in the industry are the most tangible measures. The analysts are in better positions than the individual investor to determine such less tangible elements as whether objectives are well-founded, whether management enjoys good relations with executives and employees, and how alert and determined it is. There is no mathematical computation for determining management ability; the opinions of analysts and of others in the same business are the chief available guides.

Finding Facts from Reports

A basic source for the facts you need to evaluate a potential investment in a company's stock is its financial report. You can get a copy of the current report from the company itself. The report also will provide summaries of results in the preceding five or ten years. Data for previous years is available in such compilations as *Moody's Handbook of Common Stocks* and *Standard & Poor's Corporation Records*, available usually at public libraries. Be sure also to get data on the company's latest quarterly report, and obtain brokers' estimates of expected current year profits, although these are not fully reliable.

You will acquire insight into a company's operations and prospects as you become familiar with its annual reports. There are certain cautions to observe. Some companies tend to obscure facts they would like to, well, keep obscure. In fact, many professional analysts think that annual reports are often less than candid, one survey found.[30]

Perhaps the single fact you need most is the earnings per share of common stock. But some companies have convertible bonds, warrants, and other convertible securities outstanding. These can "dilute" the per share earnings if they are converted into common stock, as they can be at specified prices. In recent years, accountants have insisted that annual statements tell what the earnings would be if these securities were converted.

Thus, you need to look for two figures: the earnings per share and the earnings per share "diluted." A large difference can affect the potential P/E ratio significantly.

Many of the respondents in the Taplinger survey also thought that the president's report, which is part of an annual statement, sometimes tended toward overoptimism or at minimizing disappointing results.

Making the Most of Your Investment Dollars 151

There also are differences in corporate accounting methods that, unfortunately, are not always simple to detect. In general there is criticism of insufficient breakdown of expenses. Some corporations tend to capitalize a larger proportion of their expenses such as research and development or start-up costs for new plants. This practice makes their current earnings look larger. Still others may amortize such expenses over a number of years. Others, more conservatively and dependably, count as immediate expenses as many of these items as they can.

Another obscurity that has affected investors involves the reporting of income. In most cases of well-established companies there usually is no problem. The most notorious problem arose in the accounting practices of some franchising companies. As noted in chapter 5, some tended to overstate their income by counting as current income the promissory notes given them by franchisees. On the strength of these overstatements they won an enthusiastic welcome from Wall Street that led to serious losses by many individuals. It was not until late in 1969 that accountants belatedly challenged this practice.

So-called generally accepted accounting principles actually have permitted a wide range of reporting choices affecting sales and profit figures on which investors must base decisions, and inaccurate data have hurt many investors, Leonard S. Silk, a leading economics writer, pointed out. A Federal Trade Commission study of corporate mergers, prepared under the direction of Willard F. Mueller and released in 1970, cited the case of the Automatic Sprinkler Corp. of America. It reported that its after-tax earnings doubled from 1966 to 1967 but did not include in the 1966 figure the earnings of companies it acquired in 1967. If it had, the comparison would have shown a 15 percent decline.[31]

Various investment guides provide additional assistance on gleaning information from reports. Noteworthy is the candid discussion in Robert D. Merritt's *Financial Independence Through Common Stocks*.

The glossary with this book provides definitions of the

various terms used in annual reports. Here is a brief summary of points to look for.

Earnings. This is given both in total dollars and in amount earned per share. The latter is of most interest to you, but beware of possible dilution through existence of large amounts of convertible securities. Besides current earnings per share, note earnings in other recent years to determine the trend.

Net profit ratio. You get this by dividing total net profit by total net sales. This figure indicates a company's efficiency and should be compared with figures for previous years, with other companies in the same industry, and with other industries.

P/E ratio. You figure this on the basis of current market price.

Retained earnings. This figure tells you how much of net profit is being held, how much paid out to stockholders. Many companies nowadays pay out less than 50 percent; growth companies, who plow back, may pay out only 20 to 30 percent. A high payout is good for immediate income; lower, for future growth and capital gains.

Book value. This is the company's net worth per share of common stock (see glossary). If not given, divide total net worth or shareholders' equity by the number of shares outstanding. Compare the book value with the market price.

Profit to net worth. This shows the return or yield the company is making on its total investment. To figure it, divide the earnings by the net worth.

Current ratio. You can find this, if not otherwise given, by dividing current assets by current liabilities. Usually the higher the ratio, the better shape the business is in; but it may not tell you whether the current assets are being used to best advantage, or whether receivables and inventory are too high.[32]

Debt to equity ratio. This figure measures the amount of debt in comparison to stockholders' equity.

Balancing Growth and Income

A small investor, who obviously can invest in only several companies at the start, can balance his beginning investment effort by choosing carefully one or two growth stocks and one or two defensive stocks (recession resistant) with a higher or gradually increasing yield. This method will provide a combination of income and moderate growth.

While some growth stocks at times are priced higher—in the opinion of conservative analysts and investment managers—than a share of any business is worth, there are possible selections among the less prominent medium-grade and smaller growth stocks and among stocks that may just miss the standard growth definition of at least 10 percent increase a year. (The latter will have shown fairly consistent increases of over 5 percent.) The best growth companies have sold at unprecedented levels in relation to earnings in recent years because, among other reasons, institutional investors and especially pension funds have been buying more stocks.

But even the popular growth stocks at times become deflated to the point where they become more realistic possibilities in terms of P/E, as shown by the table in this chapter of the market records of some of the popular growth stocks. For example, Xerox, which sold at a P/E of forty-seven at its highest price in the late 1960s, fell to a P/E of thirty in mid-1970 and recovered to a P/E of thirty-eight by January, 1971.

Smaller or young growth companies usually sell at lower multiples and a product or technology breakthrough can affect their earnings more dramatically than in the case of large companies. Such companies, however, need close scrutiny, especially in the case of new or unseasoned issues. Potential profits or projected sales sometimes do not materialize. Don't buy a new stock only because it has a scientific sounding name; don't buy it if it still has no profits or if you do not really understand the company's business or function. Make sure, too, that the company has adequate capital and will not have difficulties in a period of tight money as many young companies had from 1968 to 1970.

Ferguson Taylor, an investment counselor with T. Rowe Price and Associates, noted that many of the young growth companies are traded in the over-the-counter market. Some excellent companies started there, such as Xerox and Avon, but this is sometimes a difficult market because a few sales can push down prices.

In the case of conglomerates or companies that take over others, note whether the reported growth in earnings is external (through acquisitions) or internal (a sounder indication of growth ability).

The so-called defensive stocks often are high dividend payers too, and sometimes even have growth characteristics, both as individual companies and as industries.

Among defensive groups that also often have some growth ability are food companies, drug companies, hospital supplies, fuel and utility companies, and shoe companies.

Utility companies such as electric utilities and telephone and natural gas companies are a favorite of small investors. They provide dependable income and sometimes moderate growth in areas of expanding population. But as many investors learned during the late 1960s, there sometimes is shrinkage in market value.

The fact to understand is that utilities are regarded as an income investment. When interest rates generally are high and yields from corporate bonds, federal obligations, and tax-exempt bonds become as high or higher than those from utility shares, prices of utility stocks fall. When they have fallen, they make high-yielding and yet defensive investments for moderate-income families. As the list at the end of this section shows, many utility companies in 1970 yielded 6 to 8 percent.

When other interest rates decline, the prices of utility stocks tend to rise. But then their yields decline, and when they decline to low levels, sophisticated investors abandon them. This was the case with A.T.&T., which had increased in price to the point where it yielded only 3 percent on its high

MARKET RECORDS OF SOME OF THE POPULAR GROWTH STOCKS*

	MARKET PRICES				EARNINGS	PRICE EARNINGS RATIOS	
	1	2	3	4	5	6	7
	1962 Low	1968–70 High	Price 6-30-70	Gain 1962 Low to 6-30-70	Increase 1962 to 1970 Est.	Highest Price 1968–70	On 6-30-70
Xerox	6	116	73	1142.6%	920.8%	47.2	29.8
IBM	78	387	250	220.5	215.8	43.0	27.8
Polaroid	10	146	53	423.5	587.5	67.5	24.1
Warner-Lambert	17	76	61	252.5	125.0	28.3	22.7
Philip Morris	10	39	36	258.0	211.2	12.7	11.9
Coca-Cola	18	87	69	296.4	166.0	39.2	27.8
Texas Instruments	20	140	74	275.2	282.4	45.8	22.7
Avon Products	10	92	70	631.2	297.7	52.7	40.2
Walt Disney	9	158	117	1280.9	181.7	44.5	33.1
Eastman Kodak	20	87	64	213.6	181.9	37.3	24.0
Combined Insurance	7	72	44	525.0	440.5	54.2	21.9
Minn. Mining & Mfg.	41	120	76	83.6	111.2	40.2	22.2
Avery Products	2	42	26	1055.6	286.4	49.7	30.6
Dow-Jones Industrial Avg.	535.76	985.21	683.53	27.6	46.9	17.0	12.8

* Adapted from compilation by T. Rowe Price and Associates. Prices rounded out.

market price in the 1960s. A.T.&T. consequently fell steadily over a six-year period with resultant losses for many small investors. With the yield then high enough to attract investors again, the stock slowly recovered.

Another relatively stable defensive-type investment is bank stocks. Their protected position derives from the fact that much of their income comes from their own investments in high-quality bonds. They often have growth quality too, even more so than utilities. Banks profit whether money is tight (their loan rates are high) or abundant (they are able to expand their loans). As a group they do not, however, pay as high a yield as utilities—4 to 5 percent in most cases, although the range may be anywhere from 2 to 6.

HIGH-YIELDING ELECTRIC UTILITY STOCKS

Electric utility common stocks that yielded over 5 percent on current market price in late-1970 are listed from highest to lowest.

7–8 Percent

Eastern Utilities Associates; General Public Utilities Corporation; Ohio Edison Company; Otter Tail Power Company; Philadelphia Electric Company; New England Electric System; New York State Electric and Gas Corporation; Duquesne Light Company; Boston Edison Company; Interstate Power Company; Iowa Electric Light and Power Company; Iowa Power and Light Company; Pacific Power and Light Company; Public Service Electric and Gas Company; Allegheny Power System, Inc.; Central Maine Power Company; Commonwealth Edison Company; Consolidated Edison Company of New York, Inc.; Detroit Edison Company; Iowa Public Service; Union Electric Company; United Illuminating Company; Utah Power and Light Company; Wisconsin Electric Power Company.

6–6.9 Percent

Kansas Gas and Electric Company; Minnesota Power and Light Company; New England Gas and Electric Association; Pennsylvania Power and Light Company; Portland General Electric

Making the Most of Your Investment Dollars 157

Company; Wisconsin Power and Light Company; Wisconsin Public Service Corporation; Central Illinois Public Service Company; Cleveland Electric Illuminating Company; Dayton Power and Light Company; Delmarva Power and Light Company; Niagara Mohawk Power Corporation; Northeast Utilities; Baltimore Gas and Electric Company; Northern States Power Company; Washington Water Power Company; Central Hudson Gas and Electric Corporation; Indianapolis Power and Light Company; Long Island Lighting Company; American Electric Power Company; Central Illinois Light Company; Cincinnati Gas and Electric Company; Columbus and Southern Ohio Electric Company; Public Service Company of New Hampshire; Southwestern Public Service Company; Kansas City Power and Light Company; Illinois Power Company; Montana Power Company; Orange and Rockland Utilities, Inc.; Consumers Power Company; Duke Power Company; Kansas Power and Light Company; Puget Sound Power and Light Company; Atlantic City Electric Company; Public Service Company of Indiana, Inc.

Investment Timing

Dollar averaging reduces the need for determining the appropriate timing for buying and selling. It also limits the potential capital gains. If you buy stocks in conjunction with a dollar-averaging program, determining which to buy is not enough. It is also important to evaluate when to buy and when to reduce your holdings, even in the modified form of dollar averaging some investors develop.

As indicated in chapter 8, an alert family money manager will not become wedded to one type of investment. He would invest more money in stocks when reasonably priced but as prices rise would gradually take profits and shift into other investments. For example, as common stocks and mutual fund shares in general rise to the level of twenty times earnings or more, both value and yield diminish to the point where a realistic investor would then consider other investments such as bonds.

It is not possible usually to actually buy at the bottom and sell at the top. Bernard M. Baruch said, "This can't be done. Except by liars." It is, however, feasible to determine when prices in general and the specific stocks you already own or are considering buying meet your standards of value and personal investment policy in relation to P/E, prospects, and other yardsticks.

In relation to selling, you might ask yourself whether you would buy the stock at that price. Keeping it is like buying it.

Nor is it advisable to let losses run, unless you are convinced by actual facts, not merely unwillingness to admit a mistake, that it is worth waiting for recovery.

Some serious long-term investors make it a policy to sell on the way up, reducing their holdings while still maintaining some stake in a further rise. They also try to eliminate some of their less successful holdings or those with diminished prospects. More small investors could adapt or use in part the formula investing plan described in the glossary in this book.

The importance of timely reduction of holdings is indicated by the fact that in declines stocks tend to drop faster than they rose, especially those that have enjoyed especially sharp rises. Investors sometimes are most optimistic when stocks are unrealistically priced and most pessimistic when they are good values.

Professional investors also look for support and resistance zones. The support zone is a price level at which previous experience indicated buying interest developed and the stock started up again or, to put it another way, the level at which the other holders stopped selling. The resistance zone is the general level at which buying interest slackens. Among indications of these zones are the range of prices over the year and over recent past years, and the amount of trading activity that develops in a stock as indicated by the daily volume of trading figures published by the stock exchanges for specific stocks and the market as a whole.

These tend to be more technical measures, however, and are no substitute for the basic yardsticks of P/E and prospects.

Making the Most of Your Investment Dollars

If you follow the investment markets closely, there are signs that can indicate that stocks in general are approaching their highs. One is the average yield of industrial stocks in comparison to other yields. When yields on stocks drop as their prices rise, and yields on corporate, municipal, and government bonds and other investment sources rise well above those on stocks, you can expect that some investment funds will flow out of the stock market and into higher-yielding securities.

Another sign of danger is when the average price-earnings ratio of many stocks, or of the Dow-Jones list of industrials, reaches higher than usual levels.

A fourth is trading volume. When volume of sales on the exchanges tends to increase on days when prices are falling, and fall when prices are rising, other investors are getting cautious. Shrinking volume itself may be another clue to an aging bull market.

A fifth is increased speculation in new issues of relatively unknown companies while longer-established stocks and stable dividend payers tend to fall in price.

One experienced observer, New York Times financial writer Vartanig G. Vartan, reported that he finds that advisory services are often wrong as well as right in forecasting changes in general trends. But one remarkably omniscient recommendation by Wright Advisory Reports in December, 1968, offers an example of a realistic way to view high markets.

> The average New York Stock Exchange-listed common stock is now so highly priced that there is, in our opinion, no reasonable likelihood of a further sustained advance next year—but rather a strong probability of a sharp 1969 price decline.
>
> We therefore advise that profit-taking in any stocks which are now fully priced should be completed by not later than the first week in January . . .[33]

Also watch the stocks on the American Stock Exchange and the new issues of smaller or new companies for signs of excessive speculation that may signal a general drop. For example, while the P/E multiple for the Dow-Jones average gradually moved down from eighteen in 1964 to fifteen in 1969, the median P/E on the more speculative American Stock Exchange doubled from thirteen in mid-1966 to twenty-six at the end of 1968, and the average multiple in 1969 was actually forty.[34]

It is also important to watch the trend of corporate bond yields for their possible effect on stock prices. As previously noted, investment money tends to flow into bonds and government obligations when their yields are high. In 1958 for the first time, high-grade bond yields rose above yields from common stocks, which in 1953 were as high as 6 percent while bond yields were only 3. The gap has steadily widened most years except during stock market declines when it has tended to narrow. In 1968, just before the 1969–70 stock market decline, bond yields were heading for a modern historic level of 8 percent while average stock yields had fallen below 3.

While the fluctuations in the stock market often exaggerate general economic trends and sometimes give false signals, when the market does anticipate accurately, it usually does so four to six months in advance of the general decline or recovery.

Sometimes a stock you own may seem to churn even though the market in general is relatively placid. In that case, ask your broker or consult the various financial publications to see if any discouraging news has developed in that company's affairs or in the industry. Sometimes, however, fluctuations may develop chiefly because the trading specialist in that stock may not have the ability to maintain an orderly market as he is supposed to do. Some specialists are considered excellent and well financed; others, less capable.

Choosing a Broker

You can get names of brokers who are members of the major exchanges from your banker, lawyer, your employer's pension and union welfare fund administrators, and, possibly, business friends. But after assembling the list, the question becomes how to choose one.

You can decide either on the basis of the firm itself or on

the basis of the registered representative or customer's broker who will handle your account.

If you primarily want service and research materials for your own decisions, you may want to put the firm or house first. In that case, read the research materials provided by different firms to see which provides the most thorough and careful analyses and the most complete materials to aid your investment decisions. A good research department can be useful to you. Sometimes brokers who also service institutional investors such as pension funds and banks have the larger research departments.

If you select on the basis of the representative, be careful of the hard-selling broker. Many people switch brokers after taking losses, blaming the broker. This may not always be justified. But it is true that some customer representatives do not mind losing you after a year of fairly active trading.

You can tell a great deal about a broker by discussing possible investments with him, for example, on what bases he recommends stocks. Try to see if he really knows the stocks and in general has an awareness of business conditions.

A careful representative will not offer tips or rumors but facts on earnings, prospects, and similar data to support his recommendations. In fact, he may not make firm recommendations but will suggest a number of possible stocks that suit your investment objectives. He will discuss with you those objectives and needs: immediate high income, medium-term capital gains, long-term growth, conservation of capital. He also will sometimes advise against a stock or against buying at a particular time.

You can help him too by knowing your own objectives.

Bank trust departments also provide investment handling services of different types. These range from supervised investing including recommendations on buying and selling, to nonsupervised that include only custodian and income-collection functions.

If you do not want to do the research required for investing, bank services may be useful. There also are investment counselors and managers who perform such services. Many will accept only large investors but some accept accounts as low as $5,000. One such firm pointed out that its fee often is balanced at least partly by the savings on commissions it can make in combining clients' transactions in round lots.

You can get many of the same services that a trust department provides from your broker without the additional fee if you want to leave your stocks with him in his firm's name (called the street name). In the case of active accounts with five or six transactions a year, brokers prefer to hold the certificates to save sending them back and forth by registered mail. The broker then will accumulate dividends in your account and send them to you as designated—monthly, for example—and will give you a monthly statement of your account.

There is a clause on the back of the transaction bill (sometimes in immorally if not illegally small, light print) that says your securities held by the broker may be mingled, loaned, and so on. Some investors are reluctant to leave securities in a broker's name because they fear loss if the firm goes bankrupt. To protect investors against this possibility, Congress enacted at the end of 1970 the Securities Investors Protection Corporation to insure investors against losses resulting from failures of brokerage firms.

Sometimes investors prefer to hold their own securities because they get company reports a little sooner and because they can use the securities as collateral for loans.

If you hold your own stock certificates, keep them in a safe place, preferably a safe deposit box. Never sign a certificate until you are ready to dispose of it, and always use registered mail for mailing securities. A lost or stolen certificate that has not been signed can be replaced but at some inconvenience and expense to you for the affidavit and a surety bond costing about 4 percent of the current market value of the certificate.

Warrants and Rights

Warrants are securities that represent the right to buy shares of a corporation's stock at a preset price. Corporations sometimes offer them with a new stock issue to make the

Making the Most of Your Investment Dollars

stock offering more attractive. Thus in 1970 A.T.&T. offered warrants that permitted buyers of an issue of debentures to buy shares of its common stock. Unlike the limited life of stock rights, warrants usually are good for many years.

Some buyers of the stock issue will not exercise or hold their own warrants but offer them for sale. Thus you often will see warrants quoted on the stock exchange.

Warrants have high leverage. They represent a way to make a good deal of money with small investment of capital and also a way to lose money. You do not have to invest as much to make the same gain as if you bought the stock itself. In the case of A.T.&T., in mid-1970 you could buy the stock at $44 a share or the warrants at approximately $8 each. At that price the stock, then earning $4 a share, had a P/E ratio of eleven. If you estimated that interest rates would decline, which would enhance the market value of a utility stock, and that A.T.&T. would continue its moderate earnings growth of recent years, you might calculate that sixteen times earnings, or about $65 a share, would be a reasonable value.

If you bought 50 shares at $44, you would invest $2,200. If your estimate of $65 was realized, your gain on the rise of $21 would be $1,050. But if you used the $2,200 to buy 275 A.T.&T. warrants, your gain on the same increase in market value of the stock would be $5,775.

The risks, however, are magnified on the downside too. If the stock dropped, even as much as $8, your warrants temporarily at least would have little market value, and your $2,200 would be gone at least temporarily. If you bought the 50 shares of stock itself, you could retrieve $1,800.

Moreover, while you waited for recovery, you would lose the yield your investment could have earned by buying the stock—in this case, $130 a year.

You can of course give an investment some additional leverage without excessive risk by investing a small part of your funds in the warrants, for example, buying 40 shares of the stock and 50 warrants.

There are many warrants listed on the stock exchanges, but some are for securities of companies that have not fared well recently, including a number of jerry-built conglomerates. Not only should warrants in general be avoided unless you can accept the risk of loss and forgo the income from the stock itself, but also no warrant should be bought unless you believe the stock itself is good value.

Stock rights are yours when a company whose stock you already own issues rights to buy new securities at a price usually a little below the current market. The rights must be exercised before the expiration date (usually a brief period), either by buying the stock or selling the rights through your broker. Once expired they have no value.

CHAPTER TEN

Unloading Needless Mutual Fund Problems

The pressures upon small investors to buy shares in mutual funds have multiplied, first with the many salesmen employed by securities dealers and now with the entry into mutual fund selling of life insurance salesmen, tax services, department stores, even a big equipment-leasing company.

Even the church is no longer a sanctuary from this installment plan Mammon. Mutual fund salesmen often give talks to church as well as other groups, bearing witness to the path to financial paradise.

Unfortunately, paradise has problems too. For one, as discussed in chapter 1, investors who signed contracts to invest so much a month sometimes found that if they wanted to get back their money early, they would lose part of their original investment. For another, you may pay high sales commissions.

In theory, and sometimes in practice, a mutual fund is a sound plan for small investors. A mutual fund is an investment company that pools the investments of many people and buys stocks and other securities. For a small saver who does not have the knowledge to buy stocks outright, mutual funds do have the advantage of providing investment management and diversification. Even if the professional management is not always successful, at least it usually knows enough to avoid some of the investment schemes that can trap inexperienced investors.

Mutual funds do not eliminate all the risks of stock market investment. The value of their shares inevitably sinks when the stock market in general goes down. However, the diversification they provide is helpful so that small investors do not put all their dollars in one stock, Arnold Green, a veteran broker, points out.

The trouble is that the investment industry made a hard-sell game out of a basically good idea by charging small investors a sales commission described as 8½ percent but actually 9.3 percent. If you invest $1,000, you pay $85 in sales load and get $915 in shares at the fund's current net asset value. But $85 is 9.3 percent of the $915 you really invested. This is a bit of sleight of hand on top of an already high fee.

As noted in chapter 1, earlier efforts of the SEC and other reformers to limit the sales fee to 5 percent have been blocked at this writing by the rigid opposition of mutual fund dealers. The mutual fund industry as a whole has a surprising number of links in and around Congress, through campaign contributions and other alliances. As the head of the Eaton and Howard Funds, Charles F. Eaton, Jr., explained the industry's stubbornness in an interview, "Anything that hurts the mutual funds hurts America."[35]

Under the present commission rate charged by load-type funds, if you invest $1,000 and the sales fee is 8½ percent, you really get just $915 worth of shares. Assuming the fund pays dividends of about 4 percent, it would take over two years to recover that sales fee, without considering possible gain or loss in the value of the shares themselves.

In contrast, direct purchases of stocks involve smaller brokerage fees—$22.50 for $1,000 (forty shares at $25). In fact, a number of no-load mutual funds with performance records as good as many of the load-type funds charge no commission at all.

The large sales commission charged for the mutual funds has been shared by a whole daisy chain of sellers—wholesale distributors, securities dealers, and their salesmen.

The mutual fund investment contracts that exact a penalty

Making the Most of Your Investment Dollars 167

for early withdrawal are known in the investment trade as front-end load.

In a contractual front-load plan, even if you complete it, you would have less money accumulated than if you simply had invested the same amounts under the voluntary method of buying on which you simply pay the sales commission each time you invest. That is because a smaller proportion of your periodic investment goes to work for you right away under the contractual plan, because a large part is paid to the salesman and dealer immediately.

The SEC said that one of the worst evils of the contractual plan is that it encourages high-pressure selling by the salesmen. Naturally they are anxious to collect their potential commissions early, and to make sure they get it all, as they do under the contractual plan.

But here is what can happen to an unaware investor. The wife of a workingman wrote me:

> I was high pressured into purchasing a contract for mutual funds. Exactly twenty-six months ago my husband and I bought the contract from a salesman who came to the house in answer to our request for information. We signed a contract to pay $20 a month for 150 months. So far we have invested $520. Recently I asked what my return would be if we were to cash in or discontinue now. According to the present market price, we would lose $139 of our investment. The office of the mutual fund told me that to break even, we might have to hang on for approximately three or four more years (that is, assuming the market didn't take a sudden plunge).
>
> Now I don't know whether to hang on at least another two years or take the loss of $139. The investment really was made to help put our son through college or for whatever other unforeseen expense might crop up. I would really hate to lose all that money.

That is quite understandable. That money was wages, earned the hard way. First of all, a mutual fund is no way to save for children's education (unless possibly if the investment is started very early) because of the fluctuations in values. If the stock market drops just when the youngster is ready to go to college, he can not wait until it recovers. (Nor is insurance a good way to save for college; nor even E bonds unless bought before the child is fourteen or fifteen.)

Contractual investors such as this couple become locked in. She has to stay with the plan to avoid the penalty. If it is a reasonably well-managed mutual fund, eventually she may recover the sales fee and perhaps achieve a gain.

If an investor already in such a plan does find it hard to continue, he can ask the dealer if he would reduce the monthly investment or let the payments be interrupted for a period without a penalty. Some contractual plans also will permit you to stop payments for one year, and just one monthly payment at the end of the year can provide another year's interruption if needed.

If you actually need to get back your money for some emergency before completing the contract, some dealers will let you withdraw up to 90 percent without a penalty. If not, you can use the shares as collateral to get a low-cost bank loan. The dividends from the shares would pay most of the cost of the loan and there is still the possibility of increase in value of the shares.

Contractual plans presently are prohibited in California, Illinois, New Hampshire, Ohio, and Wisconsin, with some regulation of them in Michigan.

Mutual fund dealers typically contend that the contractual plan and overhanging penalties ultimately are beneficial to the small investor because they force him to save. This solicitude would be more convincing if the shepherd did not charge so much for his services.

Another of the fund dealers' arguments is that savings-type insurance policies such as whole-life insurance, twenty- and thirty-pay and endowment policies also have a front-end load. A policyholder forfeits some of his deposits if he withdraws before completion of the plan. If competitors for the savings dollar—the insurance companies—are permitted to do it, so should mutual funds, an official of Investors Diversified Services contended at the House hearings on mutual funds.[36]

Making the Most of Your Investment Dollars 169

The arguments that periodic investing provides dollar averaging, as discussed in chapter 9, and that the investor is permitted to reinvest dividends without additional sales commission, do have merit for intelligent investors. But these ends can be achieved by investing in some of the same mutual funds through a voluntary plan. You indicate your intention to deposit so much a month but do not sign a contract to that effect. Thus you can withdraw if employment or other expense problems develop. And you can have the same arrangements with a no-load fund with no sales fee at all.

Even a former seller of contractual mutual fund plans, Norman Dacey, the author of *You Can Avoid Probate*, now has urged Congress to ban them. In 1963 Dacey wrote me that I had done "the mutual fund industry" and "especially the contractual segment" a "grave injustice" by criticizing the withdrawal penalties and the high load. But in late 1969 he testified before the House subcommittee investigating mutual fund plans that he had gone back through the accounts of his own company and was shocked at the number of investors who had suffered losses in one of the largest mutual funds—"even those plans on which the full ten years of payments have been made."

Dacey is a diligent researcher and a vigorous advocate when aroused. He pointed out that his study included a computation of the average dividend and capital gain distributions on all of the accounts shown, and the average was 5.9 percent—"not dissimilar to what the investors would have earned in a deposit account where there would have been no risk and ... no sales charge of any kind."*

Because mutual funds are offered as hedge against inflation and because the years he surveyed were "the most inflationary in our history," Dacey noted that it is hard to reconcile the actual performance with "the proud boast" that contractual

---

* In a subsequent rebuttal, David D. Grayson, president of First Investors Corp., pointed out that most of the contractual plans covered by Dacey's study were in a large balanced fund, with 40 percent of its investments in bonds and preferred stocks, and this fund did not do as well as common stock or growth stock funds generally did in that inflationary period.

plans are "the only effective method of meeting the needs of the investor who has not yet accumulated his 'nest egg.'"

He also warned about the reducing term insurance offered with contractual mutual plans, testifying that originally a large mutual fund plan had stressed that it had arranged for coverage to be provided by three companies but derived no profits from it. Later it formed its own life insurance company to reinsure these policies, thus getting part of what Dacey called "huge profits" from the sale of this insurance.

Dacey also charged that leading mutual fund management companies whose sponsors also handle the brokerage for their stock transactions tend to churn their portfolios (buy and sell excessively) in order to generate more brokerage fees. Others, he testified, churned to generate more business to reward brokers who also sell mutual funds and who may especially push the funds that give them brokerage business.

Hamer H. Budge, chairman of the SEC, pointed out that the contractual plan's front-end load has put a heavy burden on investors unable to complete their plans, and a large number do not complete them. As the plan sponsors' own statistics demonstrate, after ten- and thirteen-year periods, between 25 and 43 percent of plan holders had paid in no more than the installments scheduled for the first three years and about half of these did not even get past the first year.

Obviously many of them lost money. In fact, only because of the rising stock market of the past twenty years have long-term contractual-plan investors been able to offset the front-end loads and show a gain. In a bear market the combination of falling prices and the high percentage of the investment that goes to sales commission is a "terrifying" prospect, Budge warned.

The contract in terms of the sales load may not be quite clear to inexperienced investors. The contract says that of, say, $40 you contract to invest each month the custodian gets $1, and $20 is deducted from each of the first twelve payments "to be paid over" to the plan company. It doesn't say outright that the $20 is for the sales commission or that, of the $40 a month the investor may think he is investing, only

$19 actually will be credited to his account for each of the first twelve months. In twelve months you will have paid in $480. But $252 would have gone to the salesman commission and custodian charge and only $228 would be invested for you.

This is the unsavory side of what should be a basically useful investment medium for ordinary families—with the unsavoriness hard to regulate effectively because of the power and influence of the big and interlocked financial and mutual fund industries.

Given these problems, is it worthwhile to invest in mutual funds?

For the family unable or unwilling to do research for selecting its own stocks, or with too little capital for any kind of diversification, or no access to an investment club, mutual funds are one of the few ways to keep one foot or at least a few toes in the inflation-hedging camp. That is, it is if you carefully select your fund and manage your investments in it with a form of dollar averaging modified for your own needs.

But you can not consider mutual funds a sure way to riches. As performance records indicate, over a long term you should do a little better than leaving the money in the bank or in E bonds. For example, *Johnson's Charts* shows that at the end of the 1960–69 period, $10,000 left in a savings and loan association had a liquidating value of $10,000 and drew dividends of $4,298. Left in a mutual savings bank the liquidating value was $10,000 and the dividends $4,328. For the Johnson mutual fund average, the liquidating value was $14,984 and the dividends, $1,979.

Over the next ten years the results could be different. Other and high-yielding investments are available at least at this time for small investors too, as discussed in the succeeding chapters of this book. And over a short term you can lose money in mutual funds, as the performance tables in this chapter show.

It is possible to use a combination of investing an extra sum in mutual funds at times when stock prices are low, with the dollar averaging available through automatic reinvestment of dividends. This method offers some of the safety of dollar averaging while retaining an opportunity to buy when prices are low. You can never be sure of exact timing in buying or cashing in of shares. But, as the Wright Investment Service pointed out, it is more important to avoid speculative buying at the highs than to sell out at the top, and more important not to sell out at the lows than to buy at the bottom.

This is not to advise the use of mutual funds for speculative investment, although some investors use them that way. But in view of the fact that the timing of some mutual fund managers themselves has not been dependable, it is prudent to reduce amounts invested after an upsurge or even while the price is on the way up.

How does investing in mutual funds compare with buying stocks?

As the chart in this chapter shows, among the leading investment funds listed by United Business Service's *Mutual Fund Selector*, the stock funds went up more in the five years from 1965 to 1969 when the market was going up, than did Standard & Poor's 500-stock average. The Standard & Poor's average comprises most of the active stocks traded on the New York Stock Exchange. The leading mutual funds also went up much more than the Dow-Jones index of thirty blue-chip stocks.

But in the sharp decline in 1969 and the first half of 1970, stock-type mutual funds did not resist the general drop in values as well as did the blue chips and also went down somewhat more than the 500-stock average.

Similarly, the Arthur Lipper Corp. analysis shows that the average for the entire mutual fund industry declined approximately 28 percent in the twelve months from June 30, 1969, to June 30, 1970, compared to declines of 22 percent for the Dow-Jones, 26 for the Standard & Poor's 500, and 28 for the American Stock Exchange index.[37]

Undoubtedly the larger gains recorded by mutual funds on the upside, and somewhat larger loss on the downside, was due to the more speculative trend among some mutual

Making the Most of Your Investment Dollars

funds with the appearance of the go-go or high-performance funds.

Dividends paid by mutual funds are a little less on the average than those paid by common stocks—3 to 3½ percent in early 1971 compared to 3½ to 4 for stocks. The main concentration of several classifications of funds described later in this chapter is on capital gains and growth, although there are income funds too, which pay higher immediate dividends.

Shopping Mutual Funds

Mutual fund shares are not bought and sold on the stock market as are stocks but are sold by dealers (who are often stockbrokers) and by salesmen representing a group of funds under the same management or, in the case of no-load funds, by the fund management itself. Most dealers handle a number of mutual funds and can help you select one with a good performance record whose investment objectives are suitable for your purpose. However, some dealers may principally represent a specific fund and may tend to emphasize that fund. It is wise to compare the suitability and performance of a number of funds before deciding on one.

Among the important criteria for selecting a mutual fund or funds are its previous performance, the suitability of its objectives for your investment purposes, and the amount of load or sales commission it charges you.

How well a fund has performed in the past is no assurance of future success, but it is an indication of effective management. Read the prospectuses of various mutual funds. By law these must state their past record of gains and earnings.

Usually the prospectus will show an illustration of an assumed investment of $10,000 in the fund over the past ten years (if the fund has been operating that long). It will show the value of the shares each year. This will give you an idea both of the long-term growth and how well the fund resisted market declines in those years. The table in the prospectus showing what happened to the $10,000 will show the dividends paid and distributions from realized capital gains. The prospectus also will tell you the size of the fund and will list its investments. From this you will be able to learn whether the fund invests mainly in seasoned blue chips, quality growth stocks, younger growth stocks, such as dynamic small companies, or the businessman's risks described in chapter 9.

You can get the prospectuses of different mutual funds by writing for them. You also can examine the current performance results of various funds in such compilations as Wiesenberger's *Investment Companies Annual,* Johnson's *Charts,* the United *Mutual Fund Selector,* the Arthur Lipper Corp. *Mutual Fund Performance Analysis, Forbes* magazine's annual fund ratings (usually published in the August issue), *Fundscope* magazine, and other guides. Some of these manuals and services are expensive but often are available at the larger public libraries.

George Frazer, who considers mutual funds to be the best medium for the small investor, advised that the buyer should study performance over the past eight years. Frazer noted that often a mutual fund will show dramatic growth in its first seven years. After that, growth depends on management skill, and the effect of that will not be revealed for another few years.

Also observe the performance of the various funds for a short recent period, such as the past year or two, and observe how they performed in periods of stress as well as in rising markets.

In reading the prospectuses, note the management fee. In some smaller funds, it may amount to as much as 1 percent; in some larger ones, as little as one-eighth of 1 percent. But some large funds have been criticized for keeping their management fees at one-half of 1 percent.

The prospectus also states the mutual fund's investment objective. The various funds usually are classified as income funds, specializing in providing more current income; growth funds, specializing in investments in companies and industries with above-average growth expectations; balanced funds,

Making the Most of Your Investment Dollars

which also invest in bonds and preferred stocks; and performance funds, which seek relatively fast gains (and are the most speculative kind).

Growth funds are more suitable for younger families seeking capital gains; income funds, for retired people. Balanced funds are less useful because you can invest part of your money in bonds and preferred stocks yourself without paying a high mutual fund sales commission to do so.

If you already own shares in one type of fund, say, a growth fund, and want to switch to an income fund, see if the same investment company has the kind you now want. You can change for a nominal fee instead of paying a new sales commission.

In fact, reputable brokers warn to beware of a salesman for a brokerage house or mutual fund dealer who may try to switch you among different funds. You then pay the high sales load both times. Scrupulous dealers do not permit their salesmen to do this.

No-Load Funds

There are a number of mutual funds that charge no or very little sales fee. They have no salesmen but offer their prospectuses through ads in newspaper financial pages and magazines.

There also are several so-called low-load funds, which charge a small sales fee such as 1, 2, or 3 percent.

The directory of no-load mutual funds in this chapter gives the addresses of these funds and also that for the Fund for Mutual Depositors sponsored by savings banks. Shares are sold only to depositors in certifying savings banks in some states (at this writing, Alaska, Connecticut, Delaware, Maine, Massachusetts, Minnesota, New Hampshire, New Jersey, New York, Oregon, Pennsylvania, Rhode Island, Vermont). A depositor at a certifying bank must get a certification of his depositor status from the bank.

The advice often is given to pick a mutual fund on the basis of its performance rather than its load or sales commission. For example, a load fund, Oppenheimer, is at or near the top of most long-term performance lists. However, the list of the forty leading funds for ten years adapted from the Wiesenberger analysis includes a number of no-load funds, such as American Investors, Johnston Mutual, T. Rowe Price Growth Stock Fund, Penn Square Mutual, Guardian Mutual and Templeton Growth Fund (shares are sold only over the counter at this writing).

Similarly, the table of performance of twenty-five leading funds under different circumstances also shows a number of no-loads, such as Johnston Mutual and T. Rowe Price Growth Stock Fund, performing well in both up and down years. The low-load Istel Fund, with a sales charge of 3 percent, also performed well. (These lists are not published as recommendations but only as examples for this discussion of how to select a fund yourself. Performances change; yesterday's mutual fund hero may be tomorrow's drone. You need to get current data on relative results and also select according to your own objective.)

Note that these are management results only. They show how well management did. The percentage changes on the Wiesenberger and Lipper lists are based on net assets per share and thus do not allow for sales charges. The lists of twenty-five leading funds derived from the United *Mutual Fund Selector* also show relative performance only and do not take the load into account. If these lists did, the no-load performance would be relatively even better because more of the investment would go to work sooner. (The annual ratings by *Forbes* do show how to adjust results for the load.) The lists do take into account dividend and capital gains distribution, because they are part of the measure of performance.

One analysis, by J. A. Livingston, nationally-syndicated financial writer, did show that if you took the sales load into account, on a $1,000 investment the average no-load fund came out $209 ahead of the average fund with an 8½ percent sales charge in a ten-year period. Nearly all of the $209 represented the compounding of earnings on the extra $85 not paid as a commission, Livingston noted.

Making the Most of Your Investment Dollars

"The only certain fact about comparative performance [of load vs. no-load funds] is that a fund with an 8½ percent sales charge must show 9.3 percent growth just to get back to the point where a no-load fund started," J. O. Richards, vice-president of Hartwell Management Corp., told the 1970 *Institutional Investor* Conference.[38]

An analysis by Ian M. Rolland, a well-known actuary and second vice-president of the Lincoln National Life Insurance, showed graphically how much better a load-type fund or variable annuity with an 8 percent load must perform to yield as much return as a no-load fund. This example assumes that the no-charge fund earns 6 percent investment return each year.

Difference in Annual Investment Return	Accumulation at End of 20 Years	
	8% Charge Fund ($920 Applied)	No-Charge Fund ($1,000 Applied)
none	$35,873.31	$38,992.73
+¼%	36,939.39	38,992.73
+½%	38,041.03	38,992.73
+¾%	39,179.48	38,922.73
+ 1%	40,355.97	38,992.73

In other words, if the return is the same, the no-charge or no-load fund accumulates $3,000 more. Even if the charge fund is able to produce an additional one-half of 1 percent higher annual return, the no-load still accumulates more money. "It would take an additional three-quarters of 1 percent annually to offset the 8 percent expense charge," Rolland told the 1970 Conference of Actuaries in Public Practice.

When looking at the quotations of mutual funds in financial pages, you can tell the no-load from the load funds this way: the load funds have a higher asked than bid price. The difference represents the load. For the no-loads, the bid and asked price are the same.

The comparison of performance of different types of funds shows that in recent years the no-loads have performed well.

Note also the greater growth of stock funds in up years compared to the balanced funds but the somewhat better resistance of the balanced funds to declines.

Closed-End Funds

Another type of investment company is called a closed-end fund. Its shares are traded on the stock market, unlike the mutual funds (called open-end) described previously, whose shares are sold through dealers or by no-load funds themselves. (Some closed-end funds are traded in the over-the-counter market.)

Closed-end funds invest in stocks just as the mutual funds do. Commissions for buying shares in closed-end funds are lower than for fee-charging mutual funds; you pay only the standard broker's fee as for any stock. But you also pay the standard commission when you sell the shares.

Shares of closed-end investment companies sometimes can be bought for less than the net asset value of the securities they own. For example, the fund may own assets worth $11.50 for each fund share. But the fund share may be quoted on the stock market at only $8. On the other hand, some closed-end funds at times are quoted at more than their asset value.

Of twenty-three closed-end funds whose prices are quoted by the Association of Closed-End Investment Companies, fifteen were selling for less than their asset values in August, 1970. The others were at or above asset value. In general, this is a more sophisticated type of investment. It may require investigation or a broker's guidance to determine why a closed-end company may be selling far below asset value or, if above, to ascertain if it is still a good choice. For example, a closed-end fund may have many outstanding rights or warrants. These would dilute the asset value if many of the holders of these rights converted them into shares. Or professional investors may not value the prospects of a particular closed-end fund highly on the basis of its record.

On the other hand, the fund may sell below its asset value only because investor interest has not yet caught up with the rise in value of the securities it owns. Sometimes the prices of closed-end funds are a little sluggish in relation

Making the Most of Your Investment Dollars

to the rest of the stock market, thus presenting a possible investment opportunity.

On the other hand, some of the more successful closed-end funds sell at a premium, which is sometimes high, over their net asset value.

As the chart comparing performance of different types of funds shows, the performance of closed-end funds as a whole has approximately paralleled that of the open-end funds, except for the better resistance to the 1969 decline.

This list of closed-end funds should not be regarded as a recommendation because value will depend on price, asset value, and general prospects at the time of purchase.

> Adams Express; American European; Carriers & General; Diebold Venture; Dominick Fund; Eurofund; General American Investors; International Holdings; Japan Fund; Lehman Corp.; Madison Fund; National Aviation; Niagara Share Corp.; Overseas Securities; Petroleum Corp.; Tri-Continental Corp.; United Corp.; U.S. & Foreign Securities.

As with open-end mutual funds, some closed-end investment funds have particular specialties; others are more diversified. Some invest more heavily in foreign corporations; others invest in shares of petroleum companies, mining, land and real estate, growth stocks, and so forth.

As with mutual funds, check the past earnings performance of the various closed-end funds in Wiesenberger, Data Digests, United Business Service, and other reports that your library or a stockbroker can supply. Some closed-end funds have excellent records and high yields in dividends and distributed capital gains. Others may have less successful records.

Some closed-end funds may be more volatile (rising further and falling harder). Specialized funds sometimes are more volatile; diversified ones, more stable.

Dual Funds

One interesting type of mutual fund, which for a few years at least may offer an unusual investment opportunity, is dual investment funds. They are closed-end now. But later (mostly in the early 1980s), when the preferred shares are paid off, they will become open-end funds. Then the shares will be redeemable at asset value just like the more traditional open-end mutual funds.

The dual funds, unlike other mutual funds, have two classes of shares. One type, the preferred shares, is called income shares. They get all the dividends and none of the capital gains. The capital shares get all the capital gains but none of the dividends. Often retired people and others in low brackets (nonworking widows, children) buy the income shares; and younger investors, the capital shares.

The income shares of some dual funds have been yielding relatively stable high immediate income, such as 6 to 7 percent. The prices of the income shares also are relatively stable. When the dual fund converts to an open-end fund, the income shareholders will get back what they paid in.

The capital shares are considered speculative because they have high leverage for capital gains—or losses. These shares can go up sharply in a general stock market rise but also down sharply in a general decline. After a decline some noticeable leverage possibilities develop because the value of the capital shares rises at a faster rate than the net asset value per share of the securities the fund owns.

When the stock market is up, the capital shares usually sell at a discount from net asset value. When the market is down, they often sell at a large premium, because of the high leverage in the depressed shares.

Comparing market prices of the dual funds over a number of years, as shown in the Lipper report, will reveal which are most volatile and which most stable. The Hemisphere Fund, for example, was $12 a share in mid-1967, and $4 in mid-1970, at which time it sold at a premium because of its high leverage. The more stable Gemini Fund moved down only from $14 to $12.

During the period before they become open-end funds, the dual funds are traded (bought and sold) on the stock exchanges just like any other stock, with transactions handled by regular stockbrokers—except for the Putnam Duo-Fund, which is sold in the over-the-counter market.

Making the Most of Your Investment Dollars

The dual funds usually are sponsored by investment companies who also manage the more orthodox mutual funds. Others besides those mentioned include American DualVest, Income and Capital Fund, Leverage Fund, and Scudder Duo-Vest.

Specialized Funds

There also are a number of specialized mutual funds.

Bond and preferred stock funds offer small investors an opportunity to invest in tax-exempt securities and in high-yielding corporate bonds and preferred stocks, and are described in chapter 11.

Real estate and mortgage investment trusts offer participation in mortgage and real estate ventures, as described in chapter 13.

Mutual funds and syndicates organized for oil and gas drillings have tax advantages described in chapter 14, but also large risks and require relatively large investments. For example, the minimum investment in White Shield, one of the largest of such syndicates, is $10,000.

PERFORMANCE COMPARISON OF DIFFERENT TYPES OF FUNDS*
(Showing results for a recent five-year period, for an up year [1967], and a down year [1969])

	5 years 1964–69	1967	1969	First 6 mos. 1970
49 Open-End Stock Funds	+44.9%	+28.85%	−11.5%	−21.4%
14 Open-End Balanced Funds	+22.6	+18.6	−11.3	−14.2
Average	+33.75	+23.7	−11.4	−19.8
10 No-Load Stock Funds	+53.7	+27.4	− 9.25	−23.4
7 Closed-End Funds	+45.9	——	− 6.2	−22.2
22 Go-Go Funds	——	——	——	−32.2
Standard & Poor's 500-Stock Average	+ 2.6	+22	− 8	−19.3
Dow-Jones Industrial Average	+ 9	+19	−12	−12.6

* Derived from *Mutual Fund Selector*, United Business Service.

25 LEADING FUNDS UNDER DIFFERENT CIRCUMSTANCES**

(Showing results for a recent five-year period, for an up year [1967], and a down year [1969])

5 years 1964–69		1967		1969	
*American Investors	+86%	Keystone S–4	+63%	Chemical Fund	+5.8%
Colonial Growth	+82	Istel Fund	+54	National Investors	+4.1
Anchor Growth Fund	+78	Colonial Growth	+53	*T. Rowe Price Growth	+3.4
*Johnston Mutual	+78	Anchor Growth Fund	+52	*Johnston Mutual	+0.4
Chemical Fund	+77	Fund of America	+50	Mass. Inv. Growth	+0.2
Windsor Fund	+77	*American Investors	+46	Putnam Investors	+0.3
Keystone S–4	+76	Keystone K–2	+45	Windsor Fund	−3.4
Istel Fund	+74	Channing Growth	+44	Broad St. Inv.	−3.7
National Investors	+74	Putnam Growth	+40	*One William St.	−3.8
*T. Rowe Price Growth	+72	*Energy Fund	+39	Dividend Shares	−4.8
Delaware Fund	+70	National Securities	+38	Mass. Investors Trust	−4.8
*de Vegh Mutual	+67	Pioneer Fund	+37	Selected American	−5.7
Putnam Growth	+67	Salem Fund	+36	*Scudder, Bal. Fd.	−5.9
National Securities	+66	Investors Variable	+33	*Scudder, Com. Fd.	−6.6
Channing Growth	+65	Keystone S–3	+33	Bullock Fund	−6.6
Pioneer Fund	+65	Chemical Fund	+31	*Fidelity Stock	−7.0
Salem Fund	+64	National Investors	+31	Loomis-Sayles	−7.2
Mass. Inv. Growth	+63	Technology Fund	+31	Life Ins. Investors	−7.2
Investment Co. Amer.	+61	United Science	+31	*Stein Roe Farnham Stock	−7.3
Keystone S–3	+61	Value Line Fund	+31	*Stein Roe Farnham Bal.	−7.5
Dreyfus Fund	+60	Windsor Fund	+31	State St. Investment	−8.3
Keystone K–2	+58	Colonial Fund	+30	Investors Stock Fund	−8.6
Technology Fund	+58	Delaware Fund	+30	Technology Fund	−8.9
*Energy Fund	+57	*Johnston Mutual	+30	*Guardian Mutual	−8.9
State St. Invest.	+53	Mass. Inv. Growth	+29	United Science Fund	−9.3

* No-load funds.
** Derived from *Mutual Fund Selector*, United Business Service.

TOP 40 FUNDS FOR 10 YEARS

(Adapted from Wiesenberger *Mutual Fund Management Results*; compares results based on net assets per share, not investment results)

	1960–69
Oppenheimer Fund	278.5
Fidelity Capital Fund	252.2
Value Line Special Situations	237.3
Winfield Growth Fund	225.8
Value Line Fund	215.5
***American Investors Fund	208.9
*First Sierra Fund	207.6
Knickerbocker Growth Fund	207.6
***Hedberg & Gordon Fund	204.9
Axe-Houghton Stock Fund	203.5
**Templeton Growth Fund	201.7
Mutual Securities Fund of Boston	201.3
Istel Fund	186.7
Vanderbilt Mutual Fund	185.8
Putnam Growth Fund	173.5
***Johnston Mutual Fund	170.8
Chase Fund of Boston	169.1
Investors Research Fund	164.5
Dreyfus Fund	162.3
***Mairs & Power Growth Fund	162.2
Twentieth Century-Growth Investors	162.0
***T. Rowe Price Growth Stock Fund	161.4
National Investors Corp.	159.2
Chemical Fund	158.6
***Penn Square Mutual Fund	158.2
Windsor Fund	154.7
Investment Company of America	154.5
Pioneer Fund	153.2
Admiralty (Morton) Growth Series	149.5
Channing Special Fund	148.7
Southwestern Investors	143.0

Delaware Fund	142.3
State Street Investment Corp.	141.6
Consumers Investment Fund	140.7
Keystone (S-3) Growth Common	134.9
Florida Growth Fund	134.9
Decatur Income Fund	134.7
Mass. Investors Growth Stock Fund	134.7
Axe-Houghton Fund A	134.3
***Guardian Mutual Fund	133.4
Average	173.85

* Insurance and bank stocks.
** Canadian and international issue.
*** No-load funds.

DIRECTORY OF NO-LOAD MUTUAL FUNDS

*Leon B. Allen Fund, 12 Broadway, New York, N.Y. 10005
Afuture Fund, 8 Pennell Road, Lima, Pa. 19060
American Enterprise Fund, 50 Broad St., New York, N.Y. 10004
American Investment Counseling Fund, 615 S. Flower St., Los Angeles, Calif. 90017
American Investors Fund, 88 Field Point Road, Greenwich, Conn. 06830
Argonaut Fund, 1545 First National Bank Building, San Diego, Calif. 92101
David L. Babson Investment Fund, 301 W. Eleventh St., Kansas City, Mo. 64105
Beacon Hill Mutual Fund, 75 Federal St., Boston, Mass. 02110
Bridges Investment Fund, 8401 W. Dodge Road, Omaha, Neb. 68114
The Burnham Fund, 60 Broad St., New York, N.Y. 10004
Columbia Balanced and Growth Funds, 409 American Bank Building, Portland, Ore. 97205
Connecticut Western Mutual Fund, 460 Summer St., Stamford, Conn. 06901
Consultant's Mutual Investments, 211 S. Broad St., Philadelphia, Pa. 19107

Making the Most of Your Investment Dollars 185

Counselors Investment Fund, 615 S. Flower St., Los Angeles, Calif. 90017
de Vegh Mutual Fund, 20 Exchange Place, New York, N.Y. 10005
Dodge & Cox Stock Fund, Crocker Plaza, Post at Montgomery St., San Francisco, Calif. 94104
Doll Fund, Thackery Lane, Mendham, N.J. 07945
Drexel Investment and Equity Funds, 1500 Walnut St., Philadelphia, Pa. 19101
East-West Fund, 9301 Wilshire, Beverly Hills, Calif. 90210
Edie Special Growth Fund, 530 Fifth Ave., New York, N.Y. 10036
Energy Fund, Inc., 55 Broad St., New York, N.Y. 10004
Farm Bureau Mutual Fund, 1000 Merchandise Mart, Chicago, Ill. 60654
Fund for Mutual Depositors, 200 Park Ave., New York, N.Y. 10017
General Securities, 133 S. Seventh St., Minneapolis, Minn. 55402
*Gibraltar Growth Fund, 2455 E. Sunrise Boulevard, Fort Lauderdale, Fla. 33304
Samuel Greenfield Fund, 25 Broad St., New York, N.Y. 10004
Guardian Mutual Fund, 120 Broadway, New York, N.Y. 10005
Hartwell & Campbell Fund, 345 Park Ave, New York, N.Y. 10022
Hedberg & Gordon, 1 Station Square, Paoli, Pa. 19301
Investment Guidance Fund, 1010 Euclid Ave., Cleveland, Ohio 44115
Investment Indicators Fund, Albert Building, 1010 "B" St., San Rafael, Calif. 94902
Ivy Fund, 155 Berkeley St., Boston, Mass. 02116
Johnston Mutual Fund, 460 Park Ave., New York, N.Y. 10022
Loomis-Sayles Mutual Funds, 225 Franklin St., Boston, Mass. 02110
Mairs & Power Growth Fund, W. 2062 First National Bank Building, St. Paul, Minn. 55101
Market Growth Fund, 1133 Avenue of the Americas, New York, N.Y. 10036
Mates Investment Fund, 1700 Broadway, New York, N.Y. 10019
Mathers Fund, 135 S. LaSalle St., Chicago, Ill. 60603
Medici Fund, 120 Broadway, New York, N.Y. 10005
Mediterranean Fund, 79 Milk St., Boston, Mass. 02109

Mutual Shares Corp., 200 E. Forty-second St., New York, N.Y. 10017
Naess & Thomas Special Fund, Arlington Building, 201 N. Charles St., Baltimore, Md. 21201
Nassau Fund, P.O. Box 629, Princeton, N.J. 08540
National Industries Fund, 1800 Avenue of the Stars, Room 525, Los Angeles, Calif. 90067
Nelson Fund, 345 Park Ave., Suite 2330, New York, N.Y. 10022
Northeast Investors Trust, 50 Congress St., Boston, Mass. 02109
Oceanographic Fund, 80 Broad St., New York, N.Y. 10004
One William Street Fund, 1 William St., New York, N.Y. 10004
Penn Square Mutual Fund, 451 Penn Square, Reading, Pa. 19603
Pension Equity Fund, 50 Broad St., New York, N.Y. 10004
Pine Street Fund, 20 Exchange Place, New York, N.Y. 10005
T. Rowe Price Growth Stock and New Horizon Funds, 1 Charles Center, Baltimore, Md. 21201
PRO Fund, 1107 Bethlehem Pike, Flourtown, Pa. 19031
Prudential Fund of Boston, 50 Congress St., Boston, Mass. 02109
Rittenhouse Fund, 2022 Two Penn Center Plaza, Philadelphia, Pa. 19102
Rochester Fund, 31 Main St., East Rochester, N.Y. 14614
Scudder Special Fund, 345 Park Ave., New York, N.Y. 10022
Scudder, Stevens & Clark Common Stock and Balanced Funds, 10 Post Office Square, Boston, Mass. 02109
Shamrock Fund, 1901 Avenue of the Stars, Century City, Los Angeles, Calif. 90067
Sherman Dean Fund, 140 Broadway, New York, N.Y. 10005
Smith, Barney Equity Fund, 42 Broadway, New York, N.Y. 10004
State Farm Growth and Income Funds, 112 E. Washington, Bloomington, Ill. 61701
Stein, Roe & Farnham Stock and Balanced Funds, 135 S. LaSalle St., Chicago, Ill. 60603
Variable Stock Fund, Ninth and Main, Richmond, Va. 23218
Wade Fund, 63 S. Main St., Suite 1213, Memphis, Tenn. 38103
Weingarten Equity Fund, 551 Fifth Ave., New York, N.Y. 10017
Wilshire Fund, Beneficial Standard Life Insurance Co., 3700 Wilshire Blvd., Los Angeles, Calif. 90052

---

* 1 percent load.

CHAPTER ELEVEN

The New Interest in Bonds, Preferreds, Governments, and Tax-Exempts

The high yields in the late 1960s and in 1970 of corporate bonds and preferred stocks, government obligations, and tax-exempt state and city bonds attracted attention among knowledgeable small investors to what once was an investment reserved for the rich.

There are opportunities here but facts you need to know. There also are new ways of investing in these securities through mutual funds and bank plans that have been developed exactly to facilitate participation of moderate- and medium-income savers.

Corporate Bonds and Preferred Stocks

When interest rates rise elsewhere, as on mortgages, government borrowings, and other debt, the prices of bonds and preferred stocks fall and their yields rise. In the early 1970s these yields often have been 7 to 8 percent.

Corporate bonds and preferred stocks differ from common stocks in that they have a prior claim on the company's earnings. The holders of these "senior securities" must be paid before the holders of the common stock. But holders of bonds and preferreds do not have the same opportunity to share in increases in the company's earnings, as do holders of the common. The interest or dividend on bonds and preferred stocks is fixed. The bond or preferred stock may be issued originally at a price, say, of $1,000 with a dividend of $7. It will continue to pay just that and no more.

Bonds and preferred stocks are not risk proof. They are bought or sold on the stock exchanges and over-the-counter market. Their market prices at various times may be more or less than the original issuing price. If the price of the security in this example fell to $900, the people who originally bought at $1,000 would take a loss if they went to sell. But people who then buy it at $900 would have a yield of almost 8 percent from the $7 dividend.

If the price fell any further, investors who bought at $900 could suffer a loss too. But the new buyers also could achieve a capital gain if tight money and interest rates relaxed and demand increased as other investors again bought bonds and preferred stocks.

You can be sure of getting your original investment back on corporate bonds if you can wait for the maturity date. Then the issuing corporation will pay the face value. For some bonds this may mean a wait of fifteen or twenty years. But there are bonds of almost any maturity date; and if you select those that will mature in a few years, you do have protection against losses if you paid little or no more than face value. In fact, if you buy short-term or intermediate-term bonds in the open market for less than face value, you will not only enjoy the yield meanwhile but also will have a capital gain, taxable at the long-term lower rate.

Corporations have issued more of the relatively short-term bonds, maturing in, for example, four to six years, during the high-interest rate of the late 1960s and 1970. Thus, more bonds with this kind of built-in protection are available.

You do sacrifice some yield for the protection of the shorter term. For example, in mid-1970, a high-quality utility bond (Pacific Gas & Electric Co.) maturing in 1978 with an original interest rate of 3¾ percent was quoted at 69, a yield of 5.4 percent. The same corporation's 1984 4½s were quoted at 75, a yield of 6 percent; and its 1995 4½s at 64, a yield of 7 percent.

But long-term bonds are more vulnerable to fluctuations,

Making the Most of Your Investment Dollars

and even shorter-term bonds should be considered only for a family's long-range savings—money it knows it will not need soon.

Bonds are issued in $1,000 denominations. This poses a problem for small investors. Most brokerage houses and bond dealers prefer that you buy $3,000 to $5,000 in bonds. One reason is that their commission on bonds is less than on common stocks and small purchases are too costly to handle. Another is that the bonds are then a little easier to resell later.

You also can buy so-called $100 baby bonds from odd-lot bond dealers. If you later sell these, you will get two points less than the prevailing quotations. Even with baby bonds, it is usually better to buy at least $1,000 in bonds to facilitate later resale. Your broker or bank can direct you to odd-lot dealers if they prefer not to handle the transaction themselves.

It also is advisable for small investors to stick to bonds listed on the exchanges. Such listed bonds offer a better market for small lots when you go to sell, and you probably will get a little better price than if a small lot must be sold through an odd-lot bond dealer. There also are bond and preferred stock mutual funds (listed at the end of this section).

When you see corporate bonds listed in the financial pages, they will be quoted at, for example, 98½. This really means $985. The listings also describe the bond by its original interest rate and its maturity date.

Actually if you are buying the senior securities of a well-established corporation with relatively stable earnings, such as a utility, there is no great yield advantage in buying bonds over preferred stocks, except for the large investor who can buy bonds in large lots more easily. Bonds are senior to preferreds and so provide a little more security. But preferreds are available in smaller lots, and at as good or better yield. For example, in mid-1970, the preferred stock of Duke Power yielded 8.7 percent and its bond 8.6. However, there is added investment safety for bonds bought below redemption value in that you ultimately can be certain to retrieve all your investment. You can not be similarly sure in the case of preferreds.

Bonds almost always have a maturity or call date. Preferreds do not usually have a maturity date and can remain outstanding indefinitely, although from time to time companies do call them in for redemption. They would then be redeemed at the face value. If you paid less, you would have a capital gain; more, a loss.

In theory the bond interest is more assured. The directors could skip a dividend on a preferred. But most outstanding preferreds are cumulative. Thus, omitted dividends would build up and must be paid before dividends can be paid on the company's common stock.

While preferred stocks are considered a security type of investment, for additional assurance, ask your broker to look up the rating in Moody's or Standard & Poor's ratings. If you buy a bond or preferred stock rated C instead of an A-rating bond, you would get greater yield but could expect more risk.

Bonds can be bought through a broker or a bank. Brokers are not anxious to handle small bond purchases but will if you are a customer. As noted, the commissions are lower—until recently, $2.50 per $1,000 bond. Now more brokers are charging $5 a bond with a minimum fee of $10.

Here are several criteria for evaluating corporate bonds suggested by the Investment Dealers' Association of Canada.

1. Do earnings provide adequate coverage to pay the promised interest rate and to repay the principal when the bond comes due? Earnings available for bond interest of public utility companies should be at least twice the interest requirements, and three times in the case of industrial companies.

2. Do the assets pledged provide sufficient security? Funded debt should not normally exceed two-thirds of the value of net tangible assets for public utilities, one-half for industrials. Is the cushion of equity capital underlying the bond issue ample enough? Market value of common and

preferred shares should be at least equal to the par value of the mortgage bonds outstanding.

Read also the section on tax handling of bonds in chapter 14.

Convertible Bonds and Preferreds

Convertible bonds and convertible preferred stocks are issued with the option of being exchanged for a stipulated number of shares of the issuing corporation's common stock. If the common goes up, its convertible securities will too because they can be converted into stock. For example, a convertible bond was issued by one company at $100, with the privilege of conversion into four shares of its common stock, then $25 a share. Subsequently when the common stock rose to $32.50 a share, the convertible bond rose to $133 a share.

You do pay a little more for the conversion privilege. You could have bought four shares of common stock for $130. But you would now have to pay $133 for a bond convertible into four shares. Many convertible securities command even higher premiums depending on the value investors place on the issuing company's prospects. The premium indicates how much the common stock must rise for the convertible to be equal in value.

If the premium is moderate and if the company has favorable earnings prospects, convertible securities lessen but do not eliminate the risk of loss while giving you an opportunity to share in growth.

Often the yield from convertible securities, while lower than from nonconvertible bonds and preferred stocks, will be more when first issued than provided by the same company's common stock. But when the convertible rises, its yield shrinks, because the dividend remains constant. In the example of the convertible bond at $100, the original yield was $5 at a time when the common stock was yielding 4 percent. But at $133, the same $5 represented a yield of less than 3.8 percent. Meanwhile, the common stock continued to yield 4 percent, due to increased dividends. Thus, the current yield needs to be compared too. Perhaps most important, it is never advisable to buy a convertible if you would not buy the same company's stock.

If the price of the common stock goes down, the market value of the company's convertible securities will go down too. But convertibles usually have some defensive quality. The drop may not be as precipitous for the convertibles because the fixed dividend then offers a higher yield and attracts other investors. This is not to say that convertibles are riskless. They do have a risk element.

The convertible should sell for less or not too much more than its redemption price. It should yield almost as much as bonds without a conversion privilege and should be convertible into the company's common stock at prices not too far above the current level of the common stock. The conversion privilege should be long enough so that the stock will have a chance to rise before the conversion date expires.

Bond and preferred stock mutual funds, with sales charge shown in parentheses, include Investors Selective Fund (7 percent), Keystone Custodian B-1 (4.15 percent), Keystone Custodian B-2 and B-4 (8.3 percent), and National Securities Bond and Preferred Stock Series (8.5 percent).

More Yield from Lending to the Government

The higher yields in recent years of U.S. government bills, notes, and bonds, and of those of other federal agencies, has attracted the interest of small investors.

Unfortunately, as noted in chapter 1, the complaints of savings associations and banks that savers were drawing out money to buy the government debt obligations led the U.S. Treasury and the agencies involved to raise the limits from the previous $1,000 purchases permitted on short-term borrowings to $10,000 (less on some agency borrowings). Uncle Sam had suddenly seemed to act more like a third cousin.

But $1,000 purchases are still available at this writing on some federal securities with maturities of one year or longer. Moreover, new mutual funds for government securities offer an even simpler way to participate in Treasury borrowings at times when they are high (they do, of course, fluctuate).

Making the Most of Your Investment Dollars

Treasury securities include short-term bills, notes, and bonds.

The short-term bills are discounted notes that reach their full interest in one year or less. An investor who has $10,000 to invest can send in his certified or cashier's check for $10,000 to any of the regional Federal Reserve offices, say he will accept the "noncompetitive average price," and state the maturity wanted.

The Federal Reserve bank or branch in your area will provide forms you can use for such noncompetitive tenders.

You get back your bill by registered mail. The Treasury also will mail you a check for the discount (the difference between the purchase price and the face value).

Three- and six-month bills are auctioned off every week; nine- and twelve-month bills, monthly (on the last day of each month).

These are bearer securities and are just like cash. That is why they must be sent back by registered mail and kept in a safe-deposit box.

Treasury bonds and notes can be registered in your name. A Treasury "bond" is defined as five years or more. However, Treasury bonds have not been issued since mid-1965 because the law says the government can not pay more than 4¾ percent on such bonds.

Some older series come in denominations as small as $500 and $1,000. On new issues of notes, the Treasury can still go down as low as $1,000.

Treasury notes are issued for one to seven years, at which time the principal becomes payable. Denominations are $1,000, $5,000, and higher. The bonds and notes bear interest payable semiannually. These are issued on a regular quarterly cycle.

Older Treasury notes and bonds can be bought in the open market, and new ones can be bought through the Federal Reserve banks and branches or through your bank. If you are interested in future issues, you can watch the financial pages of newspapers for announcements or ask your bank to let you know immediately about any announcement.

In general, the notes and bonds are more feasible for small investors than the short-term bills. They are available in registered form, and the transaction costs are spread over a longer period. Because dealers, banks, and brokers have increased their charges for handling these transactions, the cost of the transaction to buy a short-term obligation would soak up much of the yield. For example, if a broker or bank charges $5 per $1,000, or $25 for a $5,000 purchase, the round trip (buying and selling) would cost at least $50. You may also have to pay a service charge of $15 on each trip in addition. Thus, commissions of $80 on a $5,000 investment for one year would reduce a 6 percent yield to 4.4 percent. Thus, buying notes or bonds for only a year may not be feasible.

A bank may charge you less commission but then may conceal some of its real charge in a slightly higher quote to you than it paid for the bonds. But you could compare commissions among a bank, broker, and bond dealer.

In any case you pay a little more than the prices quoted in the newspaper financial tables if you buy an odd lot—under $100,000 in the case of Treasury instruments.

Other federal agencies also issue bonds, notes, and debentures with relative high yields at this writing—sometimes even higher than the Treasury borrowings. These instruments include Federal Land Bank bonds, Federal Home Loan Bank notes, Federal Intermediate Credit Bank debentures, Bank for Cooperatives debentures, and Federal National Mortgage Association issues.

These agencies too have raised their minimum purchase on new issues to $10,000 but smaller issues are available through bond dealers or through your broker. As with corporate bonds, typically, the longer the maturity, the higher the yield.

The Home Loan Bank minimum at this writing is $10,000; the Bank for Cooperatives, $5,000; FNMA, $10,000 for most of its new issues. Only the farm credit agencies still issue $1,000 notes or bonds.

The securities of the farm credit agencies pay a little higher yield because they do not have quite as good credit as the other government agencies due to certain restrictions on their instruments. Nor are they as widely traded or as liquid.

Making the Most of Your Investment Dollars

At 1970–71 yields of 6 to 7 percent, many of these agency bonds and notes, as well as the Treasury instruments, are feasible intermediate investments for small investors who can invest several thousand dollars.

You can consult *The Bond Buyer,* a financial publication, for information on future issues of both federal and municipal bonds.

Representative bank dealers who act as primary dealers in U.S. government securities include: Bankers Trust Co., New York; Chemical Bank New York Trust Co.; Continental Illinois National Bank and Trust Co. of Chicago; the First National Bank of Chicago; First National City Bank, New York; Harris Trust and Savings Bank, Chicago; Morgan Guaranty Trust Co. of New York; United California Bank, Los Angeles.

Leading non-bank dealers, most of whom have branches in major cities, include: Blyth and Co.; Briggs, Schaedle and Co.; Discount Corp. of New York; the First Boston Corp.; Aubrey G. Lanston and Co.; Merrill Lynch, Pierce, Fenner, and Smith; New York Hanseatic Corp.; William E. Pollock and Co.; Charles E. Quincey and Co.; D. W. Rich and Co.; Salomon Brothers and Hutzler; Second District Securities Co.

The Bond Buyer also has a directory of bond dealers if you want to buy directly from a dealer. The larger dealers have branches in various cities. Usually your broker or bank will go to the dealer for odd-lot purchases. You can also ask the dealer to put you on his list to receive his periodic listings of quotations for available bonds, the yields, and the smallest amounts available.

As noted in chapter 14, federal securities are fully taxable for federal income tax but exempt from state and local income taxes.

Perhaps the simplest way to participate in the high yields of government securities is through the several mutual funds and at least one bank plan organized for this purpose.

One such is Mutual Fund for Investing in U.S. Government Securities, 701 William Penn Place, Pittsburgh, Pa. 15230. The distributor is Federal Investors, Inc., 421 Seventh Ave., Pittsburgh, Pa. 15219. Shares also can be bought through brokers. The fund has a low load of 1½ percent up to $10,000; less for larger amounts. The early 1970 yield was a little over 7 percent. The yield is a little higher than Treasury bills despite the one-half of 1 percent fee for management, and a similar fee for the bank for safekeeping of the shareholder's shares. The yield can be higher because the fund invests in FNMA and other agency securities as well as federal securities to get a higher yield. The fund buys short-term securities such as sixteen months to make sure investments remain liquid and can recapture the full investment. Income is paid quarterly. Shareholders can make periodic withdrawals if they have over $5,000 in shares.

The 1½ percent load reduces the yield about one-tenth of 1 percent. A $10 unit costs $10.16 with the load. Initial investment is $250.

Another mutual fund in this category is Atlantic Fund for Investment in U.S. Government Securities, 70 Wall Street, New York, N.Y. 10004. This fund charges no sales load at this writing but may in the future. Minimum investment can be as low as one share ($25 to $26). Yield usually is approximately the yield on Treasury bills.

Amalgamated Bank of New York offers USAVE participation certificates (paying 6 percent per year in early 1971, payable at maturity and compounded yearly). Certificates are available in maturities of one year, eighteen months, or three years. The offerings may be terminated and renewed from time to time, and the yield may change with changes in the supply of available government securities and changes in yields. Minimum purchase is $500. Address of the bank is 11 Union Square, New York, N.Y. 10003.

Tax-Exempt Securities

Even taxpayers in moderate brackets have begun to take advantage of the relatively high yields in recent years of tax-exempt bonds. Such securities have a somewhat lower yield than federal securities because they are exempt from federal tax. They usually are subject to state tax unless they are the bonds of your own state.

Making the Most of Your Investment Dollars

Such tax-exempt securities include municipal, state, authority, school, toll road, sewer district, housing authority, and similar state and local bonds.

Yields on tax-exempt securities are affected directly by prevailing interest rates and the supply and demand for loanable funds. The yields are usually quoted as "current yield" and "yield to maturity." The current yield is the percentage the bond yields on the stated interest rate in relation to its current market price. The yield to maturity is the annual percentage return that will be realized if a bond is held to maturity. It is a combination of current yield and the difference between the price you pay and the face amount of the bond.

The coupon or interest rate you see quoted on a tax-exempt bond in newspaper financial pages, of course, is not the actual yield. For example, "Ohio Turnpike 3¼s 92" at an "asked" price of "74" means that $1,000 of face value bonds maturing in 1992 and with a coupon of 3¼ percent (a dollar value yield of $32.50) would cost $740. Your actual current yield thus would be 5 percent. (In a 30 percent tax bracket this would be the equivalent of a taxable yield of about 7 percent.)

Note in chapter 14 the discussion of the uses and handling of tax-exempt bonds, and read the definitions in the glossary. In general tax-exempt bonds are speculative. However, purchases of such bonds can be managed to eliminate much of the capital risk. These bonds are recommended primarily for long-term investing, but in periods when tax-exempt bonds are selling below or close to their call prices, you can choose issues that come due in specific years when you will need the cash. Thus, if you will need cash for a child's college expenses in five or six years, you can choose an issue that will come due at that time.

If you have enough cash to invest, you can even select several issues coming due at varying dates. This technique minimizes the capital risk. For example, you can combine short maturities for price stability and liquidity with long maturities for maximum yield.

Simply keep in mind that the further the due date, the

higher the yield; the closer the due date, the less fluctuation in the future market price. In 1970, a typical $1,000 school district bond maturing in 1976 would have cost about $800 and would have had a yield to maturity of about 6 percent. The same school district's bonds maturing in 1980 had an offering price of $685 and a yield to maturity of 7 percent. (Current yields may differ from this example but the relationship will be similar.)

The risks in buying tax-exempts are greatest when interest rates are relatively low and tax-exempt bonds are selling at or near face value or even at a premium above. If interest rates in general rise, the market price of tax-exempts will fall.

Tax-exempt bonds are rated by Standard & Poor's and Moody's with lower-rated bonds paying a higher yield because of their greater risk. Thus, an AA bond might yield 5 percent and a BB bond, 6.

You can buy tax-exempt bonds through your broker, who probably will buy them from an odd-lot bond dealer. Your broker will charge a moderate commission, such as $5 a bond. Others may waive the commission for a regular customer and get their commission from the bond house.

Most bonds issued since 1960 are $5,000 denominations. Earlier bonds may be $1,000 denominations. But you really may not need to invest $5,000 for a $5,000 bond at times when many bonds sell at discounts from the face value. A $5,000 face-value bond may actually cost only $3,500. Some small investors even invest $2,000 or so at a time in tax-exempts as they accumulate funds, although they may have to wait until the bond house has a suitable bond.

You can, of course, deal directly with a bond house. Some deal only with large institutional buyers. Two of the larger dealers who handle transactions directly with the public as well as with brokers are Lebenthal & Co., 1 Chase Manhattan Plaza, New York, N.Y. 10005, and Gibraltar Securities Co., 10 Commerce Court, Newark, N.J. 07102, and 9100 Wilshire Boulevard, Beverly Hills, Calif. 90212.

Several mutual funds for tax-exempt bonds also have been developed or are in process of formation. Their shares usually are sold through brokers and involve a sales fee. For example, the Nuveen Tax-Exempt Bond Fund (61 Broadway, New York, N.Y. 10006) has a sales load of 4½ percent on primary offerings, and 5½ percent on secondary distributions.

This particular fund yielded 6.8 percent on its portfolio of bonds in late 1970. The sales load reduced the yield to approximately 6.5 percent. The primary offerings require a minimum investment of fifty $100 units—a total of $5,000. But as few as ten units can be bought in the secondary offerings.

CHAPTER TWELVE

Managing Fixed-Value Savings for Highest Return

You no longer can leave savings in an account simply because the depository is convenient or you have always kept your account there.

There are too many significant differences in recent years among various savings institutions and between ordinary and long-term accounts to permit apathy even about modest funds. As noted in chapter 8, a difference of 1 or 1½ percent in yield of even moderate savings can amount to thousands of dollars over a period of years because of the power of compound interest.

Too, tax considerations become increasingly important. Some types of fixed-value savings can be used to minimize or even escape taxes, as explained in chapter 14.

The other side of the coin, literally, is that some types of fixed-value investments actually can cause you to forfeit part of your savings if you must withdraw earlier. There are deferred face certificates that will at least return your original investment or deposit if you need your money before you complete the plan. But there are others, discussed later in this chapter, that actually have a front-end load like contractual mutual funds.

Life insurance or annuities used as savings also can cause unexpected losses, if you must discontinue within the first few years.

The first need is to separate your cash holdings into short-

Making the Most of Your Investment Dollars

term and long-term funds—those you may need soon and those you are holding for future uses.

Short-Term Savings

Your short-term cash will earn less but there are still significant differences of as much as 1½ percent among various types of savings institutions such as credit unions, savings associations, mutual savings banks (in the states that have them), and commercial banks, as shown in the table of comparative yields in chapter 8. There also are differences in the way interest is paid. More institutions now pay from day of deposit to day of withdrawal. If this kind of account pays the same interest as a regular savings account, it is preferable. You do not lose interest if you withdraw during a calendar quarter.

Only cash accounts in such institutions should be used for short-term savings, not E bonds because of their lower yield if you cash them in the first year.

Long-Term Savings

You can get up to 6 percent on deposit certificates and deferred savings from many of the same institutions for funds you will not need, for example, for two to five years. In some cases the interest on these accounts is payable at maturity. But whether the accumulated yield can be tax-deferred is moot at this writing until the Internal Revenue Service finally settles this question. Depending on local practice, the minimum deposit may be $1,000. Slightly lower rates are paid on smaller amounts, for example, 5¾ percent on a minimum of $500 for one year.

On amounts of $5,000 or more, you could get as much as 7½ percent on discounted bank certificates in 1970 through deposit brokers. When these certificates are available, deposit brokers' ads giving the current rates appear in the financial pages of newspapers. These are insured certificates usually maturing in three, six, or twelve months and usually renewable at maturity.

At the 5½ percent rate enacted in 1970, E bonds are another useful medium for long-range savings because of the tax-deferral opportunities described in chapter 14. Older E bonds—those you already have—now also earn interest at the new higher rate. In buying E bonds, it is preferable to buy smaller denominations for greater flexibility in cashing, so that you do not have to pay tax on a large accrued increase in value as you would if you cashed a large bond. Since E bonds are dated the month bought, you can gain two months of extra interest by buying at the end of a month and redeeming at the beginning of a suitable month (as at the end of a normal interest period).

George Frazer points out that banks can be misleading in their advertising about interest rates. The innocent saver is penalized in some cases because the interest rate is taken on the lowest amount during the month, and often the exact day when money is drawn out or put in makes the difference.

At this writing, Canadian savers enjoy even higher interest rates. The trust companies offer the best rates for Canadians. They have more flexibility in establishing rates than do banks, which have virtually fixed rates. They may offer 6½ percent on any account over $100—allowing ten checks free as well—and as much as 8½ percent on term deposits. Wives who have a savings account and a modest check requirement can save perhaps $40 a year, Frazer estimated.

But even among the trust companies, there is a variation in rates that merits shopping.

Canadian savers also have access to higher interest rates on government savings bonds—8 percent if held to maturity. U.S. citizens can not buy Canadian savings bonds but can buy Canadian Treasury notes yielding similar rates. Branch offices of Canadian banks in the large American cities will handle such purchases but advise that on small investments the commission plus a withholding tax of 15 percent would cancel the advantage over rates on U.S. securities.

Face-Amount Certificates

Face-amount certificates also are sold by several investment companies, with a sales load. As pointed out in chapter 1, the yields on such fifteen- and twenty-two-year certificates

Making the Most of Your Investment Dollars

in 1970 were only 3½ to 4 percent, compared to 5 to 6 percent for savings accounts, bank certificates, and E bonds without a penalty for early discontinuance. These penalties imposed by the investment companies in the first three years could amount to 20 percent of the payments.

The one advantage of the certificates is that the increase in value is tax deferred (or at least at this writing).

But as with the contractual mutual funds, you sign a contract to put so much a month into what is essentially a long-term, fixed-income savings accumulation program, for example, $25 a month on a fifteen-year certificate. On maturity at the end of the fifteen years, you would get the certificate face amount of $5,500. This may seem like a real gain, because you put in only $4,500.

In contrast, if you simply put the money into other tax-deferred saving or any savings netting 5 percent, you would have $6,800.

Hundreds of thousands of people buy such certificates. The fallacy of such a long-term plan is that the largest seller of such front-load certificates, Investors Diversified Services, itself reported at a Congressional hearing in December, 1969, that there were $100 million in outstanding loans to certificate holders. They were paying more to borrow their cash value than their funds earned in interest.

Insurance and Annuities: A Frank Evaluation

Life insurance as family protection to replace your earnings in case anything happens to you is, of course, a necessity for moderate- and medium-income breadwinners.

But life insurance as an investment is truly the investment of innocents or at best of people who fear they lack the planning ability or self-discipline to save without the compulsion of getting a bill in the mail.

Life insurance as an investment suffers from the same drawbacks as contractual mutual funds and front-load certificates. A large part of your payments the first year goes for sales expense.

Such policies are really a combination of reducing term

insurance and a savings account. The first three years such policies accumulate very little cash value. In many policies the break-even point comes in the eighth or ninth year, at which time you could get back approximately what you put in, but with little or no interest earnings so far to show for eight years of saving.

Annuities bought on the installment plan ahead of retirement also suffer from this problem. Consider two men age fifty. One puts $100 a year into an annuity contract that would start paying monthly retirement benefits at sixty-five. The other puts the same amount into a cash savings account netting 4 percent after taxes. At the end of the first year, the annuity buyer has $72 in cash value. The cash saver has $103. In ten years the annuity buyer has $1,110, and at sixty-five, $1,880. The cash saver has $1,234 and $2,015 at those times.

Like insurance, annuities do fill a needed role in financial planning. An annuity is the opposite of insurance. Insurance pays only if you die. An annuity pays an income as long as you live. They play different roles: insurance protects a family when it is young, an annuity when it is old.

Both insurance and annuities have tax-deferral advantages as cited in chapter 14. But so do E bonds.

You can have the protection of insurance and then an annuity at very small cost if you plan knowledgeably. For example, for $30 a month a young family can provide a sizable amount of life insurance to protect its children and then an annuity for retirement income.

Of the $30, about $13 could go to pay for a decreasing term insurance policy. This sum could buy a policy worth about $25,000 if the breadwinner passed away in the policy's first year and reduced amounts thereafter. The other $17 a month would go into a savings account or other relatively nonfluctuating investment to buy an annuity at retirement.

How much retirement income can you buy with savings of $17 a month? A man of thirty-five who puts this much away at $4\frac{1}{2}$ percent interest (after taxes) would have $13,000 at sixty-five. A typical annuity bought at age sixty-five costs about $1,300 for each $10 of monthly income. Thus $13,000 would buy an annuity of about $100 a month. If you bought a joint and two-thirds annuity, paying the full amount while husband and wife are living and two-thirds to the survivor, your costs would be a little higher—about $1,500 for each $10 of income. Your $13,000 then would buy a joint annuity of about $90 a month. (A joint and two-thirds annuity is the preferred type.)

A man who starts saving later would have to save more or accept a smaller annuity. For example, if at age forty-five a man starts saving $17 a month, his fund at sixty-five would be about $6,700 (assuming the same 4½ percent yield).

To accumulate $13,000 the forty-five-year-old would have to save $33 a month. He would, of course, be able to spend less than the thirty-five-year-old for the life insurance part of the plan because his family would need to be protected for fewer years.

There is an exception to our recommendation to save through other methods and buy an annuity outright when you plan to retire. A group deferred annuity, bought on installment through your employer, professional or fraternal association, or union does offer a lower price than one bought individually. A leading insurance company noted that under a deferred group contract, the deduction for sales and administrative expenses is about 5¼ percent for each contribution. Under an individual contract, the corresponding expense deduction is 8¾ percent—a saving of 3½ percent of the payments. The group contract also is eligible for experience-rating refunds that provide some additional savings.

Variable annuities are quite similar to mutual funds. They can be a combination of variable units and fixed annuity units. The variable units fluctuate in value as the values of the securities owned by the annuity plan fluctuate. The purpose is to provide a hedge against inflation. If you pay into the plan before retirement, the plan has the same dollar-averaging advantage of periodic payments into a mutual fund. But it also has the same disadvantage of a fairly high sales and expense fee of 8½ to 9 percent of each payment.

Again, you can reduce this expense by doing your own

saving before retirement and buying the variable annuity contract outright at that time. For a single-payment contract the cost is only 3½ percent plus $115 for sales and administrative expense in a typical plan.

Also note that if any of your present insurance is the type that has cash value, such as a whole-life policy, you can convert it to an annuity at rates often less than buying an annuity outright. You save the salesman's commission. Some older insurance policies have unusually good annuity-conversion rates.

CHAPTER THIRTEEN

The Expanding Mortgage and Realty Trusts

The development and expansion of mortgage and realty trusts offer small investors a new opportunity to participate in this high-yielding and relatively secure type of investment.

With sufficient capital you can, of course, invest in mortgages directly, or through a local real estate broker, or by buying FHA-insured mortgages from a present mortgagee (the lender). The banks, mortgage companies, and other approved lenders offering FHA-insured mortgages to investors will continue to service the mortgage.

You can learn about such mortgage investments from the nearest field office of the Federal Housing Authority (FHA) or from local banks and savings associations. Often the yield on FHA-insured mortgages will be one or two percentage points or more higher than the yield on savings accounts and other fixed-value investments. FHA insures the mortgage against default.

Mortgages in which you invest directly are, of course, suitable for long-term investing but not for money you might need in the near future.

You also now can invest indirectly in mortgages by buying shares in a mortgage investment trust. There are a number of these. They are much like mutual funds. But the shares are sold on the stock market or over-the-counter markets without a high sales load. The shares may fluctuate just as do common stocks or mutual fund shares.

Such investment trusts, if well managed, usually have a diversified portfolio of first mortgages, sometimes in combination with direct ownership of properties.

A mortgage trust often can earn a higher return on its investments than an individual investor, because it also lends on higher-rate short-term loans, such as for land development and construction, and borrows capital from banks at lower rates than it charges on mortgages it lends.

That does not mean that you will earn more for your investment in such a trust than from direct investment in mortgages. Management expenses are deducted from the investment trust's earnings. For example, two leading mortgage investment trusts, First Mortgage Investors and Continental Mortgage Investors, yielded about 7 percent on their August, 1970, market prices and dividends.

But the growing availability of such trusts does mean that a small investor can get the advantage of relatively secure high yields on investments of even $1,000 or less. There also are, of course, possibilities of capital gains—or losses.

A number of insurance companies and banks now have launched mortgage funds or trusts, such as the MONY Mortgage Investors, Connecticut General Mortgage and Realty Investments, Wells-Fargo Mortgage Investors, and Lomas & Nettleton Financial Corp. of Dallas, the nation's largest mortgage banker.

In selecting a new and unseasoned trust, it is an added safeguard to see who the sponsors are and to make sure they can float the new venture effectively, as a large insurance company or bank probably can. Such large financial institutions also usually can find a way to direct business to a mortgage fund they sponsor.

In addition to those mentioned, mortgage trusts in operation for some years include (listed alphabetically) Associated Mortgage Investors, Capital Mortgage, General Mortgage Investors, Mortgage Investment Group, Mortgage Trust of America, Republic Mortgage Investors, and Sutro Mortgage.

Other newer mortgage trusts include BankAmerica Realty Investors, Beneficial Standard Mortgage Investors, Chase

Manhattan Mortgage and Realty, City Investing Mortgage Group, Diversified Mortgage Investors, First Union Real Estate and Mortgage Investors, Galbreath First Mortgage Investments, Guardian Mortgage Investors, North American Mortgage Investors, and Security Mortgage Investors.

Some of the mortgage trusts are partly real estate investment trusts. They also invest in direct ownership of real estate such as shopping centers, office buildings, apartments, and industrial properties.

There also are a number of predominantly real estate investment trusts, known popularly as REITS.

With many new developments, even a basically sound one like mortgage trusts, faddism may at times exaggerate the market prices, and it did on at least one occasion, in 1969, with a subsequent drop to more reasonable values.[39] By 1970 there already were over one hundred mortgage and realty investment trusts in existence or about to exist, *Fortune* reported.

As with any other stocks, it is important to evaluate the price-earnings ratio and dividend yield to make sure the first is not excessively high and the second not lower than the yield you could get from other savings and investments. Note also the trend of earnings growth among the various trusts.

Look also at the book value per share. In most stocks a market price close to book value per share is considered a safety factor, but in this case a higher ratio of market price of the stock to book value is considered a help in increasing earnings. It means that the mortgage trust is able to offer new shares at a higher price, thus providing additional loanable funds and a leverage factor.[40]

CHAPTER FOURTEEN

Tax Planning and Shelter for Small Investors

The moderate-income investor has a dual objective: maximum yield and minimum taxes. It is as important to know how to save taxes on income from savings and investments as it is to get the highest yields.

If you do not take advantage of potential tax savings, you will shoulder more than your rightful share of the tax burden. The complicated nature of our tax laws favors the wealthier investors. They can afford to hire tax experts whose ingenuity is used to find loopholes in the law. In fact, many of the loopholes are there as a result of the pressures brought upon Congress by various special interest groups seeking special provisions giving them favorable tax treatment.

Nor is it easy for Congress to close even the most notorious loopholes of the large investors. After widespread publicity about the tax advantages of the well-to-do, Congress did modify several of them in the 1969 tax amendments.

Some of the remaining loopholes or shelters are available usually only to larger investors. These include oil and gas leases and mineral ventures that have special depletion allowances, investment in livestock and hobby farms, and avoidance of inheritance taxes through gifts. As one of a number of notorious examples, H. L. Hunt, the Texas oil billionaire, was reported to have an income of roughly $1 million a week and a fortune estimated at between $2 and $3 billion, largely because of the special tax loopholes for oil and gas drilling.

Making the Most of Your Investment Dollars

In general it must be admitted that, as the AFL–CIO argued, the tax laws are still rigged in favor of income from investments and against income from work.

By knowledgeable tax planning a moderate-income investor can take advantage of some of the special tax benefits for investment income. Some are simple enough to use. Particularly take steps to tax shelter savings for children's education and your own retirement savings. Increased college costs in fact make it imperative to maximize your net yield for savings.

The more you tax shelter your savings and investments, the faster your savings grow, and at a geometrically faster rate because more money is available to go to work for you earlier.

But know the rules. My experience with a number of families I counseled has been that when they try to verify potential tax savers with personnel at local Internal Revenue Service offices, they may get varying advice. An IRS employee may answer casually that some form of tax shelter such as putting E bonds in children's names is a tax evasion when actually it is a perfectly legal tax avoidance, recommended by the Treasury Department itself.

Here is a checklist of tax-saving opportunities especially selected for moderate-income investors.

Educational savings. Under the 1969 tax amendments, your children each can have up to $1,725 income with no tax liability for 1970, $1,700 for 1971 and 1972, and $1,750 for 1973 and thereafter.

This much tax-free income is available because of the combination of the higher minimum standard deduction enacted in 1969 and increased personal exemptions.

The minimum standard deduction is $1,100 for 1970, then drops to $1,050 for 1971 and to $1,000 for 1972 and thereafter. The personal exemption is $625 for 1970, $650 for 1971, $700 for 1972, and $750 for 1973 and thereafter.

Even though your child has income and claims the personal exemption on his tax return, you still can claim him as a dependent on your return as long as he is under nineteen or a full-time student and if you do provide more than half his support.

There are two broad ways to minimize taxes on savings earmarked for children's education. One way is outright gifts to the child that he will hold in his own name. The other approach is gifts to the child with control remaining in your hands until a later date, as through the custodian accounts and trusts described in this chapter.

The simplest method of making outright gifts is to give the child cash for his own savings account.

You also can give the child E bonds in his name. Treasury regulations let a child redeem E bonds any time an adult could. But when long-term savings accounts and certificates or other investments such as corporate bonds yield more than the 5½ percent paid by E bonds at this writing (1970), the tax-deferral advantage of E bonds is less useful for children's savings because they usually don't pay taxes anyway.

E bonds do have the advantages (over cash gifts) of a rate guaranteed for almost six years and of better control by you. You can put them away to avoid diversion by the child to other uses than those you intend.

If you do use E bonds to save for children's education, to avoid taxes later they should be registered in the child's name with a parent or the purchaser as beneficiary, not as coowner (unless the child's own funds are used).

Then, at the end of the first year, a federal income tax return can be filed in the name of the child, listing the increase in bond value as income to the child. Filing this one return establishes intent. No further returns need be filed as long as the child's total income including the annual bond interest comes to less than $1,700 for 1971 and 1972 or $1,750 for 1973 and thereafter.

This way of transferring the tax liability to the child is preferable to waiting until he cashes the bonds and reporting at that time the total increase in value. The combination of accumulated interest plus his own part-time earnings could put him into a taxable bracket.

Savings bonds are not a preferred investment medium for an older child who may have to cash the bonds within a year or two, because they do not earn full interest the first year.

Making the Most of Your Investment Dollars

Children's custodian accounts. You can give securities or cash to a child and still retain control by adult members of the family. Under the Gifts to Minors acts in all states, you can give securities to a child simply by having them registered in the name of a custodian. The custodian can be a parent or another family member. For estate purposes, it may be preferable to have an adult member of the family other than the father as custodian.

The earnings from the custodian account become taxable to the child and will not be taxed at all if his income is under the amount not subject to tax previously listed (plus the $100-a-year dividend exclusion any owner of stocks or fund shares gets).

Under the custodian arrangement, the custodian retains the right to buy and sell shares and can maintain a custodian savings account to accumulate dividends and other funds for reinvestment, to be left as cash, or for the deposit of cash gifts.

For this purpose you can use a bank savings account in all states, a savings and loan account in many states, and credit unions in a few. You make these gifts of money simply by depositing the funds into a custodian savings account.

A special advantage of the custodian arrangement is that it offers leeway for short-term trading in stocks. As with dividends, gains on investments in the child's name would not be subject to tax until all his income for the year had passed the tax-exempt amounts. Even if over, the tax liability would be at a lower rate than yours. Thus, you may not be as concerned about waiting for the required six months in order to qualify for the lower capital gains rate (explained later in this chapter).

But while the custodian retains the right to manage the securities and/or savings account, once you make the gift it is irrevocable. You can not take back the securities or money or even use them as collateral for a loan. You can use the income or funds for the child's benefit and education, not for other family needs. Nor can you use the income to pay for your usual legal obligation to support the child, as for necessities such as food and clothing. If you do, the income used this way would become taxable to you.

When the child reaches twenty-one, you must turn over to him all the unexpended funds and securities. Thus, you do have a fundamental question to decide: do you really want to do this?

All brokers, mutual fund dealers, banks, savings associations, and credit unions (in states permitting them as depositories for custodian accounts) know the wording and procedures, which are as simple as opening a savings account. You do need to give the broker or savings institution the child's Social Security number, because the resulting income is taxable to him. (If he does not have a number, call the local district director of Internal Revenue and ask for an application for one.)

There is no limitation on the size of gifts that can be made for a custodian account, but in the case of large gifts, perhaps over $15,000, you might consider creating a trust instead, as described in this chapter. A trust offers greater flexibility, for example, as to the age when the child takes over or if you want to give just the income and later recapture the principal. A trust does involve legal fees for drawing it up, perhaps $100 to $200 for a simple trust, while a custodian account involves no expense at all.

Trusts can be established for each child or one trust with the income going to several children.

The question of federal gift tax also may arise. You can give up to $3,000 a year ($6,000 for a married couple) to each of your children (up to a total of $30,000, or $60,000 for a couple) without becoming liable for gift tax.

While mutual funds often are used for custodian account investments, the use of load-type funds for older children especially is questionable. You can lose a large part of your investment if you must discontinue early. Even no-load funds may not be too suitable for older teen-agers for college funds.

Insurance as savings. Insurance, such as education and endowment policies in children's names, also often is used to tax shelter the income from savings. This too is a questionable method. The relative low yield on insurance savings and the sales commission on the premiums you pay (especially high the first year) more than outweigh any tax advantage.

For example, a typical education insurance or endowment policy for a child of eight, which will pay $1,000 at age eighteen, has a net cost of about $95 a year. But the same $95 a year deposited in a credit union, bank, or savings association or invested in E bonds, even at only 5 percent yield, will total $1,255 at the end of ten years. At the 6 percent available on some savings plans and fixed-value investments, the total would be $1,330.

Obviously it is even less desirable to sacrifice higher yield for insurance tax shelter in the case of children's savings than for adults, because other ways to tax shelter are easily available.

Shelter for retirement savings. Another need—and opportunity—for tax shelter is for your retirement savings.

Tax planning for retirement should start well before retirement. Your planning should be based on these tax considerations.

——You will have double exemptions for yourself and your wife when each reaches sixty-five. By 1973 these combined exemptions will total $3,000. You also will have less taxable income, because Social Security, railroad retirement, veterans' benefits, and life insurance payments to beneficiaries are all tax exempt. Pensions, annuities, and some other forms of retirement income are partially tax exempt. A couple sixty-five or older often can have $6,000 of income and sometimes even more without owing any actual tax. Thus, you should postpone cashing in securities, fund shares, and E bonds on which you have gains until after retirement.

——Because of the higher exemptions and reduced taxable income after retirement, you should take what taxable deductions and capital losses you can before retirement. For example, if your mortgage is much over 6 percent, you may want to consider paying it off before retirement. The tax deduction for mortgage interest will be less useful to you after retirement. Too, any penalty you may have to pay for prepayment is tax deductible. But if the mortgage interest you pay is an old low rate like 5 percent, you may be better off holding on to the mortgage and putting your own cash into higher-yielding investments.

You also may want to pay off other debts before retirement while the prepaid interest still can be a tax deduction.

——The suitability of various investments changes after retirement. You should be less willing to pay a premium for the capital gains tax advantage offered by growth investments and can take advantage of those paying higher immediate income. You also will be less willing to invest in volatile or fluctuating investments and more interested in conservation of capital because you will not have as much opportunity to make up losses or offset losses against taxes as a younger person. Tax-exempt state and municipal bonds also will be less useful to you, and you can change to the higher yields of corporate bonds.

U.S. savings bonds and retirement. The tax role of E and H bonds in your retirement planning merits particular attention because these are an important part of the savings of most moderate- and medium-income couples.

At some times E bonds are useful for preretirement saving for small investors because their yield or gain is postponable for federal income tax purposes and exempt altogether from state and local income tax.

Thus, you can accumulate E bonds before retirement and defer the tax until after. At that time you can cash in the bonds and your federal tax liability on the accumulated interest would be eliminated or at least reduced because of your reduced taxable income and double exemptions.

In buying E bonds, smaller denominations provide more flexibility later. If you need some cash, you will have less tax liability by cashing a smaller bond than a large one, certainly before retirement and sometimes even after. When cashing bonds, it is better to cash in the most recent ones to protect the higher rate being earned by the older bonds (and to defer their greater tax liability).

After retirement, the tax shelter of E bonds usually is less useful, and you can get more yield from some savings accounts, corporate bonds, and mortgage investment syndicates, even though these latter do have some element of fluctuation.

If you still want to defer your tax liability on E bonds after retirement, you can convert some or all to H bonds. The accumulated interest of the E bonds applies as part of the purchase price of the H bonds and can be deferred further until the H bonds are redeemed or mature.

The H bonds pay interest by Treasury check every six months. These payments do have to be reported currently for federal income tax purposes even though the tax liability on the E bonds still is being deferred.

Whether you should use H bonds this way after retirement depends on the comparative yields being offered at that time by other tax-exempt investments such as municipal bonds.

For general family tax shelter, consider these tax-savings opportunities.

Shelter through stocks. Stocks and fund shares provide tax shelter in several ways.

——Up to $100 a year of dividends received by an individual can be excluded from tax. If shares are registered jointly or some are in the husband's name and some in the wife's, up to $200 a year of dividends can be excluded. More can be excluded if shares also are registered in names of other family members. (Note that this applies only to dividends from stocks and mutual funds, not to the so-called dividends paid by savings and loan associations or life insurance dividends, which are merely a return of part of the premium you paid.) Make sure that you and your spouse and/or other family members have enough shares in their names to take advantage of the full exclusion. You can't claim any unused portion of their exclusion.

——If you sell stocks or mutual fund shares at a profit, only one-half of the capital gain is subject to tax if the securities were held more than six months. These are called long-term capital gains.

But if the securities are held six months or less, you pay

tax on the full amount of your gain. Thus, if you want to sell stocks or fund shares that have gone up, you also should take into account whether they qualify as long-term investments. The six-month holding period begins on the day following the date you bought the securities and ends on the day you sold them.

If you have capital losses, your allowable net loss (excess over gains) can offset up to $1,000 of your other taxable income. If the loss is more than $1,000, you can carry forward all or some of the rest by applying it against capital gains and then up to $1,000 of ordinary income each year until the entire loss is used up.

Under the recently enacted rules, a couple can subtract only up to $1,000 a year of allowable capital loss whether or not they file separate returns ($500 each on separate returns).

Also as a result of the 1969 tax revision, you no longer can offset 100 percent of a long-term loss against ordinary income. Only 50 percent of a long-term capital loss now can be used in this way. For example, if you have $3,000 of long-term gains and $4,000 of long-term losses after 1969, you now can reduce your ordinary income by only $500 (50 percent of the $1,000 of net loss), instead of by $1,000 as before.

If you have both long- and short-term losses, the rules now work like this: suppose you have $600 of long-term loss and $500 of short-term loss, you can offset $800 ($300 of the long-term and the full $500 of the short-term).

Or suppose your only transaction was a long-term loss of $1,500. You could subtract only $750 from ordinary income.

Short-term losses still are balanced against short-term gains. Long-term losses still are balanced against long-term gains. Thus, a $1,000 long-term loss can offset dollar for dollar a $1,000 long-term gain, and if the long-term capital loss exceeds the long-term gain, the net long-term loss may be deducted from net short-term gains. But if the net long-term loss exceeds the net short-term gain or where there are both short- and long-term losses, your offset from ordinary income is no longer as large as it was before 1970.

There is a provision permitting carry-overs for capital losses incurred before 1970. But from 1970 on, there also is a noticeable reduction in the amount of long-term loss that can be carried over.

Here is an example cited by Robert A. Hageman of Paine, Webber, Jackson & Curtis, a national brokerage firm. Suppose you have a $400 short-term loss and an $800 long-term loss. You can subtract the full $400 of net short-term losses from ordinary income but only $400 of the $800 in long-term losses —a total offset against ordinary income of $800. Nor would you have any carry-over.

Or take this example: you have a net short-term loss of $500 and net long-term loss of $2,500. You can subtract from income the net short-term loss in full. You also can deduct $500 of the net long-term loss. But this wipes out $1,000 of the long-term loss. Thus you can carry forward only $1,500, and the offset against future ordinary income would be only 50 percent of it or $750.

As a result of the change in the amount of long-term loss that can offset other income, Hageman and other investment experts recommended these policies.

———Where there is a choice, it usually is advantageous to establish tax losses before a security is held six months. It takes only $1,000 of short-term losses to offset $1,000 of other income compared to $2,000 of long-term losses.

Of course you would have to weigh whether it may be preferable to wait for recovery or take your loss before the six-month holding period has passed. Say you bought a stock for $2,000 but several months later its value had dropped to $1,200 as sometimes happens in gyrating markets. If you sell within the holding period, you have a short-term loss of $800. In a 30 percent tax bracket, this loss can mean a tax recovery of $240.

———In cases where long-term losses already exist, it generally is useful where possible to balance these by taking long-term capital gains.

———If you have long-term gains and short-term losses, you may want to consider taking the short-term losses one year and the long-term gains another year.

Experienced investors who have losses in securities on which they want to take the loss on that year's tax return often maintain their investment position by selling those securities and reinvesting the money in similar stocks or bonds in the same industry or of the same type. Most brokers and bond specialists know how to handle this kind of tax swap.

(Note that if you sell securities to register a loss, you may not be able to deduct the loss if you buy the same stock within thirty days before or after the sale. Such a transaction is called a wash sale. The unallowed loss would have to be added to your cost basis for the new stock. But this could be useful as a tax saver later when you do sell the stock.)

Or if you have averaged purchases downward, you may be able to sell the first and costlier purchase before the six months and hold the subsequent purchase bought at a lower price. For example, you may have bought 50 shares of XYZ stock at $40 a share, watched it fall to $24, then bought additional shares at $24 to make your average cost $32. But if you still are not satisfied with the stock's performance before the end of the six months, you could sell the original shares to take a short-term tax loss, holding on to the more recent lower-priced shares for possible price improvement.

If you also own stocks that have gone up, you may want to consider the tax advantages of taking short-term losses in one year and long-term gains in another.

Of course you will have to pay another commission to buy the similar new stocks or bonds, and this fee must be weighed against the potential tax saving and also against any realistic possibility that this particular stock will recover. (On the other hand, the switch might improve your portfolio by substituting a more promising stock.)

There is less concern about the relative recovery of corporate bonds you now own against possible alternative issues. Most bonds tend to rise or fall at much the same rate because they are affected primarily by general interest rates. But in deciding whether to sell the bond or which new one to buy, you should pay attention to the call date as well as the yield. When bonds are selling below par, often the closer

Making the Most of Your Investment Dollars

the call date, the lower the yield. Thus you would have to choose between higher dividend yield or quicker capital gains, as discussed in chapter 11.

To establish a tax loss for a particular year, you can sell the securities even up to the last business day of the year. But to establish a gain, you have to sell a few days before the end of the year because the proceeds must be available by the last business day, and the New York Stock Exchange has (at this writing) a five-business-day rule. Your broker can tell you what the last day is for establishing a gain each year.

Sometimes you also may want to establish a gain for tax purposes before the end of a particular year, for example, because your other income is relatively moderate that year and you expect more income or higher rates next year, or similar reasons. But you may think that this particular stock still has further potential. In that case you can sell it and immediately buy it back without regard to the thirty-day wash sale rule. But you still should weigh the tax advantage against the additional commission you will pay on the transaction.

If you feel a stock has reached its potential but you do not want to pay tax on the gain that year because of substantial other income, you can postpone selling yet nail down your profit by selling the equivalent shares short.* (Be sure, however, that the additional brokerage commissions would not cancel out any tax advantage.)

If you then have a gain on the short sale, it would be considered a short- or long-term transaction depending on whether you or your spouse owned substantially the same securities for six months or less, or over six months.

If you have a loss on a short sale, it is considered long-term, even if the transaction took place within the six-month holding period, if you owned substantially the same securities

---

* A short sale is the sale of a security that the seller does not own but which he borrows through his broker. A seller is not deemed to have completed the short sale until he has closed out the sale by delivering the borrowed securities to the lender at which time the seller will have gain or loss depending on the difference between the sale price of the borrowed stock and the subsequent cost of the stock delivered to the lender.

longer than six months. The purpose of this rule is to keep you from converting a long-term gain on the original securities to a short-term loss, which would have greater tax value to you.

The thirty-day wash sale rule also may apply to this kind of transaction. So if you ever want to use this maneuver, be guided by your broker, both to make sure of the tax consequences and that stock will be available for your short sale. Your broker needs to be able to borrow the stock pending your subsequent purchase of stock to cover the short sale.

In calculating gains and losses for tax purposes, note that to figure your cost you add on the broker's commission and federal transfer taxes, and your proceeds are the net proceeds after deducting commission and federal tax. State transfer taxes on purchases and sales of securities are deductible from ordinary income if you itemize personal deductions.

——Another way that common stocks provide tax shelter is through stock dividends often paid by some corporations in lieu of or in addition to cash dividends. In the usual case of small shareholders these are not taxable as ordinary income, and in effect you get the advantage of the capital gains rate if and when you sell your shares.

Some companies of the growth type regularly pay stock dividends in place of some or all of cash dividends. They want to keep their cash for expansion. If you don't need the cash income now, you can increase your effective income by selecting such investments. Your broker can supply you with a list of companies that usually pay stock dividends.

Capital gains dividends often paid by mutual funds and other investment companies are another tax saver. They qualify as capital gains and should not be reported with your other dividends or you will needlessly pay full tax rates on them. Usually at the end of the year the mutual fund or investment company will notify you which dividends that it has paid qualify for capital gains treatment or may even be nontaxable.

Similarly stock rights, which give shareholders the privilege of buying additional stock in the company, often at a little

Making the Most of Your Investment Dollars

lower price than quoted on the exchange, are not taxable as ordinary income. If you sell the rights (usually they are traded on the exchanges up until the final subscription date), you treat the entire proceeds as a capital gain.

If you exercise your right to subscribe to the additional shares, you figure your holding period for tax purposes as beginning with the date you buy the new shares, and your cost is the subscription price. (If you let rights expire without selling or subscribing, you throw away money, even though you can deduct it as a tax loss.)

If you acquire stocks by turning in convertible bonds or preferred stocks for them, as discussed in chapter 11, your cost basis is the amount you paid for the original securities, and the purchase date, for purposes of determining whether a long- or short-term transaction, is their purchase date.

——"Return of capital dividends" has been a popular tax saver but will be diminished or even eliminated after 1972. These are dividends paid by some companies, usually public utilities, which are regarded as a return of capital due to accelerated depreciation and/or amortization. The portion of such dividends classified as return of capital varies from year to year.

For example, in one recent year El Paso Natural Gas paid a dividend of $1 a share. The yield on the then price of $19 a share thus was 5.2 percent. But 47 percent of the dividend was tax free. The effective yield for a moderate-income taxpayer was over 6 percent.

Other examples of tax-free percentages of dividends in recent years include Atlantic City Electric, 42 percent; Consolidated Edison, 96 percent; Puget Sound Power & Light, 80 percent, and many others.

Eventually, you will pay partial tax on the tax-free percentage. When you sell the shares, the tax-free portion of the dividends will have to be deducted from the original cost of the shares in computing the capital gain or loss. Thus, your capital gain will be larger or any loss smaller.

Investment in companies still paying "return of capital dividends" is particularly suitable for preretirement savings because in retirement you may well escape any tax liability even on the capital gains.

Tax-exempt bonds. As discussed in chapter 11, in recent years, the higher rates paid on tax-exempt bonds of states, municipalities, school districts, and other local government agencies have drawn increasing interest from moderate-income investors. A family with $10,000 to $15,000 of taxable income often will have to pay in the neighborhood of 30 percent in combined federal and state income taxes. (Municipal bonds usually are exempt from state taxes only in the state in which issued.)

If that family leaves $5,000 in savings accounts at 5 to 6 percent interest, it would earn $250 to $300, but after taxes the family would have left only $175 to $200. If the family invested $5,000 in corporate bonds at a taxable 8 percent, it would have $280 left after taxes. The same $5,000 in tax-free bonds of its own state paying 6 percent would yield, at this writing, $300 free and clear.

On higher incomes, tax-exempt bonds are, of course, even more advantageous. Despite criticisms of this loophole, which is overexploited by some wealthy individuals, the tax exemption on state and municipal bonds was not changed by the 1969 tax reform law.

As of this writing, you do not even have to report tax-exempt income from local government bonds on your tax return. You do have to pay capital gains on any increase in value when you sell or turn in tax-free municipals at maturity. For example, if you pay $4,000 for bonds and receive $5,000 when they become due, you would pay tax on 50 percent of the $1,000 gain.

Nor can you deduct any loss for a premium paid on municipals. Lebenthal & Co. cited the example of a new issue of New York City 6.4 percent bonds maturing in 1979 and selling for $1,027.50, with a yield to maturity of 6 percent. For $10,000 of the bonds in this example, you would pay $10,275. But when they came due, you would get just

Making the Most of Your Investment Dollars

$10,000 and could not take the premium of $275 as a tax loss.

You would have to consider that you got the premium back a little at a time when you cashed in your coupons and that the $275 premium was reflected in the yield to maturity of 6 percent.

Unlike state and municipal bonds, the yield on U.S. government obligations, such as Treasury bills and notes discussed in chapter 11, is not exempt from federal income tax but is exempt from state and local income taxes. Treasury bills do not bear interest, but the difference between their purchase price and the amount you get on later sale or redemption (face value at maturity) is considered to be ordinary income. This must be included in your federal income tax returns but not state or local returns.

Because state and municipal bonds escape the higher federal income tax but federal obligations escape only the lower state and local taxes, for many middle-income families not yet retired, a 5 percent yield from municipal bonds may produce more actual income than 6 percent from federal bills or notes.

Income averaging. Suppose you have sizable capital gains in a year when you have large ordinary income. You may be able to soften the tax impact by using the liberalized income-averaging provisions of the 1969 amendments. If your income, including taxable capital gains, is at least $3,000 more than 120 percent of your average income in the preceding four years, most of the excess can be spread back over the preceding years and taxed in the lowest brackets of these years.

Annuities and pensions as tax shelter. As noted in chapter 11, deferred annuities also can provide tax shelter. The interest earned by your annual deposit into an annuity is not taxable until you start getting the retirement payments. At that time, you may not be in a taxable bracket at all.

But as advised in chapter 12, nowadays you usually can build a bigger savings fund for retirement through other forms of saving or investment. Both E bonds and deferred bank certificates can be held without any tax liability during your working years. If arranged judiciously, so not too many mature all at once, you may escape tax liability completely after retirement. Similarly, municipal and state bonds are completely tax free even before retirement. Even though you would have to pay tax on the yield from corporate bonds, federal obligations such as Treasury notes, mortgage participations, and savings accounts, their higher yield usually would more than compensate for the tax liability if you are not in a high tax bracket, in contrast to paying into a deferred annuity.

Once you are retired, you need to learn thoroughly the tax rules governing annuities and pensions. Many retired people who still are in taxable brackets overpay their taxes because of the complicated nature of the tax rules governing pensions and taxes. A study of tax payments by recipients of federal Civil Service pensions found 75 percent of these tax returns reported these amounts incorrectly and two-thirds overstated their taxable income and paid too much tax, Assistant Treasury Secretary Edwin S. Cohen reported.

Here are the major tax rules governing annuities and pensions.

Payments received from annuities and pensions toward which you make no contribution or investment are fully taxable. If you did pay some of the cost during your working years, and if upon retirement will get back within three years an amount equal to what you paid in, the payments you receive during this three-year period are excludable from taxable income until you recover your original contribution. Then all your payments are fully taxable.

But if you will not get back within three years all you paid in, then you have to compute, on the basis of average life expectancy, what part is taxable. To do this you need to know the cost of your annuity and the total amount you would expect to receive during the normal expected lifetime at your age. This is called the expected return. The government has published tables showing the average life expectancy at different ages. You can consult these tables at Internal Revenue Service offices. Or your employer's personnel department or

Making the Most of Your Investment Dollars

your annuity or insurance company will provide the information on the life expectancy at the age at which your annuity or pension begins.

For example, at sixty-five the life expectancy (called the multiple) is 15; at sixty-six, 14.4; sixty-seven, 13.8; sixty-eight, 13.2; sixty-nine, 12.6; seventy, 12.1. Thus, the average man who starts getting a pension or annuity at sixty-five can expect to receive it for fifteen years. Suppose the annuity or pension is $100 a month or $1,200 a year. He could expect (in the average case) to receive a total of $18,000.

Also assume he had invested a total of $12,000 in this annuity. He then divides the expected return of $18,000 into the cost of $12,000. This gives him a figure of 66.7 percent. This is the percentage of his annuity income that he can exclude each year. The remaining 33.3 percent in this example, or $400, is taxable income.

The excludable percentage remains the same as long as you collect the annuity, even after you have excluded more than you paid in.

In the case of an annuity you bought yourself, keep in mind that your cost is your net cost after subtracting any rebates, additional premiums for double indemnity or disability benefits, and the value of any refund or guarantee feature in the contract.

If you retire early because of permanent disability and your employer pays you a disability pension, the tax rules vary. If your employer contributes the entire cost of the pension, the payments you get qualify as sick pay. They are excludable from taxable income within the same limits as other sick pay (see instructions with your tax return). If you contributed part of the cost, your cost is not taken into consideration until you reach what would be normal retirement age or the earliest age at which you have the right to retire under your employer's pension program. Then the disability pension is treated as other annuities.

Note that Social Security, workmen's compensation, and veterans' pensions are not taxable at all and need not be reported on your tax return.

If your pension or annuity provides for continuing payments or a lump-sum payment to a beneficiary after your death, these payments are considered to be a refund of a portion of your pension or annuity cost, and your cost must be reduced by its value. This increases your tax liability. The Internal Revenue Service has tables that can determine the value of this refund. But if you are the beneficiary of a deceased employee such as his widow, the pension or annuity you get from his employer may qualify for a death benefit exclusion of up to $5,000. You should add this exclusion to the cost or unrecovered cost of the annuity in calculating (at the annuity starting date) the investment in the contract. This further reduces the dependent's tax liability.

Suppose your employer gives you a lump-sum payment from a pension fund or trust when you leave his employment. Before 1970 the amount received by the employee over and above his own contributions, plus the cash value of any life insurance transferred to him and the cost to the trust of employer stock, was treated as capital gains. But under the 1969 amendments, capital gains treatment is limited to the taxable portion of the distribution in excess of employer contributions accruing after 1969. The amount attributable to the employer's contribution accruing after 1969 now is subject to tax as ordinary income. However, there is a special forward-averaging provision to avoid putting a taxpayer in an unreasonably high bracket because he receives a lump sum in a single year.

Retirement income credit. This is especially helpful to retirees who do not receive maximum Social Security or certain other types of tax-exempt income.

But many retired persons—up to one-third, Treasury officials estimated—fail to take advantage of the retirement income credit because of the complicated form they must fill out. It does not pay to neglect this potential tax saver. You file a separate Schedule T that you get with your tax forms each year, and you simply follow the step-by-step procedure. Tax guides on the market explain the procedure or your local IRS office will show you how it applies in your case.

The retirement income credit is especially valuable because

Making the Most of Your Investment Dollars

it is a deduction from the tax itself and not merely a deduction from your income, like contributions.

The main rules for qualifying are that you have retirement income and are sixty-five or older unless your retirement income is from pensions or annuities under a public retirement system. (These retirees can use the retirement income credit even if under sixty-five, but in that case only in respect to amounts received under a public retirement system.)

Retirement income for taxpayers sixty-five or older can include all amounts received from pensions, annuities, interest, and dividends (after the dividend exclusion). These must be taxable income reported on page 1 of your tax return. Gross rents are considered retirement income for persons sixty-five or older. In short, this must be income for which you performed no present service.

If both husband and wife have retirement income, both can claim the credit. In that case, you should consult the special rules outlined in the government's tax guide and other guides.

At seventy-two, any earned income you may have does not reduce the maximum amount subject to the retirement credit.

Saving taxes by giving. You can reduce your own taxes through gifts of securities that have gone up in value instead of giving cash to individuals or institutions you usually help.

Suppose that you have a relative whom you help support but whom you can not claim as a dependent on your return because you don't meet the income or over 50 percent support tests. Assume that you have securities you bought for $3,000, which now have a market value of $8,000, and yield 5 percent. If you are in a 30 percent bracket, the $400 of yield leaves you only $280. Or if you sell the securities you would have to pay $750 in long-term capital gains tax (30 percent of one-half of the $5,000 gain).

But if you give the securities to the relative you help support, who presumably has no tax liability, the gift costs you $7,250 and he gets $400. You in turn can be his heir. Otherwise, to provide $400 if it first passes through your taxable hands would require a capital of $11,400 at 5 percent.

You also can set up a short-term trust for this purpose, as

discussed for children earlier in this chapter. The trust can provide that the income is payable to the beneficiary during his lifetime, and so is taxable to him, but upon his death the principal reverts to you.

Such a trust may be desirable in the case of a beneficiary whom you feel may not be capable of managing the gift properly. A short-term trust also is useful if you are only able to part with the income and not with the principal, and want to be sure you get it back at the beneficiary's death, or that someone else you name in the trust agreement gets it.

A trust of this kind would not be suitable for only a modest principal, such as less than $10,000 to $15,000 depending on your tax bracket. You do have to pay the legal expense for establishing the trust, possibly about $150, again depending on the amount of principal. If you do not have an experienced person you can name as trustee, you also might have to pay the fee of a trust company or professional trust manager. The Internal Revenue Service might not regard you yourself as a suitable trustee for a trust you create because of the question of control. Any securities bought for or contributed to the trust need to be in the name of the trustee.

To be taxed to the beneficiary, note that a short-term trust must be in effect for at least ten years.

There also is a type of trust known as an accumulation trust designed to accumulate income for future distribution to the beneficiaries. But under 1969 amendments, the beneficiaries now must be taxed on distributions in much the same manner as if the income had been distributed to them as earned.

In the case of an accumulation trust created for a spouse, the law now also provides that the income is to be taxed to the creator of the trust, as it is earned. (But this provision, which applies to transfers to the trust after October 9, 1969, does not apply where another tax provision requires the spouse to be taxed.)

Gifts of securities or other property to charitable and educational institutions also can reduce taxes. This has been one of the loopholes most exploited by wealthier taxpayers.

Making the Most of Your Investment Dollars

But it sometimes also can be used by relatively modest taxpayers. For example, suppose you had paid $1,500 for securities now worth $3,000. If, in a 30 percent tax bracket, you sell them, you would net $2,775 after long-term capital gains tax. But if you give the stocks to an institution to whom you plan to make a sizable gift in any case, you would get a contribution deduction on the full appreciated value of the $3,000, or $900. Nor need you pay any capital gains tax on the increase in value. Thus, your $3,000 gift would really cost you $1,875.

This maneuver is even more profitable to big taxpayers and leads to many abuses, some of which were modified by the 1969 tax changes. The double benefit of a full deduction and no capital gain now is available only where the gain would have been long-term if the securities or other property were sold. The double benefit does not apply to short-term assets (held six months or less). Too, the allowable deduction for appreciated property is limited to 30 percent of the giver's income, although any excess can be carried forward for up to five years. However, a gift of capital gain property is deductible up to 50 percent of income if the donor elects to reduce his contributions deduction by 50 percent of the unrealized gain.

Never give securities on which you have a loss. Sell the securities so you can take the loss on your return to offset other gains or ordinary income, and give the cash.

Another way to give while saving taxes is the life income arrangement or trust. You may have seen these advertised by charitable organizations or other tax-exempt institutions such as colleges. You make your gift to the institution, which invests it in a pooled fund or annuity trust. Then the fund or trust pays you a percentage of the income it produces.

You can arrange to get the income for a specified period of years, for life, for your and your wife's lives, and so on. You get both the income and a contribution deduction less the value of the reserved income right. The institution gets the principal amount when you die or at the end of another specified period. Sometimes income even can be increased by the use of such an arrangement because the trust is tax exempt and its investments are professionally managed. Only a qualified annuity or "unitrust" can provide an immediate tax deduction. The old type of charitable remainder trust no longer qualifies. In fact, if you already have set up such a trust in your will, better ask your lawyer whether it still qualifies.

Tax shelter in real estate. Investing in real estate provides two kinds of tax savings: the tax liability on income is reduced by the depreciation allowance on the building (not on the land, which does not depreciate), and gains on sales of the property are taxed at the lower long-term capital gains rate. The key to the tax profitability is that the cash flow is greater than the taxable income.

In fact, modest real-estate investments often have been a favorite investment method of moderate-income families who own another house, perhaps their first home, and rent it out, or who buy a two- or even four-family house for rental income.

There are some limitations now on depreciation, which were enacted in 1969 as well as earlier amendments to curb excesses of real estate speculation. Speculators would buy a property and enjoy partially tax-free income because of the accelerated depreciation then permitted, enabling large deductions the first few years of ownership. When the depreciation was exhausted, they would sell at the higher prices made possible by persistent inflation and pay only the capital gains rate on the profit. The next investor would repeat the process. This constant milking of properties encouraged by the tax laws has contributed enormously to the deterioration of some of the larger cities and to the present inflated price of real estate, and it has also built some large and small fortunes.

Accelerated deduction now is limited in many cases. New construction acquired after July 24, 1969, except for new residential rental property, no longer may be depreciated by the rapid double-declining-balance or sum-of-the-digits

Making the Most of Your Investment Dollars

methods. Used nonresidential property acquired after July 24, 1969, may be depreciated only by the straight-line method (the same amount each year of the building's estimated life).

However, the new restrictions are harder on the in-and-out speculators and larger investors than on the small investor who may buy a residential property for long-term income. Depreciation of 125 percent of the declining balance each year can be claimed for used residential realty with a useful life of twenty years or more. Too, special fast depreciation can be used for certain specified rehabilitation expenses. And new rental housing still can be depreciated under the fast methods if at least 80 percent of the income is derived from rental of residential units.

Sometimes investors want to sell a property but wait to postpone the capital gains liability in the case of a large gain on a property bought years ago when prices were much lower. For one reason, they may want to use the full proceeds for further investment rather than pay part of it in taxes. In that case they may try to arrange a tax-free, or partially tax-free, exchange of the property with another owner. An exchange also avoids the need for financing a new property in a period of tight money. For still other investors, exchanging for a smaller property with more equity or even entirely clear, can be a way of generating additional financing.

Such exchanges usually are arranged through real estate brokers.

An exchange does not, of course, avoid capital gains tax but just postpones it. But the property then can pass into an estate on death without tax liability to the heirs on subsequent sale.

Self-employed retirement plan. Some self-employed people have been slow to take advantage of the important tax advantages available through a Keogh Act retirement investment plan.

If your plan is approved by the Internal Revenue Service, you can put in up to 10 percent of your earnings or $2,500 a year (whichever is less). This entire amount can be subtracted from your earned income for tax purposes. Too, taxes are postponed on the earnings of this investment fund. Then when you retire, payments you receive will be only partly taxable as with any annuity (described earlier in this chapter) if you are liable for any taxes at all.

An approved plan can be the special Treasury retirement bonds sold by the Federal Reserve bank or your local bank, a fixed or variable annuity, bank trust, mutual fund, insurance, or a combination of these programs. Many qualified mutual funds, both load and no-loads, now offer Keogh-type self-employed pension plans, with the shares held by a bank or trust company as custodian until you retire. (This can be as early as age 59½, earlier in case of severe disability or death, or as late as age 70½.) You even can invest in stocks under trusteed plans offered by some brokers with a bank or trust company as trustee.

Thus you can arrange for tax-sheltered savings in either fixed-value or fluctuating investments or a combination. But the plan must be approved by the Internal Revenue Service. Most banks, brokers, mutual fund, or insurance companies can help you set up a plan. Using an already approved "master plan" helps save administrative and legal expenses.

To show the value of such a plan, a self-employed person in a 36 percent tax bracket would have only $1,600 a year available for investment from $2,500 of earnings. At the end of twenty-five years at 4 percent taxable yield compounded annually, he would accumulate $55,000. But the same $2,500 left untaxed in a Keogh plan and earning the same 4 percent but tax sheltered would accumulate $104,000 for retirement.

If you still will be in a relatively high tax bracket after retirement, there is one possible flaw in using a Keogh-type plan in that you will lose capital gains treatment on possible increase in value of stocks and fund shares when you withdraw the funds after retirement. You must weigh this loss against the value of the annual savings through the deduction and deferment of tax on dividends and capital gains distributions before retirement.

Your Keogh plan must cover employees if they have been

with you more than three years and work more than twenty hours a week. But in that case, you can get another tax saving. You can contribute up to another $2,500 a year as a voluntary addition to your own fund. This additional contribution is not deductible but is tax sheltered. You also can get this additional benefit if your wife works for you, plus putting her too under this plan if you pay her a salary (except in Texas). She must, of course, actually work for you in a bona fide employee relationship.

A self-employed owner of a business can count his entire net profits as earned income if his own services as well as his capital are used in the business in a substantial way.

Professional corporations and associations formed by professionals, such as doctors, dentists, and lawyers, now are legal in most states. They offer tax advantages that in some respects may be even better than a Keogh plan because larger contributions to tax-deferred pensions and annuities are possible. For example, in many states doctors in a medical partnership can set up a corporation with an employee benefit plan in which they participate.

Oil depletion allowance. Investment in oil and gas drilling ventures has been a favorite tax-saving ploy of wealthy and even middle-income investors because of the depletion allowance. The former 27.5 percent depletion allowance has been reduced to 22 percent. This is still a large tax loophole, because an oil firm or syndicate can escape taxes on 22 percent of its gross income or 50 percent of its net profits, whichever is smaller.

This form of tax-saving investment is, however, still difficult for a moderate-income investor. While some syndicates that sell shares in oil ventures will accept investments of as little as $1,500, more typically investments are $10,000 and often $50,000 and $100,000. One syndicate organizer, David Mack, reports that the average investor is rather sophisticated and usually in a 50 percent or higher tax bracket. While highly speculative, oil ventures have a cushion for higher-income taxpayers because some drilling costs can be deducted from other income, and if the venture fails, the remainder of the investment is 100 percent tax deductible. Thus, potential gains are partly protected by the depletion allowance while losses are softened by tax deductions.

The drilling syndicates themselves must be investigated with care before you invest by checking with the local Better Business Bureau, state attorney general, your banker, lawyer, and other experienced advisers. There are some shady organizers operating with less than ethical methods, and some programs are not as potentially successful as promoters claim, people experienced in oil ventures advise.

Part-time farming. Sideline or hobby farm ventures have long been a favored tax-avoidance device of wealthy investors. They have used the special deductions available from investments in farms, standing timber, and farm property such as breeder cattle and other livestock to deduct the many expense items allowed farmers, and to deduct resultant losses from other income at the higher tax rate on ordinary income. Subsequently they recapture the income when they sell the farm property but then pay only the lower capital gains rate. The primary purpose of a hobby farm was (and is) to build up losses as an offset against other income. The primary purpose of investing in breeder livestock is to "expense" the costs and realize a capital gain on the sale.

The 1969 amendments narrowed some of these loopholes for large investors. Now they must maintain an excess deductions account to record farm losses. If the taxpayer has over 50,000 of nonfarm income for the year, and to the extent that his farm losses for the year exceed $25,000, he must add those losses over $25,000 to the EDA. When he does dispose of the property, his capital gains will be taxed as ordinary income to the extent that his farm losses have been offset against nonfarm income.

But because of the limitations (over $50,000 of nonfarm income and $25,000 of losses), smaller investors are less affected. Nowadays some working people operate part-time farms on which they live, such as small dairy, poultry, timber,

Making the Most of Your Investment Dollars 237

and farm recreation ventures. Many retired people also buy small-acreage rural enterprises to provide a retirement home and some retirement income. If your honest intent is to make a profit from your farming, you can have the benefit of deducting from other income the expense of improvements or the production costs of livestock or an orchard, and enjoy the capital gains tax saving on the subsequent sale of the property.

Operating a woodland is another venture with special tax deductions.

The 1969 amendments also closed other farm investment loopholes. Before 1970, a gain on sale of livestock, unlike gain on other depreciable personal property, was not subject to recapture of the depreciation previously deducted. Now, the portion of the gain attributable to depreciation taken after 1969 is treated as ordinary income.

Too, expenditures for soil and water conservation and land clearing are subject to recapture if the land is sold within five years after it was acquired, and partial recapture if sold within six to nine years.

APPENDIXES:

AGENCIES THAT HELP INVESTORS

APPENDIX A:

Better Business Bureaus

Better Business Bureaus are located in the following cities.

ALABAMA: 2026 Second Ave., N., Birmingham 35203; 2310 Whitesburg Drive, S., Huntsville 35801; 307 Van Antwerp Building, Mobile 36602.

ARKANSAS: Continental Building, Little Rock 72201.

ARIZONA: 4025 N. Sixth St., Phoenix 85012; 100 E. Alameda St., Suite 203, Tucson 85701.

CALIFORNIA: 705 Eighteenth St., Bakersfield 93301; 404–6 T. W. Patterson Building, Fresno 93721; 130 Pine Ave., Suite C, Long Beach 90802; 417 S. Hill St., Los Angeles 90013; 360 Twenty-second St., Oakland 94612; 1818 W. Chapman Ave., Orange 92668; P.O. Box 867, Oxnard 93030; 2321 "P" St., P.O. Box 9006, Sacramento 95816; 481 Church St., Suite 307, San Bernardino 93401; 4310 Orange Ave., San Diego 92105; 414 Mason St., Suite 500, San Francisco 94102; 1153 Lincoln Ave., P.O. Box 8110, San Jose 95125; 20 N. San Mateo Drive, P.O. Box 294, San Mateo 94401; 109 E. De La Guerra St., Santa Barbara 93101; 343 Main St., Room 420, Stockton 95202; 2 Florida St., Vallejo 94590; 14545 Victory Boulevard, Van Nuys 91401; 1327 N. Main St., Walnut Creek 94596.

COLORADO: 1230 California St., Denver 80204.

CONNECTICUT: 1 Chapel St., Bridgeport 06603; 250 Constitution Plaza, Hartford 06103; 152 Temple St., P.O. Box 1445, New Haven 06506; 733 Summer St., Stamford 06901.

DELAWARE: 1609 Delaware Ave., P.O. Box 2223, Wilmington 19899.
DISTRICT OF COLUMBIA: 507 Perpetual Building, 1111 "E" St., N.W., Washington 20004.
FLORIDA: Ingraham Building, Suite 521, 25 S.E. Second Ave., Miami 33132; Suite 201, Pan American Building, West Palm Beach 33401.
GEORGIA: 212 Healey Building, 57 Forsyth St., N.W., Atlanta 30303; Box 840, Suite 400, The 500 Building, Augusta 30903; 308–312 Martin Building, P.O. Box 1218, Columbus 31902; 512 Abercorn St., P.O. Box 10006, Savannah 31402.
HAWAII: 677 Ala Moana Boulevard, Suite 602, Honolulu 96813.
IDAHO: 201 Idaho Building, Boise 83702.
ILLINOIS: 430 N. Michigan Ave., Chicago 60611; 1108 Lehmann Building, 405 Main St., Peoria 61602.
INDIANA: 118 S. Second St., P.O. Box 405, Elkhart 46514; 716 S. Barr St., Fort Wayne 46802; 583 Broadway, Gary 46401; 30 E. Georgia St., Indianapolis 46204; 320 W. Jefferson Boulevard, Suite 303, South Bend 46601.
IOWA: 246 Insurance Exchange Building, Des Moines 50309; 314 Benson Building, Sioux City 51101.
KANSAS: Suite 24, Ramada Inn, Topeka 66607; 306 Insurance Building, Wichita 67202.
KENTUCKY: 190 N. Upper St., Fuller Building, Lexington 40507; 204 Speed Building, 333 Guthrie St., Louisville 40202.
LOUISIANA: 500 Laurel St., Union Federal Building, Baton Rouge 70801; 220 Pioneer Building, Lake Charles 70601; 301 Camp St., New Orleans 70130; 305 Petroleum Building, 619 Market St., Shreveport 71101.
MARYLAND: 401 N. Howard St., Baltimore 21201.
MASSACHUSETTS: 150 Tremont St., Boston 02111; 145 State St., Springfield 01103; 50 Franklin St., Worcester 01608.
MICHIGAN: 150 Michigan Ave., Detroit 48226; 29–33 Pearl St., N.W., 324 Federal Building, Grand Rapids 49502.
MINNESOTA: 15 S. Fifth St., Minneapolis 55402; The Osborn Building, Suite 300, Saint Paul 55102.
MISSISSIPPI: 1410 Twenty-fourth Ave., P.O. Box 1707, Gulfport 39501; 315 E. Capitol, P.O. Box 1025, Jackson 39205.
MISSOURI: Suite 400, 112 E. Tenth St., Kansas City 64106; 901 Washington Ave., Saint Louis 63101; P.O. Box 1342, S. Side Station, Springfield 65805.

Appendixes: Agencies That Help Investors 243

NEBRASKA: 1015 Stuart Building, Lincoln 68508; Redick Tower Building, Fifteenth and Harney Sts., Omaha 68102.

NEVADA: 320-B E. Charleston Boulevard, Las Vegas 89104; 500 Plumas St., P.O. Box 2932, Reno 89505.

NEW JERSEY: 21 Euclid Ave., E., Haddonfield 08033; 2 Forest Ave., Paramus 07652; 247 E. Front St., Trenton 08611.

NEW MEXICO: 514 Second, N.W., Albuquerque 87101.

NEW YORK: 238 Main St., Buffalo 14202; 131 Jericho Turnpike, Jericho 11753; 220 Church St., New York 10013; 2090 Seventh Ave., New York 10027; 731 Sibley Tower Building, Rochester 14604; 101 State St., Schenectady 12305; 1700 One MONY Plaza, 100 Madison St., Syracuse 13202; 167 Genessee St., Utica 13501; 158 Westchester Ave., White Plains 10601.

NORTH CAROLINA: 510 City National Bank Building, Charlotte 28202; 225 N. Greene St., P.O. Box 2400, Greensboro 27402; 914 First Union National Bank Building, Winston-Salem 27101.

OHIO: 5 E. Buchtel Ave., Akron 44308; 203 Market Ave., S., Harvard Building, Canton 44702; 26 E. Sixth St., Cincinnati 45202; 1720 Keith Building, Cleveland 44115; 71 E. State St., Columbus 43215; 7 E. Fourth St., Suite 2000, Dayton 45402; 214 Board of Trade Building, Toledo 43604.

OKLAHOMA: 208 Leonhardt Building, Oklahoma City 73102; 3365 E. Skelly Drive, Tulsa 74135.

OREGON: 623 Corbett Building, Portland 97204.

PENNSYLVANIA: 401 Walnut St., Philadelphia 19106; 230 Grant Building, Pittsburgh 15219; 426 Mulberry St., Scranton 18503.

RHODE ISLAND: 248 Weybosset St., Providence 02903.

TENNESSEE: 11 W. Eighth St., Chattanooga Bank Building, Chattanooga 37402; 502 Gay St., 210 Fidelity Building, Knoxville 37902; 100 N. Main Building, Suite 1210, Memphis 38103; 1006 Nashville Bank and Trust Building, Nashville 37201.

TEXAS: 341 Hickory St., Abilene 79604; 102–B Vaughn Building, Amarillo 79101; 404 Littlefield Building, Austin 78701; Suite 315, Goodhue Building, Beaumont 77701; 510 Vaughn Plaza, Corpus Christi 78401; 1505 Elm St., Dallas 75201; 700 Electric Building, El Paso 79901; 1004 Sinclair Building, 106 W. Fifth St., Fort Worth 76102; 1212 Main St., 560 Main Building, Houston 77002; 915 Texas Ave., Lubbock 79401; Air Terminal Building, P.O. Box 6006, Midland 79701; 406 W. Market St., Suite 301, San Antonio 78205; 3221 Franklin Ave., P.O. Box 7203, Waco 76710.

UTAH: 19 E. Second St., S., Salt Lake City 84111.
VIRGINIA: 114 W. York St., Norfolk 23510; 4020 W. Broad St., Richmond 23230; 410 First St., S.W., Roanoke 24011.
WASHINGTON: 538 Denny Building, 2200 Sixth Ave., Seattle 98121; 514 Columbia Building, Spokane 99204; Rust Building, Tacoma 98402; 105 N. Third St., P.O. Box 1584, Yakima 98901.
WISCONSIN: 174 W. Wisconsin Ave., Milwaukee 53203.

CANADA

ALBERTA: 630 Eighth Ave., S.W., Suite 404, Calgary, 10182–103rd St., Edmonton.
BRITISH COLUMBIA: 100 W. Pender St., Vancouver; 645 Fort St., Suite 215, Victoria.
MANITOBA: 365 Hargrave St., Room 204, Winnipeg.
NEWFOUNDLAND AND LABRADOR: P.O. Box 516, St. John's.
NOVA SCOTIA: 5555 Young St., Halifax.
ONTARIO: 237 Queen St., Ottawa; 85 Richmond St., W., Suite 900, Toronto.
QUEBEC: 1155 Dorchester Boulevard, W., Montreal; C.P. 247 Haute-Ville, 17 Rue St-Louis, Quebec.

APPENDIX B:

Securities and Exchange Commission

Headquarters Office

500 Capitol St., Washington, D.C. 20549

Regional Offices

ATLANTA, GA.: 1371 Peachtree St., N.E. 30309
BOSTON, MASS.: John F. Kennedy Federal Building, Government Center 02203
CHICAGO, ILL.: U.S. Courthouse and Federal Office Building, 219 S. Dearborn St. 60604
DENVER, COLO.: 7224 Federal Building, 1961 Stout St. 80202
FORT WORTH, TEX.: 503 U.S. Courthouse, 10th and Lamar Sts. 76102

Branch Offices

CLEVELAND, OHIO: Federal Office Building, 1240 E. Ninth at Lakeside 44199
DETROIT, MICH.: 230 Federal Building 48226
HOUSTON, TEX.: 2606 Federal Office and Courts Building, 515 Rusk Ave. 77002
LOS ANGELES, CALIF.: U.S. Courthouse, 312 N. Spring St. 90012
MIAMI, FLA.: Federal Office Building, 51 S.W. First Ave. 33130
SALT LAKE CITY, UTAH: Federal Building, 125 S. State St. 84111
ST. LOUIS, MO.: Federal Building, 208 N. Broadway 63102

APPENDIX C:

Federal Trade Commission

Headquarters Office
Sixth St. and Pennsylvania Ave., N.W., Washington, D.C. 29580
Field Offices

ATLANTA, GA.: 730 Peachtree St., N.E. 30308
BOSTON, MASS.: John F. Kennedy Federal Building, Government Center 02203
CHICAGO, ILL.: U.S. Courthouse and Federal Office Building, 219 S. Dearborn St. 60604
CLEVELAND, OHIO: Federal Office Building, 1240 E. Ninth St. 44199
HOUSTON, TEX.: U.S. Courthouse, 515 Rusk Ave. 77002
KANSAS CITY, MO.: 2806 Federal Office Building 64106
LOS ANGELES, CALIF.: 1100 Wilshire Boulevard 90024
NEW ORLEANS, LA.: 1000 Masonic Temple Building, 333 Saint Charles St. 70130
NEW YORK, N.Y.: Federal Office Building, 26 Federal Plaza 10007
OAK RIDGE, TENN.: 230 N. Purdy St. 37830
SAN FRANCISCO, CALIF.: 450 Golden Gate Ave., Box 36005, Federal Building 94102
SEATTLE, WASH.: 908 Republic Building, 1511 Third Ave. 98101
WASHINGTON, D.C.: 450 W. Broad St., Falls Church, Va. 22046

APPENDIX D:

Small Business Administration

Field Offices

ALABAMA: Birmingham
ALASKA: Anchorage, Fairbanks
ARKANSAS: Little Rock
ARIZONA: Phoenix, Tucson
CALIFORNIA: Fresno, Los Angeles, San Diego, San Francisco
COLORADO: Denver
CONNECTICUT: Hartford
DELAWARE: Wilmington
DISTRICT OF COLUMBIA: Washington
FLORIDA: Jacksonville, Miami, Tampa
GEORGIA: Atlanta
HAWAII: Honolulu
IDAHO: Boise
ILLINOIS: Chicago
INDIANA: Indianapolis
IOWA: Des Moines
KANSAS: Wichita
KENTUCKY: Louisville
LOUISIANA: New Orleans
MAINE: Augusta
MARYLAND: Baltimore
MASSACHUSETTS: Boston
MICHIGAN: Detroit, Marquette
MINNESOTA: Minneapolis
MISSISSIPPI: Jackson

MISSOURI: Kansas City, St. Louis
MONTANA: Helena
NEBRASKA: Omaha
NEVADA: Las Vegas
NEW HAMPSHIRE: Concord
NEW JERSEY: Newark
NEW MEXICO: Albuquerque
NEW YORK: Albany, Buffalo, New York, Syracuse
NORTH CAROLINA: Charlotte
NORTH DAKOTA: Fargo
OHIO: Cincinnati, Cleveland, Columbus, Toledo
OKLAHOMA: Oklahoma City
OREGON: Portland
PENNSYLVANIA: Philadelphia, Pittsburgh
PUERTO RICO: Hato Rey
RHODE ISLAND: Providence
SOUTH CAROLINA: Columbia
SOUTH DAKOTA: Sioux Falls
TENNESSEE: Knoxville, Nashville
TEXAS: Dallas, Harlingen, Houston, Lubbock, Marshall, San Antonio
UTAH: Salt Lake City
VERMONT: Montpelier
VIRGINIA: Richmond
WASHINGTON: Seattle, Spokane
WEST VIRGINIA: Charleston, Clarksburg
WISCONSIN: Madison, Milwaukee
WYOMING: Casper

APPENDIX E:

U.S. Commerce Department

Field Offices

ALBUQUERQUE, N. MEX.: U.S. Courthouse 87101
ANCHORAGE, ALASKA: Room 306, Loussac-Sogn Building 99501
ATLANTA, GA.: Home Savings Building, 75 Forsyth St., N.W. 30303
BALTIMORE, MD.: U.S. Customhouse, Gay and Lombard Sts. 21202
BIRMINGHAM, ALA.: 908 S. Twentieth St. 35205
BOSTON, MASS.: 510 John F. Kennedy Federal Building 02203
BUFFALO, N.Y.: 504 Federal Building, 117 Ellicott St. 14203
CHARLESTON, S.C.: Federal Building, 334 Meeting St. 29403
CHARLESTON, W. VA.: 3000 New Federal Office Building, 500 Quarrier St. 25301
CHEYENNE, WYO.: 6022 U.S. Federal Building and Courthouse, 2120 Capitol Ave. 82001
CHICAGO, ILL.: 1486 New Federal Building, 219 S. Dearborn St. 60604
CINCINNATI, OHIO: 8028 Federal Office Building, 550 Main St. 45202
CLEVELAND, OHIO: 666 Euclid Ave. 44114
DALLAS, TEX.: 1114 Commerce St. 75202
DENVER, COLO.: 16419 Federal Building, Twentieth and Stout Sts. 80202
DES MOINES, IOWA: 609 Federal Building, 210 Walnut St. 50309
DETROIT, MICH.: 445 Federal Building 48226

GREENSBORO, N.C.: 258 Federal Building, W. Market St., P.O. Box 1950 27402
HARTFORD, CONN.: Federal Office Building, 450 Main St. 06103
HONOLULU, HAWAII: 286 Alexander Young Building, 1015 Bishop St. 96813
HOUSTON, TEX.: 5102 Federal Building, 515 Rusk Ave. 77002
JACKSONVILLE, FLA.: P.O. Box 35087, 400 W. Bay St. 32202
KANSAS CITY, MO.: 911 Walnut St. 64106
LOS ANGELES, CALIF.: Western Pacific Building, 1031 S. Broadway 90015
MEMPHIS, TENN.: 710 Home Federal Building, 147 Jefferson Ave. 38103
MIAMI, FLA.: City National Bank Building, 25 W. Flagler St. 33130
MILWAUKEE, WIS.: Straus Building, 238 W. Wisconsin Ave. 53203
MINNEAPOLIS, MINN.: Federal Building, 110 S. Fourth St. 55401
NEW ORLEANS, LA.: 909 Federal Office Building (South), 610 South St. 70130
NEW YORK, N.Y.: Federal Office Building, 26 Federal Plaza, Foley Square 10007
PHILADELPHIA, PA.: Jefferson Building, 1015 Chestnut St. 19107
PHOENIX, ARIZ.: New Federal Building, 230 N. First Ave. 85025
PITTSBURGH, PA.: 2201 Federal Building, 1000 Liberty Ave. 15219
PORTLAND, OREG.: 217 Old U.S. Courthouse, 520 S.W. Morrison St. 97204
RENO, NEV.: 300 Booth St. 89502
RICHMOND, VA.: 2105 Federal Building, 400 N. Eighth St. 23240
ST. LOUIS, MO.: 2511 Federal Building, 1520 Market St. 63103
SALT LAKE CITY, UTAH: 1201 Federal Building, 125 S. State St. 84111
SAN FRANCISCO, CALIF.: Federal Building, Box 36013, 450 Golden Gate Ave. 94102
SAN JUAN, P.R.: Room 100, P.O. Building 00902
SAVANNAH, GA.: 235 U.S. Courthouse and Post Office Building, 125–29 Bull St. 31402
SEATTLE, WASH.: 8021 Federal Office Building, 909 First Ave. 98104

Notes

CHAPTER ONE

1. Leslie V. Dix, assistant to director, Bureau of Deceptive Practices, Federal Trade Commission (Speech delivered to the Practicing Law Institute, New York, N.Y., June 19, 1970).
2. George Hanc, "The United States Savings Bond Program in the Postwar Period," *National Bureau of Economic Research* (1962), p. 99.
3. Charles P. Landt, chairman, Subcommittee on Mortgage Finance, National Association of Real Estate Boards (Testimony before Senate Subcommittee on Housing and Urban Affairs, Washington, D.C., March 4, 1970).
4. Eileen Shanahan, *The New York Times*, October 2, 1968, p. 1.
5. Representative John E. Moss, chairman, Subcommittee on Commerce and Finance, U.S. House of Representatives (Speech delivered to Spring Meeting of Investment Bankers Association of America, White Sulphur Springs, W. Va., May 8, 1970).

CHAPTER TWO

6. Clyde H. Farnsworth, *The New York Times*, March 18, 1970, p. 40.
7. Wayne E. Green, *The Wall Street Journal*, September 19, 1968, p. 1.
8. *The New York Times*, May 15, 1970, p. 55.
9. Senator Lee Metcalf (Remarks recorded in *Congressional Record*, May 22, 1970), pp. S–7680–81.

CHAPTER THREE

10. *Masters' and Generals' Manual*, sales manual distributed by Holiday Magic Informative Cosmetics (San Rafael, Calif.), p. 20.
11. Bill Fuller, *Charlotte Observer*, February 27, 1969, p. 1–A.
12. Michael Malloy, *National Observer*, December 16, 1968, p. 30.
13. Claude Koprowski and Robert J. Samuelson, *Washington Post*, March 24, 1969, p. 22–A.
14. *Ibid.*

CHAPTER FOUR

15. David Scheen, *Akron Beacon Journal*, January 14, 1970, p. F–3.

CHAPTER FIVE

16. Curt Mathews, *St. Louis Post-Dispatch*, December 6, 1968, p. 7–B.
17. *St. Louis Post-Dispatch*, March 25, 1970, p. 12.
18. Bill Jordan, *The New York Times*, July 12, 1970, Sec. 3, p. 6.
19. R. W. Apple, Jr., *The New York Times*, May 27, 1970, p. 1.
20. Paul Troop, *Long Island (N.Y.) Commercial Review*, July 30, 1970, p. 23.
21. Dennis Duggan, *Newsday*, December 28, 1967, p. 15–A.
22. Professor Donald M. Thompson, "Franchise Operation," *New York University Journal of Retailing* (Winter 1968–69) p. 39.
23. Elmer Roessner, *Business Today*, syndicated column, April 28, 1969.
24. David England, *Christian Science Monitor*, May 23, 1970, p. 10.
25. Perma Life Mufflers, Inc., et al. v. International Parts Corp., et al., 392 U.S. 134 (1968).
26. Rufus E. Wilson, chief, Division of General Trade Restraints, Federal Trade Commission, "Antitrust Policy and Franchising" (Remarks delivered to California-Nevada Soft Drink Association, San Diego, Calif., February 11, 1969).
27. Everette MacIntyre, commissioner, Federal Trade Commission, "Franchising Developments" (Remarks delivered to the Conference of the International Franchise Association, Washington, D.C., May 8, 1969).

CHAPTER SIX

28. Theodore C. Link, *St. Louis Post-Dispatch*, August 1, 1969, p. 3–A.

Notes

CHAPTER NINE

29. Securities and Exchange Commission, *34th Annual Report* (Washington, D.C.: U.S. Government Printing Office, 1968), p. XVIII.
30. *Survey on Annual Reports*, a report compiled by Robert S. Taplinger Associates (New York, 1970).
31. Leonard S. Silk, *The New York Times*, February 8, 1970, p. 10.
32. *Understanding Financial Statements*, a guide published by the Bank of America (San Francisco, Calif., 1967).
33. *Wright Advisory Reports*, December 11, 1968, p. 1.
34. *Better Investing*, published by the National Association of Investment Clubs, May, 1969, p. 9.

CHAPTER TEN

35. Eileen Shanahan, *The New York Times*, May 18, 1966, p. 72.
36. *Mutual Fund Amendments, Part 2*, Hearings before the House Subcommittee on Commerce and Finance (Washington, D.C.: U.S. Government Printing Office, 1970), Serial No. 91-34.
37. *Mutual Fund Performance Analysis*, compiled by Arthur Lipper Corporation, June 30, 1970.
38. Quoted by George Wheeler, *Newsday*, April 13, 1970, p. 80.

CHAPTER THIRTEEN

39. J. Atwood Ives and William Green, *Commercial and Financial Chronicle*, July 9, 1970, p. 16.
40. "Sorting Out the Investment Trusts," *Fortune*, August, 1970, p. 174.

A Glossary for Small Investors

(Adapted from New York Stock Exchange material and other sources especially for moderate-income investors.)

ACCRUED INTEREST: Interest accrued on a bond since the last interest payment. The buyer pays the market price plus accrued interest. Exceptions include bonds that are in default and income bonds. (See: Flat, Income Bond)

AMORTIZATION: A generic term. Includes various specific bookkeeping practices such as depreciation, depletion, write-off of intangibles, prepaid expenses, and deferred charges.

ANNUAL REPORT: Financial statement issued yearly by a corporation showing assets, liabilities, and earnings.

ASSETS: Everything a corporation owns or that is due to it: cash, investments, money due it and inventories (current assets), buildings and machinery (fixed assets), patents and goodwill (intangible assets). (See: Liabilities)

AVERAGES: Ways of measuring the trend of securities prices. Best known is the Dow-Jones average of thirty industrial stocks listed. Another widely used average is Standard & Poor's 500 popular stocks, which may be more representative of trends than the Dow-Jones. The New York Stock Exchange Common Stock Index is a composite index covering price movements of all stocks listed on the Big Board.

BALANCE SHEET: A condensed statement showing the nature and amount of a company's assets, liabilities, and capital on a given date; what the company owned, and owed, and the ownership interest of its stockholders. (See: Assets, Earnings Report)

BEAR MARKET: A declining market.

BEARER BOND: A bond that does not have the owner's name registered on the books of the issuing company and that is payable to the holder. (*See:* Coupon Bond, Registered Bond)

BID AND ASKED: A quotation or quote. The *bid* is the highest price anyone has declared he wants to pay for a security at a given time, the *asked* is the lowest price anyone will take at that time. (*See:* Quotation)

BIG BOARD: A popular term for the New York Stock Exchange.

BLUE CHIP: Common stock in a company known nationally for the wide acceptance of its products and its ability to make money and pay dividends.

BOILER ROOM: High-pressure telephone selling of stocks of dubious value; typically a room lined with desks or cubicles, each with a salesman and phone.

BOND: Basically an IOU or promissory note of a corporation, usually issued in multiples of $1,000, although $100 and $50 denominations are not uncommon. A bond is evidence of a debt on which the company usually promises to pay a specified amount of interest for a specified length of time and to repay the loan on the expiration date. In every case a bond represents debt—its holder is a creditor of the corporation and not a part owner as is the shareholder. (*See:* Convertible, General Mortgage Bond, Income Bond)

BOOK VALUE: Determined from a company's records by adding all assets (generally excluding such intangibles as goodwill), then deducting all debts and other liabilities, plus the liquidation price of any preferred issues. The sum arrived at is divided by the number of common shares outstanding and the result is book value per common share. Book value of the assets of a company or a security may have little relationship to the market value of its shares.

BROKER: An agent, often a member of a stock exchange firm or an exchange member himself, who handles orders to buy and sell securities or commodities.

BULL MARKET: A rising market.

CALL LOAN: A loan that may be terminated or called at any time by the lender or borrower. Used to finance purchases of securities.

CALLABLE: A bond issue, all or part of which may be redeemed by the issuing corporation under definite conditions before maturity.

A Glossary for Small Investors

The term also applies to preferred shares that may be redeemed by the issuing corporation.

CAPITAL GAIN OR CAPITAL LOSS: Profit or loss from the sale of a capital asset. A capital gain, under current federal income tax laws, may be either short-term (six months or less) or long-term (more than six months).

CAPITAL STOCK: All shares representing ownership of a business, including preferred and common. (See: Common Stock, Preferred Stock)

CAPITALIZATION: Total amount of the various securities issued by a corporation may include bonds, debentures, preferred and common stock. Bonds and debentures are usually carried on the books of the issuing company in terms of their par or face value. Preferred and common shares may be carried in terms of par or stated value. Stated value may be an arbitrary figure decided upon by the directors or may represent the amount received by the company from the sale of the securities at the time of issuance. (See: Par)

CASH FLOW: The sum of all of a corporation's profits plus bookkeeping charges for depreciation, amortization of debt, and extraordinary charges to reserves, which are bookkeeping deductions but which the corporation actually keeps. Cash flow has been used increasingly as a yardstick of a company's success because it is a good indication of earning power.

CASH POSITION: The ratio of a corporation's cash or easily cashed securities to other assets.

CERTIFICATE: The actual piece of paper evidencing ownership of stock in a corporation. Loss of a certificate may at the least cause a great deal of inconvenience—at the worst, financial loss.

CLOSED-END INVESTMENT TRUST: (See: Investment Trust)

COLLATERAL: Securities or other property pledged by a borrower to secure repayment of a loan.

COMMISSION: The broker's fee for purchasing or selling securities or property for a client.

COMMON STOCK: Securities that represent an ownership interest in a corporation. If the company also has issued preferred stock, both common and preferred have ownership rights, but the preferred normally has prior claim on dividends and, in the event of liquidation, assets. Claims of both common and preferred stockholders are junior to claims of bondholders or other creditors of the company. Common stockholders assume the greater risk, but may gain the greater reward in dividends and capital appreciation. (See: Capital Stock, Preferred Stock)

CONVERTIBLE: A bond, debenture, or preferred share that may be exchanged by the owner for common stock or another security, usually of the same company, in accordance with the terms of the issue.

COUPON BOND: Bond with interest coupons attached. The coupons are clipped as they come due and are presented by the holder for payment of interest. (See: Bearer Bond, Registered Bond)

CUMULATIVE PREFERRED: A stock having a provision that if one or more dividends are omitted, the omitted dividends must be paid before dividends may be paid on the company's common stock.

CURRENT ASSETS: Those assets of a company that are reasonably expected to be realized in cash, or sold, or consumed during the normal operating cycle of the business. These include cash, U.S. government bonds, receivables and money due usually within one year, and inventories.

CURRENT LIABILITIES: Money owed and payable by a company, usually within one year.

CURRENT POSITION: A comparison of current assets to current liabilities. As *Forbes* explains, a quick but not infallible method of measuring a firm's financial health. A two to one ratio is normally considered sound, or one to one for utility companies and railroads.

DEALER: A securities firm acting as a principal rather than an agent. Typically, a dealer buys for his own account and sells to a customer from his own inventory. His profit or loss is the difference between the price he pays and the price he receives for the security. The dealer's confirmation must disclose to his customer that he has acted as principal. The same firm may function at different times as broker or dealer.

DEBENTURE: A promissory note backed by a company's credit and usually not secured by a mortgage or lien on specific property. (See: Bond)

DELIVERY: The certificate representing shares bought the regular way on the New York Stock Exchange normally is delivered to the purchaser's broker on the fifth business day after the transaction.

A Glossary for Small Investors

DEPLETION: Natural resources, such as metals, oils, gas, and timber, which conceivably can be reduced to zero over the years, present a special problem in capital management. Depletion consists of bookkeeping charges against earnings based upon the amount of the asset taken out of the total reserves in the period for which accounting is made, but it does not represent any cash outlay.

DEPRECIATION: Normally, charges against earnings to write off the cost of an asset over its estimated useful life. It is a bookkeeping entry and does not represent any cash outlay.

DISCRETIONARY ACCOUNT: An account in which the customer gives the broker or someone else discretion, which may be complete or within specific limits, as to the purchase and sale of securities or commodities including selection, timing, and price to be paid or received.

DISCRETIONARY ORDER: The customer empowers the broker to act on his behalf in the choice of security to be bought or sold.

DIVIDEND: The payment designated by the board of directors to be distributed pro rata among the shares outstanding. On preferred shares, it is generally a fixed amount. On common shares, dividends vary with earnings and available cash, and may be omitted if business is poor or the directors want to use earnings for expansion.

DOLLAR COST AVERAGING: A system of buying securities at regular intervals with a fixed dollar amount rather than by the number of shares. (See: Formula Investing)

DOW THEORY: A theory of analysis based upon the performance of the Dow-Jones industrial and rail stock averages. The theory says that the market is in a basic upward trend if one of these averages advances above a previous important high, accompanied or followed by a similar advance in the other. When the averages both dip below previous important lows, this is regarded as confirmation of a basic downtrend. The theory does not attempt to predict how long either trend will continue, although it is widely misinterpreted as a way to forecast future action. Whatever its merits, the theory is sometimes a factor in the market because many people believe in it—or believe others do. (See: Technical Position)

EARNINGS REPORT: A statement—also called an income statement—issued by a company showing its earnings or losses over a given period, and income and expenses. (See: Balance Sheet)

EQUITY: The ownership interest of common and preferred stockholders in a company.

EX-DIVIDEND: Meaning "without dividend." Every dividend is payable on a fixed date to all recorded shareholders as of a previous date. Open buy and sell stop orders, and sell stop limit orders in a stock on the ex-dividend date are ordinarily reduced by the value of that dividend. In the case of open stop limit orders to sell, both the stop price and the limit price are reduced. Anyone who bought it on and after that day would not be entitled to that dividend. (See: Delivery, Net Change)

EX-RIGHTS: Without the rights. (See: Rights)

FACE VALUE: The value of a bond that appears on the face of the bond, unless the value is otherwise specified by the issuing company. Face value is ordinarily the amount the issuing company promises to pay at maturity. It is not an indication of current market value. Sometimes referred to as par value.

FISCAL YEAR: A corporation's accounting year, which may not coincide with the calendar year.

FIXED CHARGES: A company's fixed expenses—such as bond interest, which it has agreed to pay whether or not earned—which are deducted from income before earnings on equity capital are computed.

FLAT: This term means that the price at which a bond is traded includes consideration for all unpaid accruals of interest. Bonds that are in default of interest or principal are traded flat. Income bonds, which pay interest only to the extent earned, are usually traded flat. All other bonds are usually dealt in "and interest," which means that the buyer pays the market price plus interest accrued since the last payment.

FORMULA INVESTING: An investment technique. One formula calls for the shifting of funds from common shares to preferred shares or bonds as the market, on average, rises above a certain predetermined point—and the return of funds to common share investments as the market average declines. (See: Dollar Cost Averaging)

FUNDED DEBT: Usually interest-bearing bonds or debentures of a company. Could include long-term bank loans but not short-term loans, preferred or common stock.

GENERAL MORTGAGE BOND: A bond secured by a blanket mortgage on the company's property, but which is often outranked by one or more other mortgages.

A Glossary for Small Investors 261

GILT-EDGED: High-grade bond issued by a company that has demonstrated its ability to earn a comfortable profit over a period of years and pay its bondholders their interest without interruption.

GOOD 'TIL CANCELED ORDER (GTC) OR OPEN ORDER: An order to buy or sell that remains in effect until it is either executed or canceled.

GOVERNMENT BONDS: Obligations of the U.S. government, regarded as the highest grade issues in existence.

GROWTH STOCK: Stock of a company with prospects for future growth—a company whose earnings are expected to increase at a relatively rapid rate.

HEDGE: (See: Puts and Calls, Selling Against the Box, Short Sale)

HOLDING COMPANY: A corporation that owns the securities of another, in most cases with voting control.

INCOME BOND: Generally income bonds promise to repay principal but to pay interest only when earned. In some cases unpaid interest on an income bond may accumulate as a claim when the bond becomes due.

INDENTURE: A written agreement under which debentures are issued, setting forth maturity date, interest rate, security, and other terms.

INVESTMENT BANKER: Also known as an underwriter. He is the middleman between the corporation issuing new securities and the public. The usual practice is for one or more investment bankers to buy outright a new issue of stocks or bonds. The group forms a syndicate to resell the securities.

INVESTMENT COUNSEL: One whose principal business consists of acting as investment adviser and providing investment supervisory services.

INVESTMENT TRUST: A company that invests in other companies. There are two principal types: closed-end, and open-end or mutual funds. Shares in closed-end investment trusts are bought and sold like other shares. Capitalization of these companies usually remains the same. Open-end funds sell their own new shares to investors, stand ready to buy back their shares, and are not listed on stock exchanges. Their capitalization is not fixed; they issue more shares as investors want them.

ISSUE: Any of a company's securities, or the act of distributing such securities.

LEVERAGE: The effect on per share earnings of a common stock when large sums must be paid for bond interest or preferred stock dividends before the common stock can share in earnings. Leverage may be advantageous for the common stock when earnings are good but may work against it when earnings decline. Example: Company A has 1,000,000 shares of common stock outstanding, no other securities. Earnings drop from $1,000,000 to $800,000 or from $1 to 80 cents a share, a decline of 20 percent. Company B also has 1,000,000 shares of common and $1,000,000 in earnings but must pay $500,000 annually in bond interest. If earnings fall to $800,000, there is only $300,000 available for the common, a drop of 40 percent. Or if earnings of the company with only common stock increased to $1,500,000, earnings per share would go to $1.50, an increase of 50 percent. But if earnings of the company that had to pay $500,000 in bond interest increased that much, earnings per share would jump from 50 cents to $1, or 100 percent.

LIABILITIES: The claims against a corporation including accounts and wages payable, dividends declared payable, accrued taxes, fixed or long-term liabilities such as mortgage bonds, debentures, and bank loans. (See: Balance Sheet)

LIEN: A claim against property, which has been pledged or mortgaged to secure the performance of an obligation. A bond is usually secured by a lien against specified property of a company. (See: Bond)

LIMIT, LIMITED ORDER, OR LIMITED PRICE ORDER: An order to buy or sell a stated amount of a security at a specified price or at a better price if obtainable.

LIQUIDITY: The ability of the market in a particular security to absorb a reasonable amount of buying or selling at moderate price changes; one of the most important characteristics of a good market.

LISTED STOCK: The stock of a company traded on a securities exchange, and for which a registered statement giving detailed information about the company has been filed with the Securities and Exchange Commission, unless otherwise exempted, and the exchange itself. The various stock exchanges have different standards for listing. Some of the guides used by the New York Stock Exchange for an original listing are national interest in the company, a minimum of 1,000,000 shares outstanding with at least 700,000 shares publicly held among not less than two thousand shareholders including at least seventeen hundred

A Glossary for Small Investors

round-lot stockholders. The publicly held common shares should have a minimum aggregate market value of $12 million. Normally the company should have earning power of over $2 million annually before taxes and of over $1.2 million after all charges and taxes.

LOAD: The portion of the offering price of shares of open-end investment companies that covers sales commissions and other costs of distribution. The load is incurred only on purchase, there being, in most cases, no charge when the shares are sold (redeemed).

LONG: Signifies ownership of securities. "I am long 100 U.S. Steel" means the speaker owns 100 shares. (*See:* Short Sale)

MANIPULATION: An illegal operation. Buying or selling a security for the purpose of creating false or misleading appearance of active trading or for the purpose of raising or depressing the price to induce purchase or sale by others.

MARGIN: The amount paid by the customer when he uses his broker's credit to buy a security. Under Federal Reserve regulations, the initial margin required in the past twenty years has ranged from 40 percent of the purchase price all the way to 100 percent. (*See:* Equity)

MARGIN CALL: A demand upon a customer to put up money or securities with the broker. The call is made when a purchase is made; also if a customer's equity in a margin account declines below a minimum standard set by the exchange or by the firm.

MARKET ORDER: An order to buy or sell a stated amount of a security at the most advantageous price obtainable. (*See:* Good 'til Canceled Order, Limit, Stop Order)

MARKET PRICE: In the case of a security, market price is usually considered the last reported price at which the stock or bond sold.

MATURITY: The date on which a loan or a bond or debenture comes due and is to be paid off.

MEMBER FIRM: A securities brokerage firm organized as a partnership and having at least one general partner who is a member of the New York Stock Exchange.

MORTGAGE BOND: A bond secured by a mortgage on a property. The value of the property may or may not equal the value of the so-called mortgage bonds issued against it. (*See:* Bond, Debenture)

MUNICIPAL BOND: A bond issued by a state or a political subdivision, such as county, city, town, or village. The term also designates bonds issued by state agencies and authorities. In general, interest paid on municipal bonds is exempt from federal income taxes.

MUTUAL FUND: (See: Investment Trust)

NASD: The National Association of Securities Dealers, Inc. An association of brokers and dealers in the over-the-counter securities business. The association has the power to expel members who have been determined guilty of unethical practices. NASD is dedicated to "adopt, administer, and enforce rules of fair practice and rules to prevent fraudulent and manipulative acts and practices, and in general to promote just and equitable principles of trade for the protection of investors."

NEGOTIABLE: Refers to a security, title to which is transferable by delivery. (See: Delivery)

NET ASSET VALUE: A term usually used in connection with a mutual fund or investment trust, meaning net asset value per share. Generally a mutual fund computes its assets daily, by totaling the market value of all securities owned. All liabilities are deducted, and the balance divided by the number of shares outstanding to figure the net asset value per share.

NET CHANGE: The change in the price of a security from the closing price on one day and the closing price on the following day on which the stock is traded. The net change is ordinarily the last column in a stock price list. The mark +½ means up 50 cents a share from the last sale on the previous day the stock traded.

NEW ISSUE: A stock or bond sold by a corporation for the first time. Proceeds may be issued to retire outstanding securities of the company, for new plant or equipment, or for additional working capital.

NONCUMULATIVE: A preferred stock on which unpaid dividends do not accrue. Omitted dividends are, as a rule, gone forever. (See: Cumulative Preferred)

NYSE COMMON STOCK INDEX: A composite index covering price movements of all common stocks listed on the Big Board. (See: Averages)

ODD LOT: An amount of stock less than the established 100-share unit or 10-share unit of trading: from 1 to 99 shares for the great majority of issues, 1 to 9 for so-called inactive stocks. (See: Round Lot)

ODD-LOT DEALER: A member firm of the exchange that buys

and sells odd lots of stocks—1 to 99 shares for 100-share units. The odd-lot dealer's customers are brokers acting on behalf of their customers. There are one or more odd-lot dealers ready to buy or sell, for their own accounts, odd lots in any stock. The odd-lot dealer's price is based on the first round-lot transaction that occurs on the floor following receipt at the trading post of the odd-lot order. The usual differential between the odd-lot price and the effective round-lot price is 12½ cents a share for stock selling below $55; 25 cents a share for stock at $55 or more. For example: You decide to buy 20 shares of ABC common at the market. Your order is transmitted by your commission broker to the representative of an odd-lot dealer at the post where ABC is traded. A few minutes later there is a 100-share transaction in ABC at $10 a share. The odd-lot price at which your order is immediately filled by the odd-lot dealer is $10.125 a share. If you had sold 20 shares of ABC, you would have received $9.875 a share.

OFFER: The price at which a person is ready to sell. Opposed to bid, the price at which one is ready to buy. (See: Bid and Asked)

OPEN-END INVESTMENT TRUST: (See: Investment Trust)

OPEN ORDER: (See: Good 'til Canceled Order)

ORDERS GOOD UNTIL A SPECIFIED TIME: A market or limited price order good until a specified time, after which the order or portion not executed is to be treated as canceled.

OVERBOUGHT: An opinion as to price levels. May refer to a security that has had a sharp rise or to the market as a whole after a period of vigorous buying, which, it may be argued, has left prices "too high." (See: Technical Position)

OVERSOLD: The reverse of overbought. A single security or a market that, it is believed, has declined to an unreasonable level. (See: Technical Position)

OVER-THE-COUNTER: A market for securities made up of dealers who may or may not be members of a stock exchange, usually dealing in securities of companies with insufficient shares, stockholders, or earnings to warrant a listing on a stock exchange. Such securities are traded over-the-counter between dealers who act either as principals or as brokers for customers. The over-the-counter market also is the principal buying and selling medium for U.S. government bonds and municipals. (See: NASD)

PAR: In the case of a common share, par means a dollar amount assigned by the company's charter. Par value may also be used to compute the dollar amount of the common shares on the balance sheet. Par value has little relationship to the market value of a stock. Many companies today issue no-par stock but give a stated per share value on the balance sheet. But in the case of preferred shares and bonds, par is important. It often signifies the dollar value upon which dividends on preferred stocks, and interest on bonds, are figured. The issuer of a 6 percent bond promises to pay that percentage of the bond's par value annually. (See: Capitalization, Transfer Tax)

PARTICIPATING PREFERRED: A preferred stock entitled to its stated dividend and also to additional dividends on a specified basis upon payment of dividends on the common stock.

PASSED DIVIDEND: Omission of a regular or scheduled dividend.

POINT: In the case of shares of stock, a point means $1. If XYZ goes up 3 points, each share has risen $3. In the case of bonds a point means $10, because a bond is quoted as a percentage of $1,000. A bond that rises 3 points gains 3 percent of $1,000, or $30 in value. An advance from 87 to 90 would mean an advance in dollar value from $870 to $900 for each $1,000 bond.

PREFERRED STOCK: A class of stock with a claim on the company's earnings before dividends may be paid on the common stock, and usually entitled to priority over common stock if the company liquidates. Usually entitled to dividends at a specified rate. (See: Cumulative Preferred, Participating Preferred)

PREMIUM: The amount by which a preferred stock or bond may sell above its par value. In the case of a new issue, premium is the amount the market price rises over the original selling price. May refer also to redemption price of a bond or preferred stock if it is higher than face value.

PRICE-EARNINGS RATIO: Current market price of a stock divided by twelve-month earnings per share, as explained in chapter 8.

PRINCIPAL: The person for whom a broker executes an order, or a dealer buying or selling for his own account. Principal may also refer to a person's capital or to the face amount of a bond.

PRIOR PREFERRED: A preferred stock that usually takes precedence over other preferreds issued by the same company.

PROFIT MARGIN: A measure of earning capacity before taxes; for example, if a company made 20 cents before taxes on each $1 of sales, its profit margin would be 20 percent.

A Glossary for Small Investors

PROSPECTUS: A circular that describes securities being offered for sale. Required by the Securities Act of 1933.

PROXY: Written authorization to someone else to vote your shares at a shareholders' meeting.

PRUDENT MAN RULE: An investment standard. In some states, the law provides that a fiduciary, such as a trustee, may invest the fund's money only in a list of securities designated by the state—the so-called legal list. In other states, the trustee may invest in a security if it is one that a prudent man of discretion and intelligence, who is seeking a reasonable income and preservation of capital, would buy.

PUTS AND CALLS: Options that give the right to buy or sell a fixed amount of a stock at a specified price within a specified time (thirty or sixty days or longer). A put gives the holder the right to sell the stock; a call the right to buy it. Puts are bought by those who think a stock may go down. A put obligates the seller of the contract to take delivery and pay the specified price to the owner of the option within the time limit of the contract. The price specified is usually close to the market price at the time the contract is made. Calls are bought by those who think a stock may rise. A call gives the holder the right to buy the stock from the seller of the contract at the specified price within a fixed period of time. If the buyer does not wish to exercise his option, the price he paid for the option becomes a loss.

QUOTATION: Or quote. The highest bid to buy and the lowest offer to sell a security in a given market at a given time. If you ask your broker for a quote on a stock, he may come back with something like "45¼ to 45½." This means that $45.25 is the highest price any buyer wanted to pay at the time the quote was given on the exchange floor, and $45.50 was the lowest any seller would take. (See: Bid and Asked)

RECORD DATE: Date on which you must be registered as a shareholder in order to receive a declared dividend. (See: Delivery, Ex-Dividend)

REDEMPTION PRICE: Price at which a bond may be redeemed before maturity, at the option of the issuer. (See: Callable)

REGISTERED BOND: A bond that is registered on the books of the issuing company in the name of the owner. It can be transferred only when endorsed by the registered owner. (See: Bearer Bond, Coupon Bond)

REGISTERED REPRESENTATIVE: In a New York Stock Exchange member firm, a registered representative is an employee who has met the requirements of the exchange. Also known as an account executive, customer's broker.

REGISTRATION: Before a public offering may be made of new securities or of outstanding securities by controlling stockholders through the mails or in interstate commerce the securities must be registered under the Securities Act of 1933. Registration statement is filed with the SEC, and must disclose pertinent information relating to the company's operations, securities, management, and purpose of the offering. On offerings involving less than $300,000, less information is required.

REGULAR WAY DELIVERY: Unless otherwise specified, securities (other than government) sold on the New York Stock Exchange are to be delivered to the buying broker by the selling broker and payment made to the selling broker by the buying broker on the fifth business day after the transaction. Regular way delivery for government bonds is the following business day. (See: Delivery)

RIGHTS: When a company issues additional securities, it may give its stockholders the opportunity, ahead of others, to buy them in proportion to the number of shares each owns. The piece of paper evidencing this privilege is called a right. Because the additional stock is usually offered to stockholders below the current market price, rights ordinarily have market value and are actively traded. In most cases they must be exercised or sold within a short period. Failure to do so may result in loss to the holder. (See: Warrant)

ROUND LOT: A unit of trading or a multiple thereof. On the New York Stock Exchange the unit of trading is generally 100 shares in stocks and $1,000 par value in the case of bonds. In some inactive stocks, the unit of trading is 10 shares.

SEC: Securities and Exchange Commission, established to help protect investors and administer laws regulating investments.

SECONDARY DISTRIBUTION: Also known as a secondary offering. The redistribution of a block of stock, usually a large one such as might be involved in settling an estate. The sale is handled off the stock exchange by a securities firm or group, usually at a fixed price related to the current market price.

SELLING AGAINST THE BOX: A way of protecting a paper profit. Let's say you own 100 shares of XYZ, which has gone up and

A Glossary for Small Investors

you think it may decline. So you sell 100 shares short. You keep the 100 shares you own. If XYZ declines, the profit on your short sale is exactly offset by the loss in the market value of the stock you own. If XYZ advances, the loss on your short sale is exactly offset by the profit in the market value of the stock you have retained. You can close out your short sale by buying 100 shares to return to the person from whom you borrowed, or you can send them the 100 shares you own. (See: Hedge, Short Sale)

SERIAL BOND: An issue that matures in relatively small amounts at periodic stated intervals.

SHORT SALE: A person who believes a stock will decline and sells though he does not own any has made a short sale. For instance: You instruct your broker to sell short 100 shares of ABC. Your broker borrows the stock so he can deliver the 100 shares to the buyer. The money value of the shares borrowed is deposited by your broker with the lender. Sooner or later you must cover your short sale by buying the same amount of stock you borrowed for return to the lender. If you are able to buy for less than you sold it for, you make a profit. If you have to pay more than the price you received, you have a loss.

SPECIALIST: A member of the New York Stock Exchange who has two functions. First, he must maintain an orderly market, insofar as reasonably practicable, in the stocks in which he is registered as a specialist. In order to maintain an orderly market, the exchange expects the specialist to buy or sell for his own account, to a reasonable degree, when there is a temporary disparity between supply and demand. Second, the specialist acts as a broker's broker. When a commission broker on the exchange floor receives a limit order, say, to buy at $50 a stock then selling at $60, he leaves the order with the specialist, who will try to execute it in the market if and when the stock declines to the specified price.

SPLIT: The division of the shares of a corporation into a larger number of shares. If a company split its stock two for one, the holder of 50 shares would have 100 shares. But his proportionate equity in the company would remain the same.

STOCK AHEAD: Sometimes an investor who has entered an order to buy or sell a stock at a specified price will see transactions reported at that price while his order has not been executed. The reason is that the specialist had other orders at the same price ahead of his. (*See:* Specialist)

STOCK DIVIDEND: A dividend paid in securities rather than cash, described in chapter 14.

STOCKHOLDER OF RECORD: A stockholder whose name is registered on the books of the issuing corporation. (*See:* Ex-Dividend, Ex-Rights, Record Date)

STOP LIMIT ORDER: A stop limit order to buy becomes a limit order executable at the limit price, or less. A stop limit order to sell becomes a limit order executable at the limit price or at a higher price, if obtainable.

STOP ORDER: A stop order to buy becomes a market order when a transaction in the security occurs at or above the stop price. A stop order to sell becomes a market order when a transaction in the security occurs at or below the stop price. A stop order may be used to protect a paper profit or to try to limit a possible loss to a certain amount. Since it becomes a market order when the stop price is reached, there is no certainty that it will be executed at that price. (*See:* Limited Order, Market Order)

STREET NAME: Securities held in the name of a broker instead of the owner's are said to be carried in a street name.

TAX-EXEMPT BONDS: Securities of states, cities, and other public authorities, the interest on which is either wholly or partly exempt from federal income taxes.

TECHNICAL POSITION: A term applied to internal factors affecting the market; opposed to external forces such as earnings and general economic conditions. Such internal factors include the size of the "short" interest, whether the market has had a sustained advance or decline, a sharp advance or decline on small volume, and the amount of credit in use in the market. (*See:* Overbought, Oversold)

THIN MARKET: A market in which there are comparatively few bids to buy or offers to sell or both. The phrase may apply to a single security or to the entire stock market. In a thin market, price fluctuations are usually larger. A thin market in a particular stock may reflect lack of interest or a limited supply or demand for that stock. (*See:* Bid and Asked, Liquidity)

TRANSFER AGENT: A transfer agent keeps a record of each registered shareowner, address, number of shares owned, and sees that certificates presented for transfer are canceled and new certificates issued.

A Glossary for Small Investors 271

TRANSFER TAX: A tax imposed by New York State when a security is sold or transferred. The tax is paid by the seller.

UNDERWRITER: (See: Investment Banker)

UNLISTED: A security not listed on a stock exchange. (See: Over-the-Counter)

WARRANT: A certificate giving the right to buy securities at a stipulated price within a specified time or perpetually, as described in chapter 9. Sometimes a warrant is offered with securities as an inducedment to buy. (See: Rights)

References

Brown, Harold. *Franchising: Trap for the Trusting*. Boston: Little, Brown and Company, 1969.
Continental Franchise Review, semi-monthly newsletter. (Address is 290 Fillmore St., Denver, Colo. 80206; price is $52 a year including semi-annual references.)
Diamond, Frank B. *Invest/Speculate Profitably in the Stock Market*. New York: Trident Press, 1969.
Dias, Robert M., and Gurnick, Stanley I. *Franchising: The Investor's Complete Handbook*. New York: Hastings House, 1969.
Engel, Louis. *How to Buy Stocks*. New York: Bantam Books, 1969.
Federal Trade Commission. *Advice for Persons Who Are Considering an Investment in a Franchise Business*. Consumer Bulletin No. 4. Washington, D.C.
Gross, Harry, and Levy, Robert S. *Guide to Franchise Investigation and Contract Negotiations*. New York: Pilot Books, 1967.
Investment Companies. New York: Wiesenberger Services, 1970.
J. K. Lasser Tax Institute and Shulsky, Sam. *Investing for Your Future*. New York: Simon and Schuster, 1969.
Loeb, Gerald M. *The Battle for Investment Survival*. New York: Simon and Schuster, 1957.
Mail Fraud Laws. Washington, D.C.: U.S. Government Printing Office, 1969. (Address of Government Printing Office is Washington, D.C. 20402; price of pamphlet is 15¢.)
Merritt, Robert D. *Financial Independence through Common Stocks*. New York: Simon and Schuster, 1969.

Metz, Robert. *Franchising: How to Select a Business of Your Own.* New York: Hawthorn Books, 1969.

Monthly Advisory Report and Mutual Fund Selector. Boston: United Business Service.

Moody's Handbook of Common Stocks. New York: Moody's Investors Service, 1970.

NAIC Investment Club Manual. Detroit: National Association of Investment Clubs. (Address of Association is P.O. Box 220, Royal Oak, Michigan 48068. Manual is $3 to nonmembers, $1 to members.)

Nickerson, William. *How I Turned $1,000 into Three Million in Real Estate—in My Spare Time.* New York: Simon and Schuster, 1969.

Pilot Books Staff, ed. *1970 Directory of Franchising Organizations.* New York: Pilot Books, 1970. (Address of Pilot Books is 347 Fifth Ave., New York, N.Y. 10016; price of booklet is $2.)

Pilot Books Staff, ed. *Pilot's Question and Answer Guide to Successful Franchising.* New York: Pilot Books, 1970. (Price of booklet is $1.)

Seriff, Med. *Business Building Ideas for Franchises and Small Business.* New York: Pilot Books, 1970. (Price is $2.)

Shaffer, Ivan. *The Stock Promotion Business.* Toronto: McClelland and Stewart, 1969. (Paperback edition is available at $2.50 from publisher; address, 25 Hollinger Road, Toronto 16, Canada.)

Stewart, Maxwell. *Investing for Income and Security.* Pamphlet No. 317A. New York: Public Affairs Committee, 1970. (Address is 381 Park Ave. S., New York, N.Y. 10016; price of pamphlet is 25¢.)

Understanding Bonds and Preferred Stocks. (A pamphlet, available from brokers or from New York Stock Exchange, 11 Wall St., New York, N.Y. 10005.)

Index

AAA Enterprises Inc., 77
A to Z Rental Inc., 78–80
AAMCO Automatic Transmission, 84, 86
Accountants, 150–151
Acme Missiles and Construction Corp. (ASE), 100
Admiralty Growth Series, 183
Advance-fee schemes, 105–106
Advertising Age, 68
Advertising and ads, 44, 54, 57–61, 64–70, 73, 82–87, 90, 94, 101, 115–119, 125, 175, 201–202
Advisory services, 12, 101, 134, 141, 144–145, 154, 159
AFL-CIO, and tax laws, 211
Akron Better Business Bureau, 17, 69, 108
Al Hirt's Sandwich Saloons, 86
Alabama Market Centers, 49, 51
Aldridge International Associates, Inc., 101
Allegheny Power System, Inc., 156

Amalgamated Bank of New York, 196
American Dual Vest, Income and Capital Fund, 181
American Electric Power Co., 157
American Investors Fund, 176, 182–183
American Stock Exchange, 159, 172
Anchor Growth Fund, 182
Annual reports, company, 149–152
Annuities, 215, 229, 234–235; conversion rates, 206; as savings, 200; as tax shelters, 225–227; variables, 203–205, 277
Aplo Therm, trade name, 100
Aqua-Chek, 69
Arkansas Fried Chickenbone, 74
Arkansas Loan and Thrift Corp., 101
Arthur Lipper Corp., 172, 174, 176, 180
Associated Mortgage Investors, 208

Association of Closed-End Investment Companies, 178
Association of Customers' Brokers, 148
Association of Franchised Businessmen, 82
A.T.&T., 138, 154, 156; warrants, 163
Atlanta Better Business Bureau, 51, 77
Atlantic City Electric Co., 157, 223
Atlantic Fund for Investment in U.S. Government Securities, 196
Attorney General's office, 44, 47, 58, 117, 236
Aubrey G. Lanston and Co., 195
Automatic Sprinkler Corp., 151
Automotive parts and leases, 52, 71, 75, 84, 134, 143
Avon Products, 148, 154–155
Axe-Houghton Stock Fund, 183

B-7 Laundry Compound, 48
Bait advertising, 107–109
Balanced funds, 174–175, 178
Baltimore American, 68
Bank for Cooperatives debentures, 194
BankAmerica Realty Investors, 208
Bankers Trust Company, 195
Bankruptcies, 23, 60, 67, 79, 83, 96, 103
Banks, banking and bankers, 19–20, 27, 127, 131, 134, 138–139, 156, 161, 187, 192, 194, 202, 207–208, 213–215, 234
Barrons Magazine, 64–65

Battle for Investment Survival, The (Loeb), 137
Beneficial Finance Company, 34
Beneficial Standard Mortgage Investors, 208
Bessesen, Henry, 63–65
Bestline Marketing System, 48
Better Beef Inc., 95–96
Better Business Bureau, 12, 32, 40, 43–46, 49, 58, 61, 67, 70–71, 84, 98, 107, 236; addresses of, 241–244
Better Investing Magazine, 140
Beverage cans and dispensers, 71, 102
Birmingham Better Business Bureau, 51
Blue-chip stock, 143, 147, 149, 172, 174
Bond Buyer, The, publication, 195
Bonds, 24, 156, 175, 187, 190, 195–198, 220
Book value of stocks, 149, 152
Borrowing, short-term, 192; on stocks and securities, 194, 221–222
Boston College Franchise Study Center, 89
Briggs, Schaedle and Co., 195
Broad Street Investors, 182
Broadway Joe's Restaurants, 86
Brokerage houses, 101, 132–133, 146, 162, 175, 189
Brokers, 83, 132, 134, 141–144, 149, 162, 194, 199; choosing of, 160; fees of, 22, 105, 137–138, 170, 198, 221; real estate, 207, 222, 233
Brown, Edmund, Jr., 146
Brown, Harold, 89–90

Index

Buffington, John, 91–92
Bureaucracy, 24, 27
Businessmen's organizations, 82

California, 44, 52, 62, 96, 114, 117, 168
Call dates in stocks, 221
Canada, government of, 18; distribution rights in, 99; frauds in, 104; mining promotions in, 103–104; newspapers in, 104; treasury notes of, 202
Capital, conservation of, 136, 161; formation, 124, 133; gains, 127, 133, 141, 143, 157, 161, 169, 173–176, 180, 188, 208, 217–218, 221–225, 228, 233–236; investment and appreciation, 92, 141; losses, 215, 218; mortgage, 208; risks, 90, 180, 197
Carol Lee distributorships, 62
Carriers and General Fund, 179
Cash flow, 90, 149, 222
Catch-22 (Heller), 31, 33
Celebrities, role of in franchises, 74–75, 79, 81, 86
Central Hudson Gas and Electric Corp., 157
Central Illinois Light Co., 157
Central Maine Power Company, 156
Ceramic filters, development of, 103
Certificates, stock and bond, 101, 126, 162, 175, 196, 201, 212, 226
Channing Special Growth Fund, 182–183
Charles E. Quincey and Co., 195

Charles Harold Enterprises, 118
Chase Fund of Boston, 183
Chase Manhattan Mortgage and Realty Company, 208–209
Chemical Bank New York Trust Co., 195
Chemical Fund, 182–183
Chem-Plastics Corp., 66–68
Chicken Delight, 91
Child care and education, 12, 30, 75, 213
Chinchilla breeding schemes, 107, 113
Chloratron Corp. of America, 55
Christmas Club accounts, 19–20, 33, 37
Chrysler Turbo Jet car-wash device, 113
Churning, victims of, 132
Cigarettes, self-lighting, 99
Cincinnati Gas & Electric Co., 157
City Investing Mortgage Group, 209
Civil judgment, 32, 65
Civil Service pensions, 226
Cleaning products, 41, 48, 116, 134
Cleveland Electric Illuminating Company, 157
Closed-end investment companies, 127, 137–139, 178
Closed-end investment funds, 179, 181
Cocktail Mix Industry, 62
Coffee Bar Manufacturing, 70
Cohen, Jerry S., 75, 90–92
College endowment funds, 139
Colonial Growth Fund, 182
Columbus and Southern Ohio Electric Co., 159

Commerce, Department of, 88; addresses of, 246–249
Commercial banks, 26, 127, 201
Commission fees and sales, 22, 28–29, 32, 41, 43, 49–50, 55, 105, 118, 132, 137–140, 165–166, 170–171, 175, 178, 189–190, 194, 198
Common stocks, 102, 127, 140, 152, 157, 159–160, 163, 173, 187, 190–192
Commonwealth Edison Co., 156
Commonwealth Security Investors, Inc., 75
Competition, 90–91, 93
Computerized financial services, 18, 75
Conference of Actuaries in Public Practice, 177
Conglomerates, case of, 18, 35, 134, 154, 164
Congress, actions of, 24–27, 32, 88, 136, 162, 166, 203, 210
Connecticut General Mortgage and Realty Investments, 208
Consent orders, 47, 52, 80
Consolidated Edison Company of New York, Inc., 156, 223
Consultants, 83, 101, 145, 153–154
Consumer Frauds, Bureau of, 86
Consumer marketing interests, 118, 149
Consumers Power Company, 159
Continental Illinois National Bank and Trust Company, 195
Continental Marketing Associates, 49–53
Continental Mortgage Investors, 208

Contracts, foundership, 49–50; investors, 92, 167–168, 170
Contractual mutual fund plans, 28, 37, 166–167, 169–170, 200, 203
Convertible bonds, 140, 150, 191, 223; securities, 150, 152, 191–192
Co-Op Mailing Association, 119
Corporate accounting methods, 150–151; bonds, 19, 125–127, 159–160, 181, 187, 190, 212, 217, 220, 224, 226; mergers, 151; shell game, 102
Cosmetics and toiletries, 41, 44–46, 49, 57, 67n, 148
Cotter, William J., 37
Courts, 39, 47, 49, 67, 99, 103
Credit cards, 60–61, 64–65, 77
Credit unions, 12, 127, 201, 213–215
Custodian accounts, 171, 213–214
Customer representatives, 161
Cyclical industries, 143

Dacey, Norman, 169–170
Daniel Boone Fried Chicken, Inc., 75
Data Digests *Monthly Stock Digest*, 142, 146, 179
Data processing companies and schools, 75, 134
"Day of deposit to day of withdrawal" banking accounts, 201
Debentures, issuance of, 163, 194
Defensive-type investments, 153–154, 156
Deferral tax advantages, 200, 202–204, 212

Index

Delaware Fund, 182
Delmarva Power and Light Co., 157
Department stores, 34, 165
Depletion allowances, 210, 235–236
Depreciation allowances, 231–232
Depression, 43, 124, 172
Detroit Better Business Bureau, 117
Detroit Edison Company, 156
de Vegh Mutual Fund, 182
Dias, Robert M., 59–60, 82, 88–90, 92
Diebold Venture, 179
Dill, William, 114–115
Director distributorships, 47–48
Disability benefits and insurance, 227
Discount Corporation, 195
Discount stores, 46, 49–50
Discounted bank certificates, 201
Distribution, levels of, 41, 63
Distributors, 42–45, 49–52, 54, 56–57, 68
Distributorships, purchase of, 17, 32, 40–41, 44, 47–48, 56, 66
Dividends, accumulation of, 141, 162; on bonds, 187, 191; high, 145, 154; income from, 127, 174, 222–223; on mutual funds, 173; nondeductible, 135; on preferred stocks, 190; rates, 142–144; reinvestment of, 126, 169, 172; system, 19, 176, 180, 209, 213, 229
Diversified Brokers Co., 96–97
Diversified Mortgage Investors, 209
Dollar averaging of stock purchases, 137–139, 157, 169, 171–172
Door-to-door selling, 44, 49, 98
Dow-Jones Industrial Averages, 147, 155, 159, 181
Dreyfus Fund, 182–183
Drug company business, 134, 148–149, 154
Dry-cleaning franchise, 82
duPont, Francis I., 77
Dual funds, 179–181
Duke Power Company, 157, 189
Dun & Bradstreet report, 68, 105
Duquense Light Company, 156

E Bonds, 18–19, 22, 24, 124–126, 171, 201–204, 211–212, 215–217, 225
Earnings trend, 52, 146, 148, 150; exaggeration of, 88–89
Eastern States Enterprises, Inc., 118
Eastern Utilities Associates, 156
Eastman Kodak Company, 155
Eaton and Howard Funds, 166
Edie Adams' Cut and Curl, 86
Education, financing for, 12, 30, 197, 211–215, 230
El Paso Natural Gas, 223
Electric utilities stock, 154, 156
Electronics industry, 18, 134
Electronic Shinemaster, 99
Employment placement agencies, 72, 75
Endowment funds and policies, 139, 168, 214–215
Equity capital and issues, 135, 190
Exploitation, areas of, 12, 59, 95, 106

Face-amount certificates, 202–203
Fairfax Industries of Washington, D.C., 118
Family tax shelters, 124, 217–218
Farming, as hobby tax deductions, 210, 236–237; part-time, 236
Fast-food and highway restaurants, 80–81, 83
Federal agency obligations, 125, 154, 194
Federal Distributing Company, 108
Federal Home Loan Bank, 194
Federal Housing Authority, 207
Federal Land Bank bonds, 194
Federal National Mortgage Association (FNMA), 24–25, 194, 196
Federal Reserve Bank, 193, 234
Federal Reserve Board, 20, 26
Federal securities, 192, 195–196, 216
Federal Trade Commission (FTC), 33, 44, 52, 56, 69–72, 80, 84–89, 94, 97, 117, 151; addresses of, 246; citations, 113–114; Division of General Trade Restraints, 93; general counsel, 91; hearings, 108–109
Fidelity Capital Fund, 182–183
Finance companies, 69, 71, 116, 118
Financial Independence Through Common Stocks (Merritt), 151
First Investors Corporation, 169n
First Mortgage Investors, 208
First National City Bank of New York, 20n, 145, 195
First Sierra Fund, 183

First Standard Corp., 98–100
Fixed assets and income savings, 149, 203
Fixed-value savings, 124, 126–127, 200–201, 215
Florida, 71, 102, 114; Securities Commission, 49
Florida Discount Centers, Inc., 49–50
Food stores and chains, 98, 143, 146, 149, 154
Forbes Magazine, 174
Fortune Magazine, 209
Founderships, sales of, 46, 50–51
Franchises, definition of, 58n; financial status, 83, 93, 148; fraudulent, 58–60, 63, 66–68; growth of, 71, 75, 77, 79; organization of, 11, 17–18, 23, 38, 90–91; publicized celebrities in, 75; territorial rights of, 88
Fraud and fraudulent intent, 31, 38–39, 56–60, 63, 66–68, 95, 98, 101–104, 118
Frazer, George, 145, 174, 202
Freezer-food plans, 68, 98
Front-load investment plans, 28, 34, 166–167, 170, 200, 203
Funds, 123, 177–178, 214, 218. See *also* Mutual funds
Fundscope Magazine, 174

Gabor, Zsa Zsa, 84, 86
Galbreath First Mortgage Investments, 209
Gas leases and companies, 97, 154
Gemini Fund, 180

Index

General American Investors, 179
General Electric Corp., 69, 146
General Mortgage Investors, 208
Geological evaluations, purchase of, 97
Get-rich-quick schemes, 46
Gibraltar Securities Company, 198
Gifts and taxes, 26n, 210–214, 229–231
Gifts to Minors Act, 213
Glamour industries and products, 103
Global Distributors, 109–110
Go-go high performance funds, 23, 173, 181
Goal Trading Stamp promotion, 63, 65
Government agencies, 82, 88, 94; bills, 192; bonds, 19, 159, 192, 202, 224; obligations, 160, 187, 192, 225; securities, 195; surplus, 96
Grand Union food stores, 146
Gray-area operations, 60, 74, 90
Green, Arnold, 138, 166
Greenheart Laboratories, 72
Group deferred annuities, 205
Growth characteristics, 154; companies, 143; funds, 173–175; stocks, 127, 142, 145–148, 153, 169n
Guardian Mortgage Investors, 209
Guardian Mutual, 176, 182
Gyro-Matic Safety Control, 52–53

Hamburger stands, 23, 93
Hard-sell pressures and practices, 11, 18, 34, 84, 161, 166
Hartwell Management Corp., 177
Hedberg & Gordon Fund, 183
Hedge funds, development of, 36
Hemisphere Fund, 180
High-pressure promotions, 17, 26, 56, 58, 95, 101, 116, 167; yielding investments, 25, 156, 160–161, 171, 195, 216, 221
Hildebrand, Russell Lee, 112–113
Hobby farms and tax losses, 210, 236–237
Hoffman, J. R., 58, 74
Holdiay Magic Cosmetics, 40–45, 53, 67n
Holt, Edward, 53–55
Home Loan Bank, 24–25
Homen, Manuel, 62–63
Homeowners, exploitation of, 106; improvement kits for, 67–68, 75, 118
Hong Kong Executive Fashions, 40–41, 53
Hooker, John Jay, Jr., 80, 87
Hot tips on stocks, 101, 103, 161
House subcommittee hearings on mutual funds, 168–169
Howard Johnson Distributing Co., 80, 111
Hunter, John, 61–62
Hurley Chinchilla Ranch of Omaha, 113–114
Hydro-Mite Sports Boat, Inc., 70

H Bonds, 18, 127, 216–217
Hageman, Robert A., 219
Hale, Frank C., 72, 89
Hale, Paul, 60–62

Illinois, 71, 168; banks, 95
Illinois Power Company, 157
Import business, 107, 114

Income averaging, 225, 231; funds and shares, 153, 161, 173, 180, 210, 214; part-time, 71, 108; taxes, 12, 151, 212, 215, 217, 224–225, 228
Indiana, 47, 96
Indianapolis, 61, 101, 106
Inflation, 18, 169n, 232; hedges against, 124, 136, 169, 171
Inheritance taxes, 210
Installment notes, 22, 69
Institutional investors, 19, 23, 35, 134–135, 139, 153, 161
Institutions, savings, 18, 20, 143, 200, 231
Insurance, 20–21, 28, 168, 203–204, 234; companies, 21, 34, 36, 98, 127, 131, 134, 138–139, 205, 208, 227; savings, 21, 168, 214–215. See also specific types of insurance
Interest, bond, 190, 224; compound, 125, 127; high, 95–96, 106; rates, 19, 21–22, 123, 130, 135, 142, 154, 163, 187–188, 197, 202, 215, 229
Internal Revenue Service (IRS), 201, 211, 226, 228, 230, 233–234
International Association of Machinist and Aerospace Workers, 11
International Business Machines (IBM), 148, 155
International Conference on Franchising, 90, 92
International Distribution Center, 71
International Holdings, 179
Interstate Engineering Corp., 116
Interstate Power Company, 156

Investment clubs, 123, 131, 137, 140–141, 171; companies, 123, 126, 178, 181; direct and indirect, 131, 137; diversification, 40, 81, 88, 107, 124–125, 127, 157; industry, 27, 132–133, 166; funds, 136, 138, 141, 159–161, 169n; manuals, 146; periodic, 139, 169; promotions, 32–33, 38; trusts, 207–208
Investment Company of America, 182–183
Investment Dealers' Association of Canada, 190
Investors, levels of, 53–54, 61, 154, 182
Investors Diversified Services, 22, 168, 203
Investors Research Stock Fund, 182–183
Iowa Public Service, 156
Istel Fund, 176, 182–183

Japanese and American Associates, 100
Jersey Standard Oil, 146
Johnny Carson's Here's Johnny's food shops, 86
Johnson, Lyndon B., 26–27
Johnson's Charts, 142, 171, 174
Johnston Mutual Fund, 176, 182–183

Kachena Uranium Corporation, 102
Kansas Gas and Electric Co., 156
Kentucky Fried Chicken, 80, 87
Keogh Act, 233–235

Index

Keys, James W., 114–115
Keystone Custodian Funds, 182, 192
Knickerbocker Growth Fund, 183
Koscot Interplanetary Corporation, 40, 44–47, 53

Land development, 31, 208
Large investors, 12, 18–19, 149, 162, 233
Lebenthal & Company, 198, 224
Lefkowitz, Louis, 33, 58
Legislation, 38–39; criminal, 32; false advertising, 107; regulatory, 92; remedial, 31–33, 88; security, 51; tax, 211, 224
Liberal income stocks, 127
Life insurance, 28n, 37, 135, 147, 165, 168, 170, 182, 200, 206, 215, 217
Lifetone Electronics Company, 118
Lincoln National Life Insurance Company, 177
Litter-Vac Corporation, 68
Livestock, 95, 210, 236–237
Living costs and needs, 124, 136
Load-type funds, 29, 166, 214, 234
Loans, 92, 105, 115, 162, 168
Lobbying, effects of, 27, 33, 136
Lomas & Nettleton Financial Corp. of Dallas, 208
Long-term accounts, 90, 161, 170, 176, 200, 203, 212, 221–222; bonds, 188; capital appreciation, 141, 145, 217–219, 231; income savings, 124, 127, 201, 233; investment programs, 136, 146, 158, 197, 207

Los Angeles, Cal., 66, 68, 82; Better Business Bureau, 59; investment firms in, 105
Lotteries, 44, 49

MacDonald's food stores, 80
Machinist Magazine, 11–12, 45
MacIntyre, Commissioner, 91, 94
Magazines, financial, 12, 44, 65, 68, 142, 160, 175, 195
Mail fraud, 53, 65, 95–96, 108, 110, 112, 116–119
Management fees, 29, 174, 196, 208; quality of, 12, 83, 90, 93, 145, 149–150, 153, 161, 176, 213–214
Marble, manufacture of, 65–66
Market fluctuations, 30, 54, 90, 99, 154, 173
Martin Industries, 65–66
Maryland, 47, 71
Medicine and Medicare, 23, 79
Merchandise exchange, 61, 67n
Merchandise by Mail Sales Plan, 119
Mercury Automotive Products, 72
Merrill Lynch, Pierce, Fenner & Smith, 34, 195
Miami Better Business Bureau, 37, 41, 45, 47, 70–71, 98, 100
Michigan, 47, 77, 119, 168
Mickey Mantle's Country Cookin', 86
Midas Muffler franchise, 91
Middle South Utilities, 35
Mineral and mining promotions, 103–104, 210

Minnesota, 63, 175; University of, 93
Minnesota Mining & Manufacturing Company, 155
Minnesota Power and Light Co., 156
Missouri, 51–52, 65
Moderate and middle-income families, 11, 125, 135, 141, 154, 210–211, 225, 235
Monarch Electronic Corp., 118
Montana Power Company, 157
Monthly Investment Plan (MIP), 138–139
Moody's Investors Service and *Handbook of Common Stocks*, 142, 145–146, 150, 190, 198
Morgan Guaranty Trust Co., 195
Morgan and Keys Associates, 114–115
Mortgage, 17, 25, 106, 123, 138, 187, 215–216; companies, 207, 217, 226; contracts, 20; money, 95–96, 105; trusts, 125–127, 181, 207–209
Mortgage Investment Group, 208
Mortgage Investors of Iowa, 101
Multi-level distributors, 11, 17, 37, 40, 46, 48, 52–53, 56, 67n, 98, 110
Municipal bonds, 19, 21, 125, 132, 159, 187, 195, 224–225
Murphy, Thomas H., 83, 85
Mutual Fund Selector, 172, 174, 176, 181–182
Mutual funds, 12, 18, 23, 26–30, 34, 124–127, 131–141, 157, 165, 168–175, 178, 187, 192, 195, 198, 207, 214, 222, 234
Mutual Savings banks, 127, 171, 201

Mutual Securities Fund, 183

Nabisco Snacks, 111–112
Namath, Joe, 86–87
National Association of Franchised Businessmen, 59, 75
National Association of Investment Clubs (NAIC), 140–141
National Association of Mutual Savings Banks, 25, 37
National Better Business Bureau, 58, 74
National Investors Corp., 182–183
National Marketing Association, 53, 55
National Observer, 46, 48
National Pizza Corporation, 76–77
National Securities Bond and Preferred Stock Series, 182, 192
Nationwide Industries, 78–79
Net profit ratio, 152
New Hampshire, 116, 157, 168, 175
New Jersey, 100, 175
New York, 19, 82, 98, 100, 105, 175, 224
New York Hanseatic Corp., 195
New York Post, 68
New York State Electric and Gas Corp., 156
New York Stock Exchange, 34, 132n, 138, 141, 159, 172, 221
New York Times, The, 77, 81, 87, 159
Newspapers, financial sections and ads in, 44, 47, 54, 65, 84,

Index

101, 104, 107, 142, 175, 194, 197, 201
Nitti, Victor, 78–80
Nixon, Richard, 27, 29
No-load funds, 123, 166, 169, 173–178, 181, 196, 214, 234
North American Mortgage Investors, 209
North Carolina, 51, 109
Northeast States Power Co., 157
Nursing homes, 23, 75, 134
Nuveen Tax-Exempt Bond Fund, 199

O'Brien, John L., 37, 42, 67, 97
Odd-lot purchases, 189, 194–195
Oestreicher, J. S., 19
Ohio Edison Company, 156
Ohmlac Paint & Refining Co., 70
Oil leases and companies, 95, 97, 146, 181, 210, 235–236
Oklahoma City, Okla., 53–54, 56, 71, 110
One William Street fund, 182
Open-end investment fund, 139, 179–181
Oppenheimer Fund, 175, 183
Orange and Rockland Utilities, Inc., 157
Over-the-counter market, 102, 154, 176, 178, 180, 188
Overrides, paying of, 47, 50

Pacific Power and Light Co., 156
Paine, Webber, Jackson & Curtis, 219
Paint industry, 59, 68–70
Paramount Oil Co., 97

Park Chemical Co., 134
Pat Boone's Dine O Mat, 74
Patrick, William P., 44
Payroll savings plans, 18, 24
Pearl, Minnie, 80–81, 87
Penn Square Mutual Fund, 176, 183
Pensions, and funds for, 29, 36, 131, 134–135, 153, 160–161, 215, 225–229
Pentex Distribution Co., 109n
Performance tables, 23, 133, 171, 173–179, 181
Peticare Insurance Company, 71
Petro Vend self-service pumps, 113
Petroleum Corp., 179
Pets, household, 71, 75, 92
Pioneer Fund, 182–183
Pizza parlors, 92, 102
Playboy facilities, 99–100
Politics, influence of, 26–27
Portland General Electric Co., 156–157
Post Exchange System, 34
Post Office Department, 56, 60, 66; authority of, 31–33, 67, 72, 111; fraud division, 63; investigation division, 37–39, 54, 72, 105, 108, 116–119
Preferred stock, 101, 125, 127, 140, 169, 175, 180–181, 187–191, 223
Pre-retirement savings, 216, 223
Price-earnings ratio (P/E), 142–153, 157–160, 163, 209
Pritchard, Harold, 66–67
Professional investors and managers, 22, 139, 146, 149–150, 158
Profit, element of, 149, 157, 159

Promotions, sales, 11–12, 17–18, 30–32, 40, 44, 46, 54, 59, 79, 98
Property, development of, 106, 231–234
Prospectus, company, 80–81, 99–100, 173–175
Public Service Co., 156–157
Public utilities, 142, 190, 223
Puget Sound Power and Light Co., 157, 223
Putnam Growth Fund, 180–183
Pylon Distributing Co., 66–68
Pyramid investments, 17, 40, 48

Quality Home Foods, 68
Quotations, financial, 177

Rack distributorships, 71, 107
Radios and tubes, 54, 59, 72
Realtors and real estate, 17, 25, 32, 54, 84, 127, 138, 181, 207, 209, 222, 232–234
"Reckus," definition of, 17
Recruitment of investors, 41–49, 53, 56–57
Redemption values, 189–192, 200, 202, 212
Referral selling schemes, 11, 37, 116–119
Reforms and reformers, 26–29, 94, 166
Regulatory agencies, 11–12, 18–20, 27, 31n, 36, 39, 212
Rental property, 80, 232
Research, investment, 22, 137, 143–149, 151, 161
Retirement plans, 12, 135–136, 175, 180, 204, 211, 215–216, 228–229, 233–234

Rights, stock, 35, 162, 164, 222–223
Rite Baby Pants, 72
Roadrunner Burger, 74
Robinson, Jackie, 87
Roessner, Elmer, 75, 91
Rolland, Ian M., 177
Royalties, collection of, 86, 92

Sacramento Bee, 68
Safe deposit boxes, 162, 193
St. Louis, Mo., 43–44, 65–66, 76, 96, 113; Better Business Bureau, 37, 42, 51, 67–68, 107
Salem Fund, 182
Sales charges, 27–29, 165–166, 169–170, 176, 199; parties, 45–46; programs, 38, 51, 56, 59, 64, 117, 132
Satterwaite, Samuel, 109–110
Savings accounts, 19, 20, 125–127, 162, 213, 226; associations, 24, 26, 124–125, 127, 192, 201, 207, 213–217; banks, 24–25, 175; bonds, 18, 24, 212, 216
Scott & Fetzer Company, 117
Scudder Common Fund, 181–182
Securities, gifts of, 229; sales of, 25, 44, 97–98, 101, 103, 165–166; senior, 187, 189; tax exempt, 196–198; trading in, 49, 52, 96, 102, 126, 132, 141, 180, 219–220
Securities and Exchange Commission (SEC), 26–28, 33–36, 52, 75, 80–85, 94, 98–103, 131–132, 166–167, 170, 245

Index

Self-employment, 233–235
Senate subcommittees, 27, 38, 58, 74, 78, 81, 86, 90
Shaffer, Ivan, 104
Shoe companies, 154
Short-term obligations, 90, 124, 188–189, 193–194, 201, 213, 218–222, 229–230
Small Business Administration, 88, 92, 247–248
Small investors, 12, 17, 31–33, 68, 132, 139, 153, 156, 158, 165, 171, 174, 181, 187, 189, 195, 198, 208, 233, 254–271
Smathers, Ralph, 37, 100
Snack-meal franchises, 59, 62
Soap products, 48, 54, 57, 134
Social Security, 21, 215, 227–228
South Carolina, 61; Securities Division, 49
Specialized funds and investors, 35–36, 133, 179, 181, 210, 220
Speculation, 101, 133, 139, 141, 159–160, 172, 175, 197
Sporkin, Stanley, 98–99
Standard & Poor's ratings, 141, 147, 150, 172, 181, 190, 198
State bonds, 125, 187, 197, 224–226; tax, 196
State Street Investment Corp., 35, 182
Stock exchange, 133, 158–160, 163, 188; market, 29–30, 101, 124, 133–136, 160, 166, 179–180
Stocks, investments in, 35, 124, 126, 131, 133–138, 148, 162, 178, 189, 218, 222
Stuckey, W. S., Jr., 27, 92

Success Motivation Institute, 76, 85
Susser v. Carvel case, 92
Swingers, stock market, 133–135

T. Rowe Price Growth Fund, 154, 176, 182–183
Tables and charts, 127–129, 144
Tape recorders, 41, 99
Tax advantages, 136, 141, 221; deferrals, 202–204, 234–235; exemptions, 19, 123, 125, 127, 135, 154, 181, 187, 196–198, 215, 224, 227, 230–231; liabilities, 224, 229; loopholes, 97, 210–211, 235–236; losses, 220–221; planning, 20, 124, 210–211; on properties, 20, 232–234; laws, 123, 211, 218, 224, 226; savings, 123, 145, 212, 235; services, 77, 165; shelters, 26n, 125, 214–217, 225–226, 232–234
Television (TV), 50, 54, 59, 66, 71, 72, 79, 84, 113, 118
Templeton Growth Fund, 176, 183
Tennessee, 49, 51, 81, 102
Term insurance, 170, 204
Terrific (Turific) Products Co., 53–55
Texas Bank & Trust Co., 62
Texas Gulf Sulphur Co., 34
Texas Instruments, 155
Texas Southern Distributing Co., 111
Thompson, Donald M., 88
Thompson, Fletcher, 27
Tight money, 105, 154, 188
Timber woodlands, 236–237

Toombs, Jean, 11, 38, 93, 104, 110
Toronto, Can., 104–105
Trading, specialists, 160; stamps, 63–64; suspension of, 103; volume, 159
Training, nature of, 94, 114–115
Treasury, Department of, 25, 192, 211; securities, 24, 193–196, 212, 225–226, 234
Tri-Continental Corp., 179
Trusts, 125–126, 161–162, 181, 202, 207–209, 228–234
Turner, Glenn, 45–46

Ultra Jet Industries, 103
Union Electric Company, 156
Unions, 12, 160, 205
United Business Service, 133, 141, 172, 179, 181–182
U.S. Electronics, Inc., 71–72
U.S. Sonics Corp., 103
Universal Credit Card Inc., 61–62
Universal Fiberglass Co., 17
United Illuminating Co., 156
Utah Power and Light Co., 156
Utility investments, 127, 144, 154, 156, 163, 188

Vacation clubs, 19–20
Vacuum cleaners, 116–118
Value, standards of, 142, 158
Value Line Fund, 182–183
Vartan, Vartanig G., 159
Vel-Vett process, 76

Vending machines, 107–109
Veterans Administration, 21, 215, 227
Virginia, 46, 48, 51
Vitamin products, 41

Wall Street, 18, 30, 39
Wall Street Journal, The, 68, 87
Warner-Lambert Company, 155
Warrants, 150, 162–164
Wash sales, 220–222
Washington Water Power Co., 157
Water softeners, 118
West Virginia, 48, 106
Western Testing Inc., 95–96
Westex Enterprises, 72
Wiesenberger Mutual Fund Management Results, 174, 176, 179, 183
Wig shops, 75–76
Williams, Harrison, 86, 92
Williams, John J., 24, 77–78
Wilson, Rufus E., 93
Windsor Distributing Co., 109
Windsor Fund, 182–183
Winfield Growth Fund, 183
Wisconsin, 47–48, 168
Wolmart Discount Corp., 69
Wonder Bar products, 62–63
World Executive, Inc., 72
Wright Advisory Service, 159, 172

Xerox Corp., 148, 153–155
You Can Avoid Probate (Dacey), 169–170
Youngstown Spectrum Corp., 71